Critical Reflections on Career Education and Guidance

Around the globe, career education and guidance is being presented as the answer to social exclusion, ensuring economic competitiveness and prosperity. The profile of career education and guidance has never been higher. Yet, current policy discussions have centred on individuals' development of 'self-managed' careers within a global labour market, placing employability skills above all other concerns.

This book goes beyond the rhetoric of the 'self-managed' career and 'employability skills' by exploring career education and guidance from critical and radical standpoints. The contributors question the economic underpinning that has driven social agendas, arguing that career education and guidance needs to place greater emphasis on developing socially just practices. The views expressed help to open up the debate around the impact of globalisation as consideration is given to the ways in which career professionals might actively enable, empower and promote the democratic engagement of all in the shaping of their world(s). The authors consider the issues within a range of contexts including 'race', gender, disability and social class.

Critical Reflections on Career Education and Guidance is essential reading for students, academics, practitioners and researchers who wish to achieve a greater understanding of the contexts involved.

Barrie A. Irving is Senior Visiting Research Fellow, Department for Career and Personal Development, Canterbury Christchurch University College.

Beatriz Malik is Professor in Educational Guidance at the National University of Distance Education (UNED) in Madrid.

Critical Reflections on Career Education and Guidance

Promoting social justice within a global economy

Edited by Barrie A. Irving and Beatriz Malik

RoutledgeFalmer
Taylor & Francis Group
LONDON AND NEW YORK

First published 2005
by RoutledgeFalmer
2 Park Square, Milton Park, Abingdon, Oxon OX14 4RN

Simultaneously published in the USA and Canada
by RoutledgeFalmer
270 Madison Ave, New York, NY 10016

RoutledgeFalmer is an imprint of the Taylor & Francis Group

Typeset in Times by Wearset Ltd, Boldon, Tyne and Wear
Printed and bound in Great Britain by MPG Books Ltd, Bodmin

British Library Cataloguing in Publication Data
A catalogue record for this book is available from the British Library

Library of Congress Cataloging in Publication Data
A catalog record for this book has been requested

ISBN 0-415-32453-X

Contents

Acknowledgements vii
Notes on contributors ix

Foreword xiii
PETER PLANT

1 **Introduction** 1
BARRIE A. IRVING AND BEATRIZ MALIK

2 **Social justice: a context for career education and guidance** 10
BARRIE A. IRVING

3 **Welfare to work: economic challenges to socially just career practice** 25
FIONA DOUGLAS

4 **Liberté? Futilité? . . . Autonomé! Careers education as an emancipatory activity** 41
BILL LAW

5 **Cultural diversity and guidance: myth or reality?** 56
BEATRIZ MALIK AND TERESA AGUADO

6 **Career education for Muslim girls: meeting culture at the crossroads** 72
VIVIENNE BARKER AND BARRIE A. IRVING

7 **(En)gendering socially just approaches to career guidance** 86
WENDY PATTON AND MARY MCMAHON

8 Women, work and career development: equal employment opportunity or employment equity? 100
MARIA HUMPHRIES AND SUZETTE DYER

9 The career education curriculum and students with disabilities 114
PAUL PAGLIANO

10 Social class, opportunity structures and career guidance 130
KEN ROBERTS

11 Working with youth at risk of exclusion 143
NURIA MANZANO SOTO

12 Social justice and equality of opportunity for Mexican young people 158
JULIA HERNÁNDEZ HERNÁNDEZ AND BERNARDO ANTONIO MUÑOZ-RIVEROHL

13 Beyond the toolbox: integrating multicultural principles into a career guidance intervention model 172
HAZEL L. REID

14 Challenging careers: perspectives from auto/biographical research 186
LINDEN WEST

Index 199

Acknowledgements

The editors would like to thank all of the contributors to this collection for their willingness to share their thoughts and ideas in the development of this book. Their dedication and professional commitment to the project has been greatly appreciated by the editors.

We also wish to acknowledge the financial assistance given by the Spanish Distance Education University (UNED) Vicerectorate for Research for supporting the translation of Chapter 11 by Nuria Manzano Soto from Spanish into English.

Finally we are indebted to Priyanka Pathak at RoutledgeFalmer for her timely comments, helpful advice, encouragement and ongoing support throughout the publication process.

Contributors

Barrie A. Irving is a Senior Visiting Research Fellow at the Department for Career and Personal Development, Canterbury Christ Church University College, England, and now lives in New Zealand. He has written widely on social justice and career-related issues, and recently co-authored, *In Good Faith: Schools, Religion and Public Funding*, published in 2004 by Ashgate.

Dr Beatriz Malik is an Assistant Professor in Educational and Career Guidance at the National University of Distance Education (UNED) in Madrid, Spain. Her fields of research and teaching include intercultural education, social mediation and counsellor qualifications. She is also interested in multiculturalism in guidance, career guidance programmes (specifically how they address cultural diversity), students with disabilities, and the promotion of social justice.

Fiona Douglas has spent many years lecturing in higher education. Her current PhD research explores the implications of governmentality on public service providers, comparing the New Zealand and English Careers Services. She has also published widely and presented papers at national and international conferences.

Dr Bill Law taught for 12 years, and is now an independent consultant. He is a Senior Fellow with NICEC; Visiting Associate at The Centre for Guidance Studies, University of Derby; and Senior Visiting Research Fellow at the Department for Career and Personal Development, Canterbury Christ Church University College, England. Bill writes extensively on theory, policy and practice useful to career and citizenship education, and to career guidance. His website, the Career-learning Café is at www.hihohiho.com.

Dr Teresa Aguado is Professor at the National University of Distance Education (UNED) in Madrid, Spain. Her fields of research include intercultural education and social mediation in educational contexts. Several of her publications address cultural diversity and equity issues, and she has recently authored *Pedagogía intercultural* (McGraw-Hill 2003). She is currently coordinating the *Inter Project: A guide to implement intercultural education at schools* (Socrates Programme 2002/2005).

Vivienne Barker is a Senior Lecturer in Education at the Department for Career and Personal Development, Canterbury Christ Church University College, England. Her research and teaching interests include social exclusion and adult guidance, equal opportunities and social justice. She has co-authored articles and presented papers at national and international conferences.

Dr Wendy Patton is a Professor in the Faculty of Education at the Queensland University of Technology where she co-ordinates the Masters of Education (Careers Guidance). She has published extensively in the field of career development and is an editorial advisory board member for a number of journals.

Dr Mary McMahon manages a portfolio career in which she combines teaching, writing, research, and career counselling. She has published a number of journal articles and book chapters. In addition, she has co-authored and co-edited books on career development theory and programs (with Wendy Patton).

Dr Maria Humphries is an Associate Professor in the Waikato Management School (WMS), University of Waikato in New Zealand. She teaches and researches on issues pertaining to career development and women in organisation(s). Currently, her main responsibility at the WMS is the stewarding into existence of a teaching and research agenda in Not-for-Profit or Third Sector organisation and management.

Dr Suzette Dyer lectures at the University of Waikato, New Zealand, in the area of management studies. Her interests include the implications of globalisation and flexibility on careers. She is also interested in notions of management and discipline and the work experiences of women.

Dr Paul Pagliano is a Senior Lecturer in Education at James Cook University, Townsville, Australia. He has dual teaching responsibilities and research interests in career development and special education. His work has been published by the UK Institute of Career Guidance, and he has authored books on multisensory environments published by David Fulton.

Professor Ken Roberts is Professor of Sociology at the University of Liverpool, England. Since his work in the 1970s on opportunity structure theory, he has conducted investigations into the impact of changing economic conditions and new educational and training initiatives. Since 1990 most of his research has been how the transformation of East-Central Europe and the former USSR is impacting on young people.

Dr Nuria Manzano Soto is an Assistant Professor in Educational Assessment and Counselling Techniques at the National University of Distance Education (UNED) in Madrid, Spain. She has worked in a range of different areas of careers counselling. Her current research interests are counselling and working with youth at risk of exclusion, developing and evaluating comprehensive counselling programmes, and counsellor qualification standards.

Julia Hernández Hernández works at the Departmento de Extensión de la Dirección General de Orientación y Servicios Educativos, Universidad Nacional Autónoma de Mexico (UNAM). She has been working in careers counselling in different areas, and is currently involved in career counsellor training and refresher courses.

Dr Bernardo Antonio Muñoz-Riverohl is a researcher and postgraduate instructor in education and career counselling at universities in Mexico.

Hazel L. Reid is Principal Lecturer at the Department of Career and Personal Development, Canterbury Christ Church University College, England. She teaches in the subject area of career and guidance theory and application. She has written for career and guidance publications, presents papers at conferences and is currently undertaking a doctorate researching the meanings associated with support and supervision.

Dr Linden West is Reader at Canterbury Christ Church University College, England. His publications include *Beyond Fragments* (about adult learner motivation) and *Doctors on the Edge* (about stress and subjective learning). He co-ordinates a European Biographical Research Network and teaches on a Masters programme in career development.

Foreword

Mind the Gap

> 'Mind the Gap': this is the sonorous voice in the London Underground reminding us of the Gap along the platform, societally and otherwise, no doubt.

A number of current concepts emphasise the positive sides of globalisation. Freedom and flexibility are such a pair. Freedom to choose, and flexibility of choice, in relation to, for example, lifestyle, workplace, working hours. This is the bright side, and it applies to some, but not the majority. It represents what the authors of this book call a 'neo-liberal economic rationalist rhetoric, in which everything is subservient to the needs of the market . . . (and) presents a restricted picture of how things could, and possibly should be, if the interests of justice and democracy are to be served'.

But every coin has a flip side. Change, for example, may be seen as a positive challenge, as opposed to tedious routine, but on the other hand, the call for employees to be flexible and enhance their employability as a result of constant changes, may equally be perceived as a threat and a stress factor. Similarly, the world of education reflects the pressure on each individual to take responsibility for their own learning and to take up the challenge of lifelong learning. Remember the time when 'education, education, education' was the mantra? Now it is learning. For some, this is paradise: they thrive on the plethora of learning opportunities, formal as well as informal; they find it easy to plan; they have the cultural capital that is needed to be flexible. For others, it feels less like the Promised Land: to them, lifelong learning sounds much more like lifelong imprisonment. In short, the result is a polarised society in which those 'who have' get more, and those 'who don't have' lose what little they may have; a society with social imbalance, social exclusion and little social cohesion: the Gap. The ensuing downward spiral of a de-skilled and disfranchised labour force add to this gloomy picture of marginalisation. No economic growth here. On the contrary. Yet, the official rhetoric salutes growth figures of the economics, disregarding, by the way, that the natural base for affluent lifestyles is deteriorating. It takes no great scientist to see that fish and oil are running out. There is a huge gap between rhetoric and reality in terms of sustainability. Mind the Gap.

Clearly, in terms of career education and guidance, one of the credos has been, and is, that of choice. Free choice, however, was never free for all. But guidance has been seen as a lubricant to facilitate transitions from learning to working life on precisely the basis of choice. In this picture the 'right' choice has often been closely related to what is pictured as the realities of the economic world. In this context, guidance these days has to prove its economic benefits to secure public funding. Yet paid work cannot be, and is not, the only yardstick by which to measure career paths. Moreover, the emphasis on the individual aspects of choosing mainstream paid careers tends to shift the focus away from the forces of 'underemployment, poverty, homelessness, under-funded welfare services and a degenerating environment', as mentioned in this book.

Career education and guidance will have to take a stand. This will challenge the myth of neutrality and impartiality in guidance. Exposing the ideologies of the global labour market to scrutiny gives the users an opportunity to explore alternative visions and develop their own understanding of what 'career' means to them. It may not be a nice, straightforward paid career in the formal labour market. Voluntary work, part-time work, and even work in the informal economy may turn out to be more promising career pathways, or indeed, the only possible ones. Empowerment is a key concept there. Thus, the role of the guidance practitioner goes beyond that of exploring self and opportunity. It poses questions to globalisation, and it questions economic growth as an end in itself. We could call this Green Guidance. Thus, career guidance enters into the risky areas of social change. How far can guidance go in terms of being an agent for social and economic change, a Trojan Horse in a society that salutes globalisation and capitalism?

This important book, with its highly stimulating chapters, questions the present paradigm. Critical reflections are especially important at a time when one ideology is prevailing. We need this intellectual counterflow.

Mind the Gap.

Peter Plant
'Rojlegaarden', Torup
Denmark

Chapter 1

Introduction

Barrie A. Irving and Beatriz Malik

Critical reflections in context

Governments around the world appear to have been captured by narrow economic imperatives driven by the desire to win in the global competition for business, jobs and profit. It is argued that the gains made will ensure the economic health of successful nation states resulting in social cohesion, individual well-being and benefits for all. In response to demands from employers for a work-ready labour force the function of education is coming under ever-closer scrutiny to ensure that the 'right' attitudes, skills and behaviours are being inculcated in the young. Compulsory schooling is given the task of ensuring that the needs of an emerging high skills labour market will be met by pupils who understand the benefits of a 'free market' and the need to become lifelong learners. Further, young people and adults are being made aware of their responsibilities as productive citizens, yet also encouraged to recognise the potential prizes on offer to those individuals who make a 'success' of their lives. In recent years the provision of career education and guidance has been presented as a panacea for social exclusion, the key to individual aspiration, and an essential component in ensuring that labour demands are met.

Yet whilst the discourse of the market and triumphalist cry of capitalism currently rings loud, there is increasing unease about the ways in which globalisation is impacting on the lives of people in economically and politically powerful western nation states, and the relatively impoverished developing world. The emergence of a re-invigorated political 'right' in Europe and elsewhere, evidence of increasing social disadvantage and poverty, the hysteria associated with asylum seekers and refugees, concerns about increasing occurrences of racism, and negative portrayals of anti-capitalist and environmental protest, has led many to question the prevailing wisdom.

Think global: act local

In a rapidly changing labour market increased demands are being placed on employees to be flexible, continually enhance their employability skills, and be responsive to change (Rajan *et al.* 1997; Smith 2002). Teachers meanwhile are given the responsibility of ensuring their students are prepared for new challenges and opportunities by becoming lifelong learners (Irving 1999). Beneath the glowing picture of choice, opportunity, and economic rewards however lies a neo-liberal individualist conception, which belies the notion of social belonging or collective rights. Further, it is these aspects of life that have been increasingly undermined as the global capital message stakes its claim as the core ideology in many western states. The neo-liberal economic rationalist rhetoric, in which everything is subservient to the needs of the market, presents a restricted picture of how things could, and possibly should, be if the interests of justice and democracy are to be served.

Colley (2000) argues that the ongoing mantra concerning the benefits of globalisation is disingenuous at best as many workers in advanced western capitalist countries have experienced a decline in living standards, reduced employment rights, and a contraction in opportunity. She asserts that:

> The tendency of globalization is not to create an economy requiring high skill levels and reward these with prosperity for all, but the opposite: greater inequalities in income, weakened trade union protection, casualised work with low skills and low pay.
>
> (Colley 2000: 19)

If Colley is correct in her analysis, then there is a need to ask why there has been widespread acquiescence to such an individualistic and deterministic model. Whilst reality may take many forms, it appears clear that particular versions have greater power to influence public policy. At the current time, a managerialist form dominates, reinforced through government intervention (Offer in Gothard *et al.* 2001: 91) legitimated by the need to fundamentally change labour market practices in response to global competition (Bradley *et al.* 2000, cited by Offer in Gothard *et al.* 2001: 90).

Meanwhile the gap between the richest and poorest in society continues to grow as structural inequalities remain hidden from view. Individuals are increasingly held responsible for their futures, regardless of 'race', gender, social class or (dis)ability. An inverse approach to redistribution appears to be taking place in Britain today based on a meritocratic view of achievement and success. Talk of reducing the tax burden, removing restrictive labour practices, and enforcing participation in learning and work can be regarded as a means whereby greater economic rewards are given to those deemed to be 'successful' by taking away resources from those who have least (Darom 2000). Tomlinson (2001) identifies the emergence of a post-welfare society in which the work ethic and competition, whether in education or the labour market, dominates. In pursuit of economic efficiency, she argues, welfare benefits are being restructured or removed as they are perceived to be an economic drain on the nation's wealth. This is reflected in Coffield's observation in the United Kingdom.

> The government's stated aim of rebuilding the welfare state around work (DSS, 1998), by which is meant 'paid employment', has created a climate where learning is judged according to 'rates of return', and people are evaluated according to their employability and their capacity to deliver added value to the economy.
>
> (Coffield 2000: 12)

Yet the restructuring of the welfare state, alongside the economic insecurities and uncertainties in this new order of globalised business, also has a cost reaching far beyond that of individual aspiration and opportunity. The impact on family, community and social cohesion is at stake as the pursuit of neo-liberal economic rationality overshadows any discussion of the collective good. Moreover, social worth is increasingly couched in the language of responsibility and economic participation, thereby marginalising the contribution made by those engaged in 'alternative work' activities. It is interesting to note the changing language as we move from a discourse of citizens' rights to that of responsibilities. Responsible citizenship is primarily evidenced through an individual's engagement in the formal labour market, thereby avoiding the spectre of social exclusion. Tony Blair, British Prime Minister, notes in the foreword to a key report produced by the Social Exclusion Unit, 'The best defence against social exclusion is having a job and the best way to get a job is to have a good education with the right training and experience' (1999: 6).

This discourse also pervades the educational arena, where emphasis is placed on the individual, and on 'self-determination'. A clear example of this is the importance of 'personal effort' and 'rigour' to attain school success which permeates throughout the recently enacted Spanish education law (LEY ORGÁNICA 2002). The 'culture of effort' is considered an essential quality assurance element in education, besides evaluation and adequate teacher training.

The implication is clear, the needs and desires of society as a whole are subservient to the economic goals of capital accumulation. Failure or reluctance to make an economic contribution is therefore construed as deviant or disruptive behaviour. Yet what does this say to those who are not actively engaged in paid labour due to family responsibilities, cultural/religious beliefs, disability, age, or a decision to commit their life to socially useful work such as volunteering in the community or participation in protest movements? If the social conscience is to be recaptured, a restructuring of economic relations will be required to ensure a critical citizenship emerges that engages with individuals and members of diverse communities in a holistic way, recognising the value and worth of all, whilst also embracing the collective good.

Challenging career education and guidance

Clearly, career education and guidance is part of a wider political arena through which participants explore and examine multiple possibilities concerning their potential pathways through life. However, these pathways cannot be regarded as free, unfettered and equally available to all, as access to opportunity is subject to individual desires, social expectations and structural constraints. It is influenced by a range of particular discourses of power relations, and saturated by competing conceptions of social and economic reality. For some observers, the primary role of career education and guidance has been identified as a mechanism through which smooth transitions from education to work are facilitated, thereby enabling the labour market to function efficiently and effectively (Bridges 1998; Offer in Gothard *et al.* 2001: 83; Douglas 2004). In this scenario, career education and guidance adopts an instrumentalist role by ensuring that education and counselling provides '(R)ealistic, impartial information and advice – *embedded in the realities of the labour market*' (Stokes 1994, cited in Colley 2000: 17, emphasis added).

Career educators and guidance counsellors ultimately become duty bound to mediate in the aspirations of their clients to ensure that the 'right' choices are made within the context and realities of an inequitable, yet ostensibly acceptable, economic world. The need to demonstrate the economic benefits accruing from career education and guidance in order to secure government funding and support (Bysshe *et al.* 2002) further entrenches the view that its primary goals should be narrowly related to labour market productivity and participation. The uncritical acceptance of such goals acts to move discussion away from a wider exploration of the concept of work in advanced capitalist countries, consideration of inequality and justice, and ways in which human value and worth are socially derived (Irving and Marris 2002). Perpetuating the view that individuals are solely responsible for their actions and situations helps to '(S)hift the political focus away from the structural problems of underemployment, poverty, homelessness, under-funded welfare services and a degenerating environment' (Franklin 1998: 2).

Watts (1996) makes a profound, yet in many respects self-evident, statement in his identification of the political nature of career education and guidance. He writes that, '(w)ithin a society in which life chances are unequally distributed, it faces the issue of whether it serves to reinforce inequalities or to reduce them' (p.351). Not only is the myth of the neutral state exposed but the concept of impartiality is also brought into question (Young 1990). As discussed earlier, career educators and counsellors must seriously question whether professional impartiality or neutrality is ever possible; to consider which realities are to be presented; and to decide whether their practice will work to reinforce or reduce inequality. Assisting in the development of employability skills, helping with job search activity and identifying opportunities in the labour market is only a partial aspect of career education and counselling, and is of most relevance to those clients seeking to secure employment. There is a wider role, however, concerning the provision of support and encouragement to those 'Others' who are not engaged in paid employment, or wish to transgress from the economic doctrines of the state. This is especially pertinent if career educators and guidance counsellors are to provide effective support to clients who may 'have experiences of feeling lost, bewildered, confused, angry, stupid, rejected, misunderstood and redundant' (West 2003: 22). Moreover, asking young people in particular to uncritically develop the skills to self-manage uncertain, insecure, yet potentially boundaryless careers in isolation of a social context or the development of a broad understanding of this concept, paradoxically may lead to a heightened sense of powerlessness, with their lives constructed in relation to the vagaries of economic toil. This is noticeable when we begin our examination of the prevailing dominant economic ideology from the position of the least advantaged. Presenting the perspectives of already powerful and privileged groups in normative and neutral ways can serve to silence dissenting voices, or demean the experiences of oppressed individuals and groups (Young 1990), doing little to enable them to recognise their individual and collective power to influence and enact change. This is of particular importance for those engaged in the practice of career education and guidance counselling. Exposing the value-laden ideologies of the global labour market to scrutiny serves to ensure that the recipients of career learning are given an opportunity to explore alternative visions and develop their own understanding of 'career' within a lived context.

Giroux (1992) emphasises the importance of an empowering approach within education, defining this term as the ability to think and act critically. When applied to career educators and guidance counsellors, it requires them to become transformative intellectuals, concerned not only with state sanctioned knowledge (Apple 2000) but also the promotion of alternative and critical perspectives. As Apple (2001) asserts, 'the best way to understand what any set of institutions, policies, and practices does is to see it from the standpoint of those who have the least power' (p.197). Agreeing with Giroux's perspective on education, career educators and guidance counsellors must:

> explore the complexity of culture within power relations that both enable and silence students from diverse traditions. They must also address issues of inequality as they are structured within racial, gender and class relations and recognize the limitations of the politics of separation in waging collective struggle against various relations of oppression in their complexity and interrelatedness.
>
> (Giroux 1992: 246)

Whilst it is important to acknowledge that even the best intentioned career educator and guidance counsellor is likely to experience restrictions and limitations in pursuit of socially just outcomes from their work, this does not imply that there is no scope for action. As Beyer (2000) suggests, 'If education is a social practice, and responsible for social continuity, then it must also be seen as having a critical perspective, one that is open to social change as well as continuity' (p.37). Clearly, finding space to question dominant discourses is not always easy as it exposes professionals to reactionary claims that the presentation of alternative world-views is an act of naiveté based on simplistic assumptions, or prompted by self-interest (Young 1990). Yet failure to respond positively to this challenge leaves career education and guidance open to the charge that is has a strong tendency to act, albeit unintentionally perhaps, as a state agent.

Whilst much career theory has focused on the concept of self and opportunity, it is now timely to think more deeply about the need to embed a social justice philosophy that begins to 'overcome the deficiencies associated with a sanitized, depoliticized and ... neutralized perspective of social relations [and is] explicit about the sites of oppression ... and their interlocking nature...' (Irving *et al.* 2000: 176). A more holistic view of career education and guidance that not only works to improve the life of individuals, but also acknowledges its wider social responsibilities, is an essential prerequisite. This will require career professionals to become social activists (Irving and Marris 2002), moving beyond the relative safety of the school, college or counselling situation to expose and challenge social injustices within the wider community. By openly taking a critical stance as career educators and counsellors it will help to clarify our role in relation to choice and opportunity, and reassure those for whom we have a responsibility to educate, inform support and guide that we are working in the interests of both individuals and groups to secure just futures.

Exposing inequality: promoting social justice

By taking critical standpoints, the contributors in this book explore a range of issues in relation to inequality, injustice and social exclusion. The views expressed help to open up the debate around the impact of globalisation on individuals and diverse groups. Consideration is given to ways in which career education and guidance might actively enable, empower and promote the democratic engagement and inclusion of all sections of society in the shaping of their world(s). The chapters engage with both macro/global perspectives, and micro/local issues that affect the life chances and opportunities of young people and adults in increasingly uncertain times.

In Chapter 1, Barrie Irving focuses his attention on the concept of social justice and seeks to make sense of this in relation to career education and guidance. He argues that the adoption of a critical–recognitive social justice approach will help to ensure that those working within the career arena are able to engage with the lived realities of their clients. Whilst advocating fairer and more just society he also considers how this perspective may be put into practice. In the following chapter Fiona Douglas builds on this theme, looking more closely at career guidance and ways in which it is influenced by dominant models of welfare capitalism. She puts forward the view that both practitioner and manager need to be aware of how the wider socio-economic climate impacts on their work and, as a result, the need for them to become astute policy interpreters. Bill Law probes ideas about freedom, and finds some ideas more useful to career education and guidance practice than others. He also finds that the most useful ideas offer the most serious challenges to current practice.

The next two chapters look more closely at issues of cultural diversity and ethnicity, outlining how difference is presented and accommodated within career guidance and education. In Chapter 5, Malik and Aguado discuss the various ways in which schooling transmits dominant cultural norms to the detriment of those who hold different affiliations or values, and consider alternative courses of action. Concepts of ethnicity and culture are outlined and considered by Barker and Irving in Chapter 6. They then focus on the particular needs of Muslim girls in Britain in relation to choice and opportunity, and present a career education approach that is educationally sound and culturally sensitive.

Chapters 7 and 8 explore the dynamics of gender, focusing on the career needs of women. Patton and McMahon explore current definitions of women's careers and key issues that are relevant to a fuller understanding of women's career behaviour. Social justice concerns are discussed and implications for the practice of career education and guidance presented. Following on from this, Humphries and Dyer discuss equal opportunities and human rights discourses and the development of ethical capital practices, relating this to their own research on aspects of gender division within New Zealand society. They identify the need for critical theorists to propose and promote alternatives to market driven practices.

Paul Pagliano discusses ways in which children with disabilities risk being excluded and marginalised from the experiences enjoyed by those regarded as able-bodied. In his chapter he explores the potential for the development of an inclusive career education curriculum that accommodates students with disabilities. In the following chapter issues of social class, and how these contribute to the structuring of opportunity, are outlined and discussed by Ken Roberts. He questions whether career guidance professionals can have any real impact on class-based opportunity structures, arguing that they lack the power and influence to challenge dominant ideologies.

Social exclusion is the theme of the next two chapters. Nuria Manzano Soto considers some conceptual definitions of social exclusion and how these are constructed. She argues that the language of inclusion and social integration presents a more positive message and relates these to current debates within Europe concerning citizenship, and the need for effective comprehensive counselling programmes. The chapter by Hernández and Muñoz Riverohl focuses on current conceptions of equality and social justice promoted by the current Mexican government. They argue that it fails to meet the needs of its youth and consideration is given to the potential role of the guidance counsellor and educator in supporting and promoting a socially just agenda.

In Chapter 13, Hazel Reid discusses the concept of multiculturalism in the context of career guidance. She argues that career guidance training needs to adopt a more complex view of social justice and multiculturalism, and embed it in all of its practices. Current approaches towards the training of career guidance practitioners are examined, and changes suggested. Linden West, in the final chapter, draws his perspectives from auto/biographical research and argues for new meaning to be attached to the concept of career. He also advocates an approach towards the concept of career and guidance counselling that is culturally sensitive, narratively based and multi-disciplinary, grounded in notions of learner empowerment and critical awareness.

Bibliography

Apple, M.W. (2000) *Official Knowledge: Democratic Education in a Conservative Age*, 2nd edn, London: Routledge.

Apple, M.W. (2001) *Educating the 'Right' Way*, London: Routledge.

Beyer, L.E. (2000) '"Teacher education" and the "new professionalism": the case of the USA', in A. Scott and J. Freeman-Moir (eds) *Tomorrow's Teachers: International and Critical Perspectives on Teacher Education*, Canterbury: Canterbury University Press.

Bridges, W. (1998) 'Career development in a new key', *Careers Guidance Today*, 6(3): 9–14.

Bysshe, S., Hughes, D. and Bowes, L. (2002) *The Economic Benefits of Career Guidance: A Review of Current Evidence*, Derby: Centre for Guidance Studies.

Coffield, F. (2000) 'The three stages of lifelong learning: romance, evidence and implementation', in F. Coffield (ed.) *Differing Visions of a Learning Society: Research Findings. Volume 2*, Bristol: The Policy Press.

Colley, H. (2000) 'Deconstructing "realism" in career planning: how globalisation impacts on vocational guidance', in Institute of Career Guidance (ed.) *Constructing the Future: a Global Perspective*, Stourbridge: Institute of Career Guidance.

Darom, D. (2000) 'Humanistic values education: personal, interpersonal, social and political dimensions', in M. Leicester, M. Modgil and S. Modgil (eds) *Education, Culture and Values. Volume 6: Education and Citizenship*, London: Falmer.

Douglas, F. (2004) *Public Service: Private Agendas*, unpublished PhD thesis, London: Brunel University.

Franklin, J. (1998) 'Social policy in perspective', in J. Franklin (ed.) *Social Policy and Social Justice*, Cambridge: Polity Press.

Giroux, H. (1992) *Border Crossings: Cultural Workers and the Politics of Education*, New York: Routledge.

Gothard, B., Mignot, P., Offer, M. and Ruff, M. (2001) *Careers Guidance in Context*, London: Sage.

Irving, B.A. (1999) 'The role of initial teacher training in the promotion of a lifelong learning culture: a conflict of ideals?', *Education and Training*, 41(9): 416–424.

Irving, B.A., Barker, V., Parker-Jenkins, M. and Hartas, D. (2000) 'In pursuit of social justice: careers guidance provision for Muslim girls in England', *Revista Española de Orientación y Psicopedagogía*, 11(20): 173–186.

Irving, B.A. and Marris, L. (2002) 'A context for connexions: towards an inclusive framework', in Institute of Career Guidance (ed.) *Career Guidance: Constructing the Future. Social Inclusion: Policy and Practice*, Stourbridge: Institute of Career Guidance.

LEY ORGÁNICA 10/2002, de 23 de diciembre, de *Calidad de la Educación* (LOCE). Ministerio de Educación, Cultura y Deporte (MECD): Boletín Oficial del Estado (BOE) núm. 307 de 24/12/2002. Available on 'PDF' format at http://www.mecd.es/leycalidad/index.htm (last visited: 15 December 2003).

Rajan, A., Van Eupen, P. and Jaspers, A. (1997) *Britain's Flexible Labour Market, What Next?*, Southborough: Centre for Research and Technology in Europe.

Smith, C.S. (2002) 'A stocktake on the economics of vocational education and training in Australia', *Australian Journal of Career Development*, 11(2): 22–24.

Social Exclusion Unit (1999) *Bridging the Gap: New Opportunities for 16–18 year olds Not in Education, Training or Employment*, London: Stationery Office.

Tomlinson, S. (2001) *Education in a Post-Welfare Society*, Buckingham: Open University Press.

Watts, A.G. (1996) 'Socio-political ideologies in guidance', in A.G. Watts, B. Law, J. Killeen, J. Kidd and R. Hawthorne (eds) *Rethinking Careers Education and Guidance: Theory, Policy and Practice*, London: Routledge.

West, L. (2003) 'Challenging auto/biographies: careers and guidance in a 5 to 9 world', in A. Edwards (ed.) *Challenging Biographies: Re-locating the Theory and Practice of Careers Work*, Canterbury: Canterbury Christ Church University College.

Young, I.M. (1990) *Justice and the Politics of Difference*, Princeton: Princeton University Press.

Chapter 2

Social justice

A context for career education and guidance

Barrie A. Irving

Introduction

In a world characterised by technological development, the power of global capital, employment insecurity and the primacy of economic goals, the value and worth of individuals is increasingly measured in relation to their economic productiveness and contribution. This chapter questions the accepted realities of the global labour market, and ways in which human value and worth are measured against economic output. The concept of social justice is explored, and its varied interpretations outlined. Consideration is then given to the construction of career education and guidance in relation to compulsory schooling, and whether it serves to promote or restrict a socially just agenda. It is argued that career education and guidance places too much emphasis on the instrumentalist values associated with the demands of employers in a global labour market. The embedding of a critical–recognitive social justice philosophy that embraces difference and encourages critical and reflexive inquiry is explored, and it is asserted that by advocating for social change career education and guidance will contribute to the promotion of just outcomes for all. Finally, there is discussion about the extent to which the practices of career educators and guidance counsellors are constrained in their role as state agents, and the potential for them to become social activists is explored.

Making sense of social justice

Wherever they stand on the political spectrum, all parties lay claim to a belief in social justice. This in itself is evidence of the confusion and lack of cohesion that tends to surround this concept. The term social justice is used freely in a range of contexts and situations, yet what is meant by the term social justice, and where does it fit in relation to notions of equality? These key questions must be addressed if the veil of innocence is to be removed from the economic imperatives that underpin distributive models of social justice in contemporary western society.

Current political policy is ostensibly couched within a distributive model of social justice that encompasses:

> Two main principles, liberty, or individual freedom (to the extent that this is compatible with others); and the equal distribution of material and social goods (except where an unequal distribution would contribute to the well-being of those who have unfavourable starting positions).
>
> (Gale 2000: 254)

In practice, this is founded on a strong belief in the responsibilities and obligations of the individual, the adoption of meritocratic principles that reward success, and a free and unfettered working of the labour market. Any redistribution of wealth or removal of inequalities is only regarded as legitimate if the interests of the most vulnerable in society are affected, identified by Jordan (1998) as the Blair–Clinton orthodoxy. What comes through clearly is the view that social wellbeing is primarily a product of economic and individual success, therefore the welfare state must be restructured to reflect this reality. This is evident in government rhetoric through which justice is located within the language of economic efficiency and employability. Any radical redistribution of wealth is regarded by the Commission on Social Justice (CSJ) as a 'detrimental and inhibiting force ... in taking away things from successful people and giving them to the unsuccessful' (1994: 19). Further to this, the CSJ (1998) hold an interesting view concerning the relationship between society and the workings of the labour market. Whilst acknowledging that 'Social justice has a part to play in deciding how a market is constructed' (p.47), paradoxically perhaps they also assert that 'there is only one criterion of a just outcome of society, namely that it should be the product of the free market' (p.37). Interestingly, the CSJ do not propose that the labour market should be the product of, and its practices subject to, a democratic, inclusive and equitable society.

Lister (1998) observes a paradigm shift in UK government thinking as the discourse of equality is replaced with that of social inclusion and equality of opportunity. Conceptually, the distributive model of social justice has been constructed within the context of a global economy that emphasises competitiveness, compliance and compulsion. Active participation in the labour market, a re-iteration of the importance of family values (Jordan 1998), and a move away from a reliance on social mutuality and state-sponsored provision is occurring. The human capital and productive potential of individuals is given pride of place in the new economically driven social order. Attention is drawn to those aspects of social welfare that are regarded as a drain on the economic resources of the state, with particular reference to those recipients who are not economically productive. Further, emphasising social obligations rather than social rights is increasingly shifting attention away from the responsibilities of the state to safeguard, protect and promote the welfare of all of its citizens.

Within this world of shifting boundaries, legislative anti-discrimination procedures are put in place by governments to create the conditions through which inequitable practices in education, the labour market and elsewhere are influenced and challenged in a 'just' way. Justice, however, is translated as the provision of equality of opportunity, whereby the primary onus is placed on individuals to compete; to prove their ability; to challenge discrimination as it affects them personally; and to engage in the race for success in an open market for jobs. When considered alongside the prevailing discourse of social inclusion, which asserts that a good education, appropriate training and participation in paid employment is the best way to avoid exclusion (Social Exclusion Unit 1999), a meritocratic theme and normative modes of behaviour based on morality, employability and employment are evident (Jordan 1998). The role of the state becomes that of a benevolent umpire, there to manage the economic benefits accruing from the free market, mediating conflict between labour and employer; ensuring a steady supply of appropriately skilled labour; and redistributing wealth in a way that rewards success.

Yet it remains questionable as to whether the creation of a level playing field, or the adoption of a narrowly defined social inclusion agenda that is limited to labour market participation, can accommodate different needs and desires, and facilitate socially just outcomes that are fair and equitable for all. As Branson (1991) highlights with regards to education, 'Equality of opportunity, success through individually-based intelligence and aptitude, achievement through free and equal competition, these are the ideologies . . . which blind people to the structural inequalities fundamental to capitalist production' (p.92). Inequality remains, as issues of oppression and disadvantage centred on class, gender, race-ethnicity, disability and so forth (Young 1990; Branson 1991; Irving and Marris 2002) are embedded within social, political and economic institutions, and continue to be acted out in all aspects of everyday life. An ideological reinforcement of inequalities in wealth, influence and power, resulting from unfettered capital practices and meritocratic reward, serves to ensure that those who control any redistribution of goods and services are able to do so secure in the knowledge that their own interests are preserved.

Alternative visions of social justice that start from the standpoint of the least advantaged (Gale 2000), engage with critical perspectives (Apple 2000, Irving *et al.* 2000), and focus on concepts of oppression and domination rather than distribution (Young 1990) are possible however. Such visions embrace the view that diverse groups must be included in all major social institutions, and provided with opportunities to participate in decision-making processes, without giving up their values and beliefs (Gale and Densmore 2000). Young asserts that there should be 'the socially substantive opportunity for all to develop and exercise their capacities and realise their choices' (1990: 34). This impacts both on the individual and members of diverse cultural and social groups. Gale and Densmore (2000: 19) advocate a recognitive form of social justice that requires three necessary conditions:

- The fostering of respect for different social groups through their self-identification.
- Opportunities for their self-development and self-expression.
- The participation of groups in making decisions that directly concern them, through their representatives on determining bodies.

There is a risk, however, that social and cultural difference could become essentialised and reified, thereby creating an aura of impassability. For some individuals, such as those with learning difficulties, this may also be particularly problematic 'partly because of their difficulty in developing a shared sense of identity and solidarity and also because it is not evident that learning difficulties lend themselves to celebration' (Riddell *et al.* 2001: 44). Hence the limitations associated with the imposition of a universal or one-dimensional view of social justice. The politics of difference acknowledges that individuals construct a fluid self-identity in a lively interplay with their membership of diverse social groups, in relation to gender, religious beliefs, class and such like. Drawing on the work of Gale and Densmore (2000), Irving *et al.* (2000) take a more critical stance, arguing that social justice is not only dialogical and based on group recognition and self-respect within and between groups, but that it is also relational. Explicitly acknowledging sites of oppression, removing the gap between the privileged and the oppressed (Young 1990), requires us to identify fractures within and between groups that share a common label, such as women, or have a sense of belonging based on cultural practices. Diverse social and cultural groups, including those of the majority culture, must be open to, and be prepared to engage in, internal and external critique (Parekh 2000). It is also important to note that membership of these groups is not fixed, individuals may choose to identify with one or more at the same time, and in relation to context. This can be seen in the work of Parker-Jenkins *et al.* (1999) who studied the career guidance needs of Muslim girls.

It is this complexity that adds to the richness of the critical–recognitive social justice perspective. As Irving and Marris assert:

> For social justice to be meaningful it cannot be reduced to acts of retribution, which punish individuals who fail to conform, or which

> position people as gracious beneficiaries who remain thankful to others for a redistribution of goods – a mechanism by which the powerful retain a paternalistic responsibility for the 'masses'. Nor can reliance be placed on tokenistic methods of consultation which fail to include the views of diverse groups in the formulation of policy and action.
>
> (2002: 140)

If a democratic and participative form of social justice is to be achieved, there will be a need to create the conditions that allow for a widening of participation and openness in dialogue to ensure that the voices and concerns of all are not only heard but also acknowledged. We all have a responsibility for creating the conditions to allow this, academic and professional alike. Regarding democratic engagement, this will require the development of a critical political citizenship. Engaging in critique, questioning and challenging the policies and actions of the state, and discussing and exploring our own culturally derived practices, should provide real evidence of a well-informed inclusive society that is working for the collective good. The introduction of a form of communicative dialogue will complement and aid this transformative process, thereby facilitating a healthy discussion and debate about social, political and economic goals, and how these might be achieved. By giving due recognition to varied experiences, embracing cultural differences, accepting competing perspectives, and respecting all contributions equally (Young 1995), a consensus might be reached that is acceptable to, and accommodates, the views and desires of diverse groups. The agenda therefore can no longer be driven by economic rationalist arguments if a holistic view of social existence is to be adopted. Incorporating all aspects of living, not only those activities that are economically valued, will contribute a broader understanding and valuing of social and human worth.

Shifting boundaries: (re)constructing career education and guidance

Traditionally the concept of career has been constructed around 'progression up an ordered hierarchy within an organization or profession' (Watts 1991: 1), as distinct from entry into a job with few or no prospects. Within the realms of career theory, recognition is increasingly being given to the interrelationship between the individual and society (Patton and McMahon 1999) in the shaping of career and decisions taken about present and future possibilities. The notion of individual choice, which is ideologically bound in liberal and psychological explanations, is slowly giving way to an acceptance that cultural and structural influences are also at play (see Chapter 13 by Reid). For Peavey (2001), the understanding of self and the creation of our life-plan occurs through our interactions with others as we move in a social world, develop new capacities, and engage in activities to which we ourselves ascribe meaning. This is a significant shift away from dominant psychological constructs that have tended to view choice, opportunity, and change in relation to individual attributes and self-focused goals (Harris 1999).

The breakdown of traditional employment routes has helped to create a climate in which career can be reconceptualised in a holistic way, incorporating all aspects of the messy cycle of life. As the public world of employment and private world of family and community become intertwined, career is taking on a lateral, boundaryless form (Collin 2000), through which a broader understanding of work and opportunity is emerging. Ruff observes, 'there is a growing recognition that our understanding of career needs to be both inclusive, embracing the multiple dimensions of the lives of individuals, and exclusive, promoting learning about the world of work, community and adult life' (in Gothard *et al.* 2000: 97).

Career education has enjoyed an elevated status in recent years as it is seen to have an important role in preparing young people to self-manage their career in a changing and uncertain world (McCowan and McKenzie 1997; Ruff in Gothard *et al.* 2001). It is clear that career education operates in a highly political arena (Watts 1996; Harris 1999), and in its current form faces contestation on a number of fronts. Firstly, there is a distinct lack of clarity in this curriculum area (Harris 1999) as it wavers between preparation for work and preparation for adult life. Secondly, it continues to focus on individual aspiration and self-awareness within a monocultural educational framework (NIACE 1997; Gundara 2000; Lievano 2000) that tends to neglect social and cultural dimensions. Finally the educational aspect is overshadowed by competency-based behaviourist approaches that, for example, give primacy to preparation for, rather than a critical exploration of, the labour market (Mignot in Gothard *et al.* 2001).

With reference to the first contestation, career education exists as a fuzzy concept, lacking clarity with regards to what its assumptions and practices are based on. Whilst McCowan and McKenzie (1997) assert that career education is underpinned by a strong theoretical base heavily informed by career theory, this is challenged by both Ruff (in Gothard *et al.* 2001) and Harris (1999). Ruff argues that, in the UK, career education is not only ill-defined and lacking a body of knowledge, but also has no national programme of study that would help give it some clear sense of direction. This is advanced further by Harris (1999) who identified from her research in English schools that career education is primarily defined by government through policy statements and interventions. Moreover, she argues, government-sponsored definitions of career education are riddled with ambiguity, which leaves both the knowledge base and practitioner uncertain and confused. Preparation for work, by which we might read employment, cannot be regarded in the same way as preparation for adult life that might encompass a multiplicity of pathways and experiences only tangentially related to labour market participation.

Concerning the continued focus of career education on the development of self-awareness and self-esteem, this is influenced by humanistic psychology, whereby self as individual takes precedence over self as collective (Kerka 1998). Whilst there are few who would challenge the view that an understanding of, and positive regard for, self is of value, the construction of self-identity does not occur in a vacuum. Consideration of self and career must be considered alongside the social and cultural influences that shape subjective realities (Ruff in Gothard *et al.* 2001, Pouwhare and Mortlock 2002) and inform the stories we tell to ourselves, about ourselves. Moreover, with reference to self-esteem, biased interpretations as to what counts as 'positive' reinforces the values of the dominant culture at the expense of those with different or collective ways of being. As Gale and Densmore observe, 'Anglo perceptions of sex roles, conditioned by the emphasis that western societies place on individualism, can effectively undermine the self-esteem that Indo–Chinese females in Australia derive from their family roles and traditional networks of support' (2000: 131). Structural inequalities and the effects of discrimination can remain hidden as feeling good about *yourself* may serve to mask the reasons that lie behind the social positioning of the 'Other' (Young 1990), and fail to provide the insights that enable dominant discourses to be exposed and challenged.[1]

Finally, and most crucially, there is a need to question the extent to which career education embraces an educational perspective, as opposed to the application of competency-based behaviourist approaches that seek to instil ideologically loaded values regarding learning and work. The work of McCowan and McKenzie (1997) helps to illuminate this ongoing debate. Whilst they explore the concept of work in society, and acknowledge that employment should be set within the context of personal development, career is ultimately defined in relation to progression in learning and work. They are not on their own – the current consultation draft from the Department for Education and Skills (2002) in England defines career education as helping 'young people develop the knowledge and skills they need to make successful choices, manage transitions in learning and move into work' (p.2). Colley (2000) observes, however, that career education and guidance in schools has given weight to 'behaviourist models of competence-based education and training justified by the demands of the globalized economy' (pp.16–17). There is little to suggest that current career education approaches expose young people to alternative opportunities and ways of being; prepare them to become critical learners and workers;

connect with active citizenship; provide space to question inequitable labour market practices; promote democratic engagement; or advocate the pursuit of critical–recognitive socially just goals.

Agreeing with Tomlinson, for career education to lay claim to educational credentials it should be 'help[ing] people to make sense of global changes, combat[ting] any resurgent nationalism and mov[ing] beyond tawdry subservience to market forces' (2001: 171). This will enable students to learn to act both in and on their worlds. Skills, knowledge and attitudes (Killeen and Kidd 1991) are not the total sum of education, and are more akin to competency-based models of training, more so if lacking a critical edge. Knowledge cannot be considered to be neutral as it is politically, economically and socially derived (Apple 2000), steeped in particular values and ideologies. There is therefore need to remain constantly vigilant concerning the prominence given to particular issues if we are not to promote versions of reality constructed in the narrow instrumental interests of capital (Colley 2000), that are then presented as incontrovertible truths. As Giroux (1992: 18) asks, 'are schools to uncritically serve and reproduce the existing society or challenge the social order to develop and advance its democratic imperatives?' If career education remains primarily focused on the development of employability skills that reflect the 'social norms of behaviour and self-presentation which are strongly gender, ethnic and class specific' (Mignot in Gothard *et al.* 2001: 128), the answer is painfully clear.

Whilst much of the discussion has focused on career education, career guidance has also been subject to the same shifting discourses concerning the concept of career, and policy rhetoric of the state. The artificial divide between the two, however, serves to weaken any understanding of the inextricable relationship between career education and career guidance. A particular strength of career guidance within compulsory education is the unique position it occupies, operating at the interface between school, community and the labour market. However, it faces considerable challenges in establishing its credentials as a champion of social justice.

> Career guidance has become trapped between two worlds ... On the one hand it seeks to provide support to individuals who are attempting to find their own pathways within the world, and on the other has become hostage to the economic vagaries of the labour market, charged with ensuring that the wheels of industry continue to turn unimpeded.
>
> (Irving 2001: 11)

The introduction of the Connexions initiative in England, based on an influential report by the Social Exclusion Unit (1999), has seen a restructuring of career guidance provision. In response to concerns that some young people are at risk of social exclusion or marginalisation, career guidance activity is now focused on ensuring that they receive the help they need to overcome personal barriers that restrict their opportunities in the labour market (Irving and Marris 2002). As Watts (2001) identifies, social exclusion has placed a moral obligation on those without jobs to participate in formal learning, education and training. This mirrors the prominence given to preparation for work and learning in career education, and reflects a model of equality of opportunity that implies that the only barrier to success is yourself. Ultimately such limiting viewpoints restrict opportunities for the client and guidance counsellor to explore meaningful alternatives to formal learning and work, question labour market practices, identify structural inequalities and devise strategies to challenge these.

Putting social justice into practice

Whilst the rhetoric of career education and guidance appears to reflect a desire to prepare young people for work and adult life (Harris 1999), or as workers and citizens (DfEE/QCA 2000), the reality is somewhat different. Career is currently constructed in a narrowly defined manner that stresses the development of career management skills (SCAA 1996), and emphasises continued engagement in formal learning or labour market participation. From a critical–recognitive social justice perspective, little room is left for any deep and meaningful examination about what actually constitutes work, how its value is measured, and who decides what (and who) is worthy. This serves the function of restricting exploration of alternative possibilities, distancing those who, for whatever reason, do not engage in paid employment and formal learning. Moreover it acts to reinforce a normative social framework derived from the demands of global capital.

If career education and guidance is to create 'an environment to enable individuals to learn about themselves, and to connect their developing ideas, needs and aspirations to the adult world' (Ruff in Gothard *et al.* 2001: 99), it will also need to engage in something much more socially and educationally relevant. What is missing in the current discourse is the relationship between career learning and the development of active citizens who are able to locate their understanding of self, work and opportunity within a socially just and relevant critical educative framework. This will enable them to assess and evaluate the influences at play in the wider society (Darom 2000).

A radical rethink of the overall aim and purpose of career education and guidance is urgently required therefore to enable it to respond positively to a rapidly changing social, political and economic landscape, and prepare young people appropriately for life in an uncertain world. Building on the writings of Irving and Raja (1998), Harris (1999) and Ruff (in Gothard *et al.* 2001), a reconstructed model of career education emerges, encompassing three key dimensions:

- opportunity awareness (that looks wider than progression in education and employment through the inclusion of alternative pathways);
- self and social awareness (concerned with the development of a sense of individual, collective and cultural being);
- critical understanding (that examines and interrogates the various political, economic and social discourses that influence the construction and distribution of work, and impacts on how we might shape our collective futures and live out our lives).

In this scenario, career education does not simply link with, or overlap, a number of other curriculum areas such as citizenship, PSHE (personal, social and health education), work-related education and work experience (Ruff in Gothard *et al.* 2001). Career education becomes the defining rationale as all of these aspects are incorporated into a holistic broad-based curriculum area. Career is no longer reduced to employability, jobs, training and education, but reflects the changing nature of modern day living, along with opportunities for the creation of multiple identities, recognition of diversity, positive regard for difference, and potential for social action. Adopting such a framework may go some way in redressing the traditional representations of career that continue to dominate in the everyday world.

Overcoming the theory–practice divide by creating opportunities for academics and practitioners to spend more time listening to and learning from each other (Darom 2000) will serve to make theory useful, and ensure practice is informed. By broadening this activity beyond those who work in the current career arena, through the inclusion of others from related professions (such as health, social welfare, the police and youth work), an insight into differing philosophies and practices can be gained, leading to greater understanding and the identification of possibilities for collaborative action. Added to this, the development of communicative partnerships and relationships (Young 1990) and active networks (Douglas 2002) which enable career education and guidance professionals to work more proactively within and alongside communities (Jordan 1998: Irving and Marris 2002) in pursuit of shared initiatives, objectives and struggles, will also help to establish a deeper sense of belonging. Engaging in dialogue and debate at the local level, within schools, with parents, community groups, employers and others, can also provide a mechanism through which issues of equity and social justice can be exposed, explored, and debated, and also used to inform institutional and national policies and practices (Donnison 1998).

Career education and guidance, therefore, must be founded on clearly established moral and ethical principles, set within a critical socio–political context, and informed by the lived realities of young people and their communities (Beane and Apple 1999). For this to be effective, career educators and guidance counsellors will need to align themselves more closely with an educational philosophy that broadens the mind, encourages exploration, inquiry and reflexivity, and aids 'the development of actively informed citizens' (Parker-Jenkins *et al.* forthcoming). Moreover, greater importance must be attached to their professional role as transformative intellectuals who are striving to progress equitable and socially just outcomes, if they are no longer to be viewed as state agents with a primary role of upholding or defending the values and ideologies of the status quo. This fits comfortably with Mignot's argument that:

> Anti-oppressive practice is based on a conscious awareness of the various forms of oppression and discrimination present within society. It involves practitioners in actively seeking opportunities to challenge and undermine sexism, racism, ageism, disablism and other forms of oppression that may be encountered in their day-to-day practice. This requires the practitioner to adopt a critical view of their own and other practice, and of the institutions within which they work.
>
> (in Gothard *et al.* 2001: 117)

This particularly powerful statement serves to reinforce the moral and ethical responsibilities of career educators and guidance counsellors to actively promote socially just imperatives in the collective and individual interests of their clients.

Just deserts?

Current government policy rhetoric places significant emphasis on lifelong learning, the importance of self-directed career management, the acquisition of employability skills, and the need to acquire appropriate training and relevant qualifications. Whilst education has been given the responsibility of ensuring that tomorrow's workforce is steeped in the 'right' virtues, values and behaviours, careers work is regarded as a key player in the reinforcement of this. Somewhat paradoxically, Hughes and Peck (2002) comment that young people expect career advisers to have 'a wide range of knowledge of jobs and those who succeed in them' (p.14). Continued emphasis on individual choice, opportunities for all, the importance of success, and fair competition within the context of a free and open labour market, feeds into this reductive turn. Everyday explanations and limiting perceptions will be hard to shift until the concept of career, and role of career education and guidance, is clearly articulated and accepted by all sections of society. This will require a move away from humanistic liberal discourses that position the individual as an isolated actor, primarily unaffected by social experience and structural constraints.

The language of equality of opportunity has served to mask deeper social divisions and injustices, presenting simplistic individualistic solutions to complex socially located problems. Current conceptions of social justice, steeped within the values of liberalism and benevolence, have shown themselves to be ineffectual in the creation of a democratic, participative and inclusive society. Whilst career educators and guidance counsellors may be subject to the discourses of the state, they do not necessarily need to be ensnared by the rhetoric. The lack of clarity surrounding the role of career education and guidance, resulting from the confusion and contradictions in current policy, provides spaces for those who wish to build their programmes and practices around a critical–recognitive socially just framework.

By opening up discussion, facilitating participative dialogue, ensuring in particular that the interests of those with least power are progressed, and actively exposing and challenging injustice and inequality, an environment is created whereby career is no longer regarded as an aspect of life, but encapsulates how lives are lived. Reconstructing career education and redefining guidance will not sit easily with some. Yet if we fail to engage with this debate, and seek to inform and effect change wherever we can, what hope is there for the citizens of tomorrow?

Note

1 For more on the ways in which culturally dominant values can impact on self-esteem see the work of Young (1990) with regards to people of Chinese and Puerto Rican backgrounds in America; Cornwall (1995) in relation to young people with physical disabilities; Haw (2000) in her discussion of social exclusion and Muslim girls in Britain; and Pouwhare and Mortlock (2002) concerning the Maori community in New Zealand.

Bibliography

Apple, M.W. (2000) *Official Knowledge: Democratic Education in a Conservative Age*, 2nd edn, London: Routledge.

Beane, J.A. and Apple, M.W. (1999) 'The case for democratic schools', in M.W. Apple and J.A. Beane (eds) *Democratic Schools*, Buckingham: Open University Press.

Branson, J. (1991) 'Gender, education and work', in J. Ahier and G. Esland (eds) *Education, Training and the Future of work 1: Social, Political and Economic Contexts of Policy Development*, London: Routledge in association with the Open University Press.

Colley, H. (2000) 'Deconstructing "realism" in career planning: how globalisation impacts on vocational guidance', in Institute of Career Guidance (ed.) *Career*

Guidance: Constructing the Future, a Global Perspective, Stourbridge: Institute of Career Guidance.

Collin, A. (2000) 'A reconceptualisation of career: implications for careers guidance and education', in Institute of Career Guidance (ed.) *Career Guidance: Constructing the Future, a Global Perspective*, Stourbridge: Institute of Career Guidance.

Commission On Social Justice (1994) *Social Justice: Strategies for National Renewal*, London: Vintage.

—— (1998) 'What is social justice?', in J. Franklin (ed.) *Social Policy and Social Justice*, Cambridge: Polity Press.

Cornwall, J. (1995) *Choice, Opportunity and Learning: Educating Young People who are Physically Disabled*, London: David Fulton.

Darom, D. (2000) 'Humanistic values education: personal, interpersonal, social and political dimensions', in M. Leicester, M. Modgil and S. Modgil (eds) *Education, Culture and Values. Volume 6: Education and Citizenship*, London: Falmer.

Department for Education and Employment/Qualifications Curriculum Authority (2000) *The National Curriculum: Handbook for Secondary Teachers in England*, London: DfEE/QCA.

Department for Education and Skills (2002) *National Specification for Careers Education and Guidance: Consultation Draft*, June, London: DfES.

Donnison, D. (1998) *Policies for a Just Society*, Basingstoke: Macmillan.

Douglas, F. (2002) 'Making connections: developing networks for effective practice', in Institute of Career Guidance (ed.) *Career Guidance: Constructing the Future. Social Inclusion: Policy and Practice*, Stourbridge: Institute of Career Guidance.

Gale, R. (2000) 'Rethinking social justice in schools: how will we recognize it when we see it?', *International Journal of Inclusive Education*, 4(3): 253–269.

Gale, T. and Densmore, K. (2000) *Just Schooling: Explorations in the Cultural Politics of Teaching*, Buckingham: Open University Press.

Giroux, H. (1992) *Border Crossings: Cultural Workers and the Politics of Education*, New York: Routledge.

Gothard, B., Mignot, P., Offer, M. and Ruff, M. (2001) *Careers Guidance in Context*, London: Sage.

Gundara, J.S. (2000) *Interculturalism, Education and Inclusion*, London: Paul Chapman.

Harris, S. (1999) *Careers Education: Contesting Policy and Practice*, London: Paul Chapman.

Haw, K. (2000) 'Border tensions: skirmishes around the term exclusion', in G. Walraven, C. Parsons, D. van Veen and C. Day (eds) *Combating Social Exclusion Through Education: Laissez-faire, Authoritarianism or Third Way?* Leuven: Garant.

Hughes, D. and Peck, D. (2002) 'Removing barriers: extending the boundaries', *Career Guidance Today*, 10(6): 14–15.

Irving, B.A. (2001) 'Transforming career guidance training: towards a socially just approach', paper presented at an education staff seminar, James Cook University, Queensland.

Irving, B.A., Barker, V., Parker-Jenkins, M. and Hartas, D. (2000) 'In pursuit of social justice: careers guidance provision for Muslim girls in England', *Revista Española De Orientación Y Psicopedagogia*, 11(20): 173–186.

Irving, B.A. and Marris, L. (2002) 'A context for connexions: towards an inclusive framework', in Institute of Career Guidance (ed.) *Career Guidance: Constructing the Future. Social Inclusion: Policy and Practice*, Stourbridge: Institute of Career Guidance.

Irving, B.A. and Raja, S. (1998) 'Career education in a changing world of work', *Australian Journal of Career Development*, 7(3): 28–31.

Jordan, B. (1998) *The New Politics of Welfare*, London: Sage.

Kerka, S. (1998) 'Career development, race and class', *ERIC Digest no. 19*, Ohio: EDRS.

Killeen, J. and Kidd, J. (1991) *Learning Outcomes of Guidance: A Review of Recent Research*, Research paper no. 85, London, Department of Employment.

Lievano, B.M. 'Intercultural competencies and strategies in guidance: tools for intervention in schools', Paper presented at the International Association of Educational and Vocational Guidance Conference, Berlin, August–September 2000.

Lister, R. (1998) 'From equality to social inclusion: new labour and the welfare state', *Critical Social Policy 55*, 8(2): 215–225.

McCowan, C. and McKenzie, M. (1997) *The Guide to Career Education*, North Sydney: New Hobson.

National Institute of Adult and Continuing Education (1997) *Learning to Live in a Multi-cultural Society*, Leicester: NIACE.

Parekh, B. (2000) *Rethinking Multiculturalism*, Basingstoke: Macmillan.

Parker-Jenkins, M., Hartas, D., Irving, B.A. and Barker, V. (1999) *The Careers Service and Young Muslim Women*, Sheffield: Department for Education and Employment.

Parker-Jenkins, M., Hartas, D. and Irving, B.A. (forthcoming 2004) *In Good Faith: Schools, Religion and Public Funding*, Aldershot: Ashgate.

Patton, W. and McMahon, M. (1999) *Career Development and Systems Theory: A New Relationship*, Pacific Grove, CA: Brooks/Cole.

Peavey, V. (2001) 'New visions of counselling in the 21st century', *Australian Journal of Career Development*, 10(2): 15–22.

Pouwhare, M. and Mortlock, S. (2002) 'Career Intelligence – Alternative Ways of Knowing', paper presented at New Zealand Careers Services/rapuara conference on the Heightened Role of Career Planning in Knowledge Societies, Wellington, November.

Riddell, S., Baron, S. and Wilson, A. (2001) *The Learning Society and People with Learning Disabilities*, Bristol: Policy Press.

Schools Curriculum Assessment Authority (1996) *Skills for Choice*, London: SCAA.

Social Exclusion Unit (1999) *Bridging the Gap: New Opportunities for 16 to 18 Year Olds Not in Education, Training or Employment*, London: Stationery Office.

Tomlinson, S. (2001) *Education in a Post-welfare Society*, Buckingham: Open University Press.

Watts, A.G. (1991) 'The impact of the "New Right": policy challenges confronting careers guidance in England and Wales', *British Journal of Guidance and Counselling*, 19(3): 230–245.

—— (1996) 'Socio-political ideologies in guidance', in A.G. Watts, B. Law,

J. Killeen, J. Kidd and R. Hawthorne (eds) *Rethinking Careers Education and Guidance: Theory, Policy and Practice*, London: Routledge.

—— (2001) 'Career guidance and social exclusion: a cautionary tale', *British Journal of Guidance and Counselling*, 29(2): 1–30.

Young, I.M. (1990) *Justice and the Politics of Difference*, Princeton: Princeton University Press.

—— (1995) 'Communication and the other: beyond deliberative democracy', in M. Wilson and A. Yeatman (eds) *Justice and Identity: Antipodean Practices*, Wellington: Bridget Williams Books.

Chapter 3

Welfare to work

Economic challenges to socially just career guidance practice

Fiona Douglas

Introduction

Career guidance in the west has a clear underpinning ethos of individual choice and defends the concept of the practitioner as 'honest broker'. Guidance theory draws predominantly upon psychological models emanating from America, but guidance practitioners and recipients exist in varying political, economic and social environments and work–welfare relationships. This influences the content and process of guidance in overt and covert ways. Managers and practitioners must help the individual and coincidentally meet objectives set by the state.

This chapter explores this contradictory and paradoxical role by examining the affect on guidance practice of models of welfare capitalism and the implications this has for socially just guidance practice.

The term 'guidance practitioner' encompasses all aspects of career work including guidance, counselling and education.

Economic demands and social justice

Late twentieth and early twenty-first century capitalism deifies business over the needs of citizens and communities. This 'business ethic' percolates through to countries that have different values and is part of a homogenising globalisation process.

This process can be explained as:

1 The end of organised capitalism caused in part by the ascendance of large monopolies and consequent demise in 'control and regulation by individual nation states' (Lash and Urry 1987: 5).
2 A response to economic boom–bust cycles by the New Right who introduced market-driven, anti statist policies (Clarke and Newman 1997) aimed at reducing public spending on welfare, passing this cost and responsibility over to individuals. Lemke (2000: 6) calls this an economic reality, 'a triumph of capitalism over the state'.

3 Part of 'Third Way' ideology, moving away from the Washington Consensus that equated effective economic management with free markets (Eichbaum and Harris 1999) towards alliances or 'partnerships' with 'big business' particularly to pay for capital-intensive welfare projects.

Each seeks to shift responsibility for welfare provision from the state to the individual, with access to benefit dependent on self-help and labour market participation. These *economic* demands translate into social policy. This is welfare capitalism and this affects significantly the relationship between career guidance and social justice.

The critical framework

In order to establish the relationship between career guidance and the political, economic and social issues of welfare capitalism, I have devised a framework that brings together three key elements: the *activity*, *context*, and *macro-environment* of career guidance (see fig. 3.1). The *activity* of guidance encompasses the interaction between guidance practitioner and client, using skills based on a body of theoretical knowledge. The *context* of guidance is the influence of the client's life stage, family, school, peers, employment etc. and of internal organisational issues such as management and staffing levels. These make up the micro-environment of guidance. The *macro-environment* comprises political, economic, social and technological influences. This chapter explores the macro-environment and examines its influence on the micro.

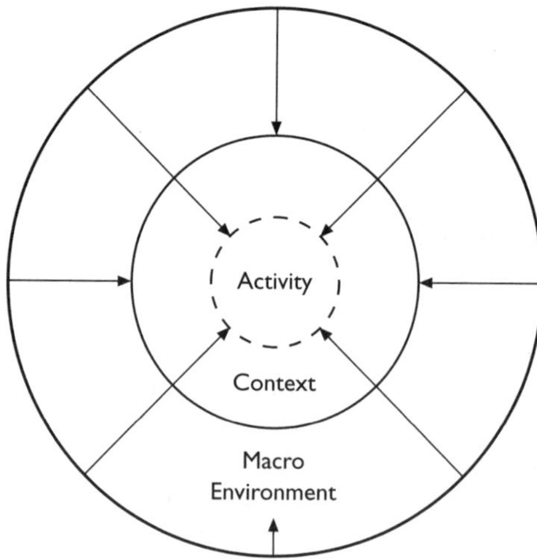

Figure 3.1 The critical framework.

Guidance practitioners and managers operate at the micro level, preoccupied with the activity of guidance and organisational survival. Outcome-driven funding mechanisms encourage this. Macro level issues may leave practitioners and managers feeling inadequate, unable to influence, and uncomfortable engaging with wider political issues. The framework outlined above enables an examination of overt and covert influences affecting career guidance practice and its management, allowing the reader to engage critically with the wider influences on career guidance.

Influences on career guidance practice

Career guidance has strong social origins, used by educationalists, social workers and philanthropists to help pupils, particularly those from less socially advantaged backgrounds, make the most of their lives (Heginbotham 1951). Despite this, the predominating influence is psychological, particularly in matching traits to occupations.

The *activity* of guidance (see fig. 3.1) requires first-class interpersonal skills, since practitioners must engage easily with a wide range of clients. The use of counselling techniques and methodology predominates, and increasing internationalisation (OECD 2002a) homogenises and standardises the process.

The *macro-environment* (see fig. 3.1) of career guidance is less homogeneous. Significant differences exist between national cultures, economies and social policies, all of which impact on the *context* and *activities* of career guidance. Practitioners and managers may experience co-incidental pressure to meet the individual's needs and those of the state, but their influence focuses predominantly on the individual 'client' rather than on policy or policy-makers.

Within this environment, the concept of career choice has become increasingly individualistic, preoccupied with individual interactions based on individualistic psychological models. Why is this? Killeen (1996) identifies three elements present in career theory: the *agent*: 'the person who acts' (p.24), the *environment*: the place 'where careers are made' (p.27) and *action*: 'what the agent does' (p.29). I contend that much of guidance practice focuses around the agent and the action, or the *activity* of guidance (see fig. 3.1), drawing heavily upon psychological models (see for example Rogers 1951; Super 1957; Holland 1985; Egan 1997).

The focus on the individual emphasises the undoubtedly essential interpersonal skills practitioners require. This introspective nature of career guidance is both encouraged and facilitated by the uni-directional pressure on the *activity* of guidance (see fig. 3.1) from the *macro-environment*. This comes via social policy, which is in turn influenced by international economic decisions such as the Washington consensus.

Two different and sometimes opposing paradigms exist. Psychological models imply that intellect, aptitude and ability are the most significant career choice and achievement factors. Sociological perspectives recognise the impact of the wider socio-political environment on career 'choice' (Roberts 1971, 1984, 1993). Killeen (1996) argues that these two 'environmental dimensions' dominate the guidance discourse in western countries, and good practitioners are aware of the interaction between them. This interaction between the *context* and the *macro-environment* requires practitioners to identify and understand their own standpoint.

Self-determination is central to many psychologically based guidance models, which assume freedom of *choice* in an environment that enables choice to be realised. The ideal outcome of career intervention from a western perspective is for individuals to control their choice. In England, the introduction of *personal* advisers who facilitate *individual* solutions to *individual* problems is a response to such individualism. Whilst career guidance seeks to perpetuate the ethos of individualism and defends its perceived role of the 'honest broker', the whole process is problematised. Particular individuals are targeted as having problems that the guidance practitioner helps to rectify. From a political and economic perspective, arguably, the goal is to have conforming, compliant citizens. Behind the guidance practitioner's role is a conformist agenda based on models of welfare capitalism that calls into question the whole 'honest broker' concept.

Psychological approaches function within politically, economically and socially constructed paradigms, emanating from capitalist economic systems of the west. Preoccupation with the individual disregards this wider political, socio-economic environment allowing it to develop unquestioningly and unchallenged. Essential work by Roberts (1971, 1984, 1993), amongst others, demonstrates how this affects career guidance clients.

This situation induces a culture of *practitioner* and *managerial* compliance with social policy. Guidance managers receive instructions from governmental ministries or agencies; these remain largely unchallenged in order to ensure organisational survival. This inhibits a culture of dialogue with policy-makers and prevents practitioners or managers from informing them. Strong, socially aware and articulate *professional* bodies could counter this, but they are marginalised or sidelined; there is no place for professional questioning and dissent. This is discussed later.

Welfare capitalism and career guidance

This section examines why governments are interested in career guidance work. It identifies economic reasons as predominating and examines the relationship between welfare capitalism and career guidance work. It introduces the factors present in the macro-environment and paves the way for more in-depth evaluation of career guidance and welfare capitalism.

Career guidance operates in a complex and changing environment where economic issues and world markets predominate. The cyclical boom–bust economies in the west and Asia, the fall of the iron curtain, the west's increasing economic interest in China and technological developments all influence labour markets and, eventually, career choice.

Recent interest in career guidance emanates from national economic benefits, not the 'helping' motive. The 'economic value' of career guidance (Killeen *et al.* 1992) prompted intense UK governmental interest and intervention. The writers price tagged guidance, or rather the lack of it, proposing the national cost of the 1.2 million people under the age of 30 who 'lack useful labour market qualifications' was '£350 million per annum' without lost tax revenue or production (p.24). Such figures, combined with increasingly complex and competitive global labour markets (Beck 1992; Bauman 1999) fuelled government interest.

This is not just a UK phenomenon. On an international level, a ministerial adviser in New Zealand spoke of career guidance as a means 'to help us get more from the population' ensuring better matches between not only skills and opportunities, but also aspirations and economic development (Douglas 2004). The OECD is interested in career guidance and economic development for similar reasons, stating that 'effective career education and guidance systems ... can help to make the best use of human resources in the labour market as well as in education' (OECD 2002a: 1).

Governments are increasingly interested in the relationship between employment and welfare provision. In many Anglo-American countries, welfare is becoming increasingly liberalised, with governments adopting active policies for citizens to work rather than claim benefit. Career guidance systems have an important place here, as the OECD comments, '*They [career guidance systems] are important elements in active welfare to work policies*' (OECD 2002a: 1, emphasis added).

Watts (2002) identifies that fourteen member states of the OECD are involved in a career guidance policy review. The purpose is to set benchmarks for all member countries, and produce a 'rationale statement which will outline the role of career guidance in relation to lifelong learning and to active labour market and to *welfare to work* strategies'. OECD interest is unequivocal: 'to encourage lifelong learning and sustained employability for all' (Watts 2002: 4; emphasis added).

Whilst this sounds laudable, what does this mean in the context of welfare capitalism? To use the UK as an example, the predominance of output-driven funding regimes signals greater state involvement in guidance delivery: what is done to whom, and what the expected outcomes of guidance interventions are. Career guidance work is low profile and largely non-controversial yet subjected to a disproportionate level of state intervention, that has increased significantly over the past two decades.

This unprecedented level of state interest changes publicly funded career guidance from a one-to-one interaction focused on the individual's needs to an economically driven interaction between an agent of the state and a citizen who is expected to take responsibility for functioning in an uncertain environment, (caused by globalisation and technological change) and *to avoid welfare dependency*. There is an inevitable time and knowledge lag between market, policy and guidance practice. The state is also vulnerable and Castells (in Bauman 1999: 19) identifies that 'while capital is flowing freely, politics stays hopelessly local'. Yet, state intervention is too important to dismiss as 'hopelessly local'; the nature of state involvement in education and employment affects guidance providers, practitioners and clients alike.

Economics and welfare capitalism intertwine, with ensuing policy, including that relating to career guidance, dependent upon the perspective of welfare taken by the state. During the past two decades, the UK has adopted increasingly minimalist welfare-provision models, seeking inspiration from the USA, encouraging people to take out private welfare insurance and pensions cover. Career guidance needs redefining in these terms.

Since welfare capitalism is central to this debate, I examine models identified by Esping-Andersen (1990), Goodin *et al.* (1999), and Goodin (2001). This will challenge preconceptions that the OECD and the Anglo-American models are the only choices, and examine whether career guidance can be socially just.

Advanced capitalist democracies provide some form of welfare for their citizens, but Esping-Andersen (1990) identifies tensions and attitudes that shape the nature of such provision. He studied welfare systems in eighteen nations and identified three welfare regimes: liberal, corporatist and social democratic. These occur in clusters depending on the inter-relationship between the state, market and family.

The liberal welfare state

This provides benefits for 'low income, usually working class, state dependants' (Esping-Andersen 1990: 26). It emphasises strongly the work ethic, i.e. work *not* welfare. The state encourages market influence. People are caught in a welfare trap and forced into low paid work. Benefits are low and welfare claimants are stigmatised. This produces 'a class-political dualism' i.e. a society of 'haves' and 'have nots'. Examples of this are found in the United States, Canada, United Kingdom and Australia.

The corporatist approach

The 'new post industrial class structure' (Esping-Andersen 1990: 27) influences welfare provision. This approach is deeply conservative, never having 'the liberal obsession with market efficiency and commodification' (Esping-Andersen 1990: 27). It emphasises welfare *through* work and strong influences from church, class, status and family maintain a particular form of society. Labour market participation by women is subjugated. Private organisations, labour relations and the Church particularly, dominate welfare provision. The corporatist approach reinforces a static labour market, with low female participation rates and low flexible work-patterns. Austria, Germany, France and Italy are examples of this.

The social democratic regime

This regime, notes Esping-Andersen (1990), has a different intent, aiming to 'promote an equality of the highest standards' (p.27). The gulf between the 'haves' and 'have nots' is not tolerated, and is resolved through high-level benefits and guaranteeing workers' rights. 'All benefit, all are dependent and all will presumably feel obliged to pay' (p.28). In contrast to the corporatist approach, this regime addresses and promotes the emancipation of women by providing social services to facilitate female labour market participation. Scandinavian countries have adopted this regime, which is summarised as 'work *and* welfare'.

Implications of these models for career guidance

These models form an essential basis from which to examine implications for the future of career guidance. Goodin *et al.* (1999) and Goodin (2001) subject these models to stringent analysis, replicating and updating Esping-Andersen's work. Goodin *et al.* (1999) identify a different agenda in each model, which, I contend, influences guidance practice significantly.

The liberal model sees redistribution of wealth via welfare as 'parasitic upon the productive sector of the economy' (Goodin *et al.* 1999: 260) emphasising the need for economic efficiency. This reflects the driving force behind the UK careers service privatisation in the early 1990s (Carley 1988) and in promoting government training schemes as alternatives to employment. This also underlies New Labour's welfare to work schemes. The British welfare state, founded by social democratic consensus after the Second World War, has proved expensive and unwieldy in an environment where politicians are reluctant, even afraid to tax the affluent to spend on the needy. Like other countries, Britain has striven, through such schemes as welfare to work, to ensure individuals are increasingly self-supporting and less reliant upon state welfare provision. To ensure 'a smooth supply of labour to the productive centres of the formal economy, and ... the welfare state should not get too badly in the way of that' (Goodin 2001: 14).

The corporatist approach relies on a stable and traditional society. The goal is security and stability. Access to welfare provision is via group membership (e.g. firm or church). Those excluded must be 'inserted into the natural economic life of the community' (Goodin *et al.* 1999: 54). Liberal individualism is a threat to this system. Nevertheless, the corporatist system is itself under threat. The recent OECD review of career guidance in Germany observes 'The somewhat bureaucratic guidance structures [which] may not always attend to the needs of the individual' (OECD 2002b: 4), signalling a preference for the liberal system. Germany is also currently revising its welfare provision, with Deutsche Welle reporting meetings between church and employers in order to reduce welfare benefits (DWTV 2003).

Goodin *et al.* argue that the social democratic approach is probably 'the best of all possible worlds' (1999: 260). It minimises inequality, is more successful at reducing poverty and is better at promoting equality. What Goodin *et al.* do not address is Esping-Andersen's perceptive identification of the inter-relationship between the state and the ability of women to work. Essentially, the state provides welfare provision to enable women to work, but jobs occupied by women are predominantly in the welfare sector. The system is self-serving.

Each of these models is 'productivist', aiming to provide producers with labour. This is a demand-led approach; employers want skilled employees on tap, to be turned on and off as they wish, and want to pass on the cost and responsibility of training to the supply side; hence the recent promotion of 'lifelong learning', where the individual takes responsibility.

The UK provides a clear example of how profoundly the liberal approach affects career guidance provision. The privatisation agenda of the 1990s sought to ally the careers service with business agendas (Morrison 1983; Department of Education and Science and Education Department 1991). The liberal model retains popularity with New Labour as the Blair administration continues the 'Work *not* welfare' approach. This economically driven agenda underpins initiatives that promote 'inclusion' via employment and training. Within days of the 2001 election, Alistair Darling, Minister for the Department of Work and Pensions, announced significant changes in welfare provision commenting that 'We are increasingly looking at tightening up conditionality; so that people get their rights, but there is a tighter regime to make sure people can, and actually do help themselves' (BBC News 11. 6. 2001).

Collective policies relating to social inclusion, such as 'New Deal' and 'New Start', emphasise and promote the importance of the link between employment, wealth creation and self-supporting citizens. The Prime

Minister stated: 'those who can work but at present don't,... we must try to help off a life on benefit and into productive work' (BBC News 11.6.2001). On the surface, this sounds reasonable. The UK's unemployment rates are 'among the lowest in Europe' (Learning and Skills Council 2001: 5). Nevertheless, the underlying agenda of 'work not welfare' seeks to reposition the responsibility or burden of financing welfare from state to individual, and needs further consideration.

This agenda is accepted increasingly in the UK, Australia, New Zealand and other Anglo-American countries, frequently without challenge. People become vociferously resentful of supporting welfare beneficiaries, whom they view as scroungers. No favourable environment exists for social democratic approaches to develop.

The flaw in this argument is that the success of the liberal approach depends upon high levels of employment and, in an individualistic society, *everyone* must actively participate. This local perspective dares to defy the predictions of writers and thinkers such as Bauman (1999: 20), who envisages that 'only 20 per cent of the global workforce will suffice to keep the [global] economy going'. What happens to the superfluous 80 per cent of the able-bodied population of the world? Bauman's view is bleak: 'Behind the expanding insecurity of the millions dependent on selling their labour, lurks the absence of a potent and effective agency which could, with will and resolve, make their plight less insecure' (1999: 20).

Personal insecurity is thus compounded by technological change, globalisation *and* by increasing state withdrawal from welfare provision. The affluent west's 'I'm alright Jack' approach ignores the plight of many within its own society and of most in third world countries. Yet the emergent cheap labour markets of these countries are precisely what capitalist organisations want in order to increase the returns to their shareholders, at a cost to western domestic labour markets.

Career guidance practitioners must be aware of the social implications of this form of welfare capitalism. As the state rolls back statutory welfare provision of pensions and other benefits, and as employment becomes more flexible, the pressure on the individual to earn increases, regardless of local employment opportunities. In order to survive, the individual must be employed within the boundaries of the capitalist system, or work outside of it in the informal economy. Effective career choice becomes a luxury for the 'haves' able to secure well-paid jobs with the benefits of pension and health provision. For many, choosing what they want to do is less likely to be about intrinsic self-determination and personal fulfilment, but more about being driven by the need for *economic* security. Career guidance becomes financial planning not facilitating self-fulfilment.

This wider picture, which constitutes both the *macro-environment* and *context* of guidance, *must* inform the guidance *activity* because of the long-term implications of people's choices. These are not only financial, but also include the social injustices that remain hurdles for many people in society, including most women, members of ethnic minorities and those with disabilities.

Is there an alternative?

Increasing globalisation, flexible labour markets and decreasing workplace security call into question the appropriateness of traditional approaches to welfare capitalism. The fractured nature of 'career' and the prolonged transitions experienced by young people in western societies (Roberts and Foti 2000) increase, rather than decrease, dependency. This requires support rather than censure.

Goodin (2001) identifies the 'post-productivist' approach as an alternative to the work–welfare relationship. This requires a serious attitudinal re-think. He argues 'economic productivity can be sustained at moderately high levels on the basis of far less than full employment, full time for absolutely everyone of working age' (p.15). Post-productivism argues against conditional welfare provision, believing that economies *can* afford to pay benefits to those who cannot or *choose not* to work. Goodin acknowledges this 'welfare *without* work' approach, 'is an impossible ideal' (p.38) if taken literally, nevertheless it challenges the increasingly relentless drive to get all of employable age, and beyond, active in the formal labour market. He cites the Netherlands as a 'post-productivist' example because of high male and female demand for part-time employment, high voluntary non-employment, social autonomy and low poverty rates. This approach provides an 'alternative welfare future, in which time matters as much as money' (Goodin 2001: 39).

Ultimately, this model weakens governmental control and is already threatened; Goodin found that Dutch political leaders are pulling back from it. 'Third way' politics continues the hegemonic drive by the 'new right' towards marketisation and enterprise 'as a means of allocating resources and distributing welfare' (Ferlie *et al.* 1996: 23). The Netherlands report from the OECD review of career guidance reflects this, identifying as a strength the 'still fragile' emergent market in career information and guidance 'created by the policy of decentralization and marketisation', and 'the lack of clarity regarding the role of government within a decentralized market system' (OECD 2002b: 3) as a weakness.

Post-productivism recognises other definitions of 'work' neglected in productivist models as of value to society, e.g. the non-financial contribution of carers and the experience and knowledge of the elderly. In New Zealand, this is central to Maori culture where voluntary work for the good of the whanau (family), hapu (sub-tribe) and iwi (tribe) is valued. This is pivotal to the development of a Maori perspective of career guidance 'Te Whare Tapa Wha', which contains four dimensions adapted very briefly here:

- Hinengaro – relevance to thoughts, feelings and behaviour.
- Wairua – when confronted with a career problem Maori do not seek to analyse its separate components or parts but ask in what larger context it resides, incorporating ancestors or future generations to discussions.
- Tinana – distinct personal space, boundary or distance is generally maintained until terms of the relationship are negotiated or agreed upon.
- Whanau – explores family relationships, attitude and preference to work as extended family members shape attitudes of the client.

Koligi *et al.* (2002)

This perspective expects the guidance practitioner to recognise and work with the whole person, respecting spiritual, emotional and social values. It contradicts economic imperatives behind much 'social' policy relating to career guidance work, and challenges the productivist view that economic outcomes are the only ones that matter.

An alternative model of welfare capitalism exists and there is a model of guidance appropriate to it. However, promoting such a holistic approach is difficult in the increasingly neo-liberal macro-environment affecting career guidance, and tends to be contrary to mainstream liberal sentiments held by many.

Can career guidance practice be socially just?

The liberal model co-opts career guidance as a mechanism for surveillance and social control through client tracking and monitoring systems. Guidance organisations must adhere to external agendas and practitioners must meet targets to avoid personal censure. The rise of globalisation and of powerful corporations weakens the nation state, which responds by strengthening internal surveillance, which Foucault (1978) named 'Governmentality'. Guidance organisations exert pressure: not meeting targets means funding is not forthcoming, so employees' jobs are threatened. Organisations dependent upon government funding face pressure to provide guidance for social compliance. Organisational survival predominates. Within this scenario, the mindset becomes, 'There is nothing we can do to change things'.

The corporatist model has significant implications for gender, age and career choice. In Germany and Italy for example, social policy 'actively discourages women from re-joining the workplace after giving birth' (Power 2003: 28). Research by the University of Turin cited by Power shows that Italian women have responded by giving up having children. The situation is similar in Germany, and the resultant demographic skew will have profound effects on retirement, with the likelihood of widespread poverty in old age (Theil 2003). The expense of welfare provision is currently under scrutiny.

The social democratic model appears to address gender differences, but it marginalises them by corralling women into gender-typical roles. It is inclusive, and everyone appears to buy into it. However, to liberals, it is unthinkably expensive and burdensome on the 'haves'. Chances of this model spreading from Scandinavia are remote in the current liberalising climate.

None of these models of welfare capitalism is socially just, and guidance practitioners operating within each model must be aware of the inherent injustices.

The post-productivist model, whilst offering the most choice to people, and a forum to promote social justice is, ironically, too individualistic even for the liberals. It appears too expensive and burdensome, calling on the 'haves' to contribute more to the welfare coffers. This approach seems to have been strangled at birth, with proponents of liberal capitalism influencing policy-makers heavily to comply with this model.

Career guidance work is now less concerned with the 'social good', and is more focused on ensuring the success of the 'work not welfare' approach. This is apparent in attitudes towards single parents (predominantly women), urged away from full-time child rearing supported by benefit, towards self-supporting but frequently low paid employment. The irony of the situation should not be lost; there is a paradoxical juxtaposition of politically imperative 'family values' and this liberal approach.

Protagonists of market forces tacitly support an inequitable labour market. Long-term financial disparities result from gender and race inequality, unequal pay, poor education, social class, maternity career-breaks, long-term financial consequences of marriage and divorce (Women's Unit 2001). These are *social* not individual problems, and policy makers, employers and even guidance practitioners have fudged their resolution for too long.

In order to obviate these inequities, the *context* of guidance can intercede. Some parents provide their children with competitive advantages: choosing schools, paying for education and effective career guidance, facilitating a head start. For the less fortunate, the emphasis is on financial self-sufficiency from any available job, rather than on freedom of career choice. Liberal governmental intervention in the macro-environment challenges the developmental 'me' centred career guidance approaches because 'social inclusion', which sounds laudable, necessitates wage earning in order to survive, regardless of ability or ambition. Local opportunity structures will determine career choice, which, for many could be a luxury.

Behind these models lies a complexity within which the most vulnerable must survive. It is caused by liberalising financial and labour markets, increasing global competition (whilst retaining protective trade practices) and decreasing state welfare support, or no state support at all, linking back to Bauman's (1999) observations on the expanding insecurity of millions.

Transient 'social inclusion' initiatives seek to promote labour market participation as social justice. The underlying assumption is that clients subscribe to, or will have their needs met by the mainstream political, economic and social hegemony. Career guidance managers and practitioners are central to these initiatives. They must acknowledge the extent to which welfare capitalism influences what they do and why they do it. The systemic nature of such influence means the term 'honest broker' for career guidance practitioners is wholly inappropriate.

Changing the framework

The uni-directional nature of economic and political influences (as shown in fig. 3.1) on the activity of guidance challenges practitioners' 'professionalism'. Policy-makers frequently lack understanding of the academic and professional body of knowledge that underpins career guidance, but weak or non-existent professional representation means practitioners have no voice with which to lobby.

Whilst chief executives and senior managers may find a forum for dialogue, their vested interests generally differ from professional ones. Professionalism means examining and sometimes challenging the context and macro-environment within which work is located. A 'professionalism' that is independent of the employing organisation is required. This means identifying and valuing the academic body of research and knowledge that underpins career guidance, developing and conferring professional qualifications that are not rendered insensitive and meaningless through international homogenisation, and fostering a dialogic model of interaction with policy-makers and business interest groups (see fig. 3.2). We live in a 'quick fix' age that is both suspicious and sceptical of things intellectual, seeking easy answers to complex questions, and uncomfortable with deconstructing and questioning issues. In order to overcome this, career guidance workers need to create a meaningful dialogue with policy-makers. Influence must be outward as well as inward (see fig. 3.2) and a collective voice is stronger and more able to lobby. Professional institutions are therefore essential.

Increased knowledge and understanding of the effects of social and economic policy, as identified in this chapter, could cause two major and divergent ways forward for career guidance. The first is the Acceptance Model, fuelled by a sense of powerlessness and insecurity, in which guidance managers and practitioners collude with policy-makers, who seek to minimise welfare responsibility and in turn are doing the bidding of 'big

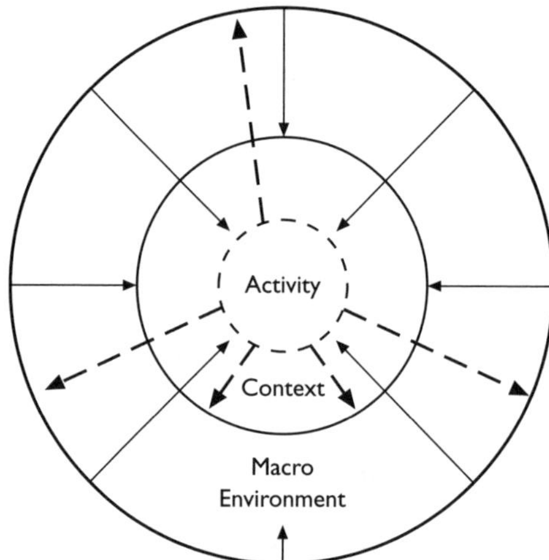

Figure 3.2 The dialogic critical framework.

business'. The second is the Dialogic Model, which endeavours to open communication channels in the opposite direction through strong professional representation, seeking to influence policy and promote social justice, causing greater sensitivity of the needs of those it seeks to help.

Conclusion

Practitioners and managers are at the interface of the paradox between individual need and the collective complexities of labour markets and social policy. Psychologically based models of guidance provide important skills, but are insufficient. Guidance practitioners and their managers need to cultivate an on-going understanding of the complex macro-environment within which guidance operates and recognise the impact this has on their work, and on their clients' lives. Guidance recipients need their practitioners to be astute policy interpreters.

If career guidance is to work towards achieving social justice, it must strive to obviate inequities through informing policy; strong professional bodies, to which all who practice are required to belong, must be cultivated in order to achieve this.

Bibliography

Bauman, Z. (1999) *In Search of Politics*, Cambridge: Polity.

BBC News (2001) Online. Available HTTP. www.http://news.bbc.co.uk (accessed 18 June 2001).

Beck, U. (1992) *Risk Society: Towards a New Modernity*, London: Sage.
Carley, M. (1988) *Performance Monitoring in a Professional Public Service*, London: Policy Studies Institute.
Clarke, J. and Newman, J. (1997) *The Managerial State*, London: Sage.
Department for Education and Science/Employment Department (1991) *Education and Training in the 21st Century*, London: HMSO.
Douglas, F. (2004) 'Public service, private agendas' unpublished PhD thesis, London: Brunel University.
DWTV (2003) *Journal*, viewed 23 September 2003.
Egan, G. (1997) *The Skilled Helper*, Belmont: Brooks/Cole.
Eichbaum, C. and Harris, P. (1999) 'Preface: why this book?' in S. Chatterjee, P. Conway, P. Dalziel, C. Eichbaum, P. Harris, B. Philpott and R. Shaw (eds) *The New Politics: A Third Way for New Zealand*, Palmerston North: Dunmore Press.
Esping-Andersen, G. (1990) *The Three Worlds of Welfare Capitalism*, Cambridge: Polity Press.
Ferlie, E., Ashburner, L., Fitzgerald, L. and Pettigrew, A. (1996) *The New Public Management in Action*, Oxford: Oxford University Press.
Foucault, M. (1978) 'Governmentality', in G. Burchell, C. Gordon and P. Miller (eds) *The Foucault Effect*, Chicago: University of Chicago Press.
Goodin, R.E. (2001) 'Work and welfare: towards a post-productivist welfare regime', *British Journal of Political Science*, 31: 13–39.
Goodin, R.E., Headey, B., Muffels, R. and Dirven, H. (1999) *The Real Worlds of Welfare Capitalism*, Cambridge: Cambridge University Press.
Heginbotham, H. (1951) *The Youth Employment Service*, London: Methuen and Co Ltd.
Holland, J. (1985) *Making Vocational Choices: A Theory of Vocational Personalities and Work Environments*, Englewood Cliffs, NJ: Prentice Hall.
Killeen, J. (1996) 'Career theory', in A.G. Watts, B. Law, J. Killeen, J. Kidd and R. Hawthorne (eds) *Rethinking Careers Education and Guidance*, London: Routledge.
Killeen, J., White, M. and Watts, A.G. (1992) *The Economic Value of Careers Guidance*, London: Policy Studies Institute.
Koligi, M., Pohe, J., Reid, L., Rewi, P. and Hawkins-Stirling, C. (2002) 'Career development from a Maori perspective', paper presented at New Zealand Careers Services/rapuara conference on the Heightened Role of Career Planning in Knowledge Societies, Wellington, November.
Lash, S. and Urry, J. (1987) *The End of Organized Capitalism*, Cambridge: Polity Press.
Learning and Skills Council (2001) *Labour Market Quarterly Report*, Sheffield: Skills. and Enterprise Network.
Lemke, T. 'Foucault, governmentality and critique', paper presented at the Rethinking Marxism conference, University of Amherst, September 2000. Online. Available HTTP. http://www.thomaslemke.de/engl.texte/foucault,governmentality,andcritique.iv.pdf (accessed 20 January 2003).
Morrison, P. (1983) 'Speech to the institute of careers officers', *The Times Educational Supplement*, 7.10.83, cited in Ranson *et al.* (1986) *The Management of Change in the Careers Service*, Birmingham: Institute of Local Government Studies.

OECD (2002a) *Country and Thematic Policy Reviews in Education, Career Guidance Policy Review*, Online. Available HTTP. http://www/OECD.org/els/education/careerguidance/ (accessed 2 December 2002).

OECD (2002b) Country Notes. Online. Available HTTP. http://www/OECD.org/els/education/careerguidance/ (accessed 2 December 2002).

Power, C. (2003) 'Mommy economy', *Newsweek*, June 30: 28.

Roberts, K. (1971) *From School to Work*, Newton Abbot: David and Charles.

Roberts, K. (1984) *School Leavers and their Prospects*, Milton Keynes: Open University Press.

Roberts, K. (1993) 'The social conditions, consequences and limitations of careers guidance' and 'Postscript' in W. Dryden and A.G. Watts (eds) *Guidance and Counselling in Britain: A 20-Year Perspective*, Cambridge: CRAC.

Roberts, K. and Foti, K. (2000) 'Europe's choice: regulation or deregulation of youth labour markets? Old alternatives and new test cases', in J. Bynner and S. Silberreisen (eds) *Adversity and Challenge in Life in the New Germany and in England*, Basingstoke: Macmillan.

Rogers, C.R. (1951) *Client Centred Therapy*, London: Constable and Co.

Super, D. (1957) *The Psychology of Careers*, New York: Harper Row.

Theil, S. (2003) 'A heavy burden', *Newsweek*, June 30: 26–28.

Watts, A.G. (2002) *Career Guidance and Public Policy: Global Issues and Challenges*, paper presented to the New Zealand Careers Services/rapuara conference on the Heightened Role of Career Planning in Knowledge Societies, Wellington, November.

Women's Unit (2001) Online. Available HTTP. http://www.womens-unit.gov.uk/voices/work/a.htm (accessed 29 April 2001).

Chapter 4

Liberté? Futilité? ... Autonomé! Careers education as an emancipatory activity

Bill Law

Introduction

Careers work, we tell ourselves, is to enable choice. It has been argued that it is a distinctive feature of 'free societies'. But there are two underpinning assumptions:

1 we help people, 'in here', to make choices;
2 they are then free, 'out there', to implement them.

Both may be greeted with knowing nods and affirming murmurs by careers workers. Who doesn't want to be associated with the enablement of choice in a free society?

Paradoxes

We nod and murmur too easily. Speaking of 'free societies' usually means ignoring the socially-stratified facts of working life (Davies 1998). Stratification means that a person's position at birth has significant impact on the position reached by career development. The families of 'higher' levels transmit their advantages to their children; and families at 'lower' levels transmit what they have.

The careers-work implications based on decade-on-decade evidence have been set out by Ken Roberts (see Roberts 2003). They re-affirm the original position of his opportunity-structure theory, 'people do not choose careers in any meaningful sense, they take what is available' (Roberts 1977). This is a social-class framed account of limitations on choice. But there are also gender, race and ethnicity-framed accounts. And, despite all our hopes and expectations, social class, in the UK anyway, appears still to be as significant an inhibitor of freedom as any (see for example, OECD 2003).

Within such frames of thought, whatever the dictionary says, degrees of 'choice' are markers for degrees of wealth, well-connectedness and social sequestration. The highest concentrations of choice occur in what Galbraith (1992: 1) has called 'a culture of contentment'. And the further liberation of the already well-positioned would hardly count as a major achievement by careers work.

If careers work is serious about speaking of choice it would be useful to rethink the associations between choice and privilege. We might also look for the differences between choice and impulse.

There are some signs of rethinking. Until recently British policy statements about careers work often sported the word 'choice'. But the flagship of British policy for this work is now called 'Connexions'. It is an interesting, and significant, shift of focus: while 'choice' speaks of an unfettered self, 'Connexions' suggests links to something, or somebody, else. The structure of Connexions programmes requires that we understand career as enmeshed with social and cultural influence (Law 2001).

Ideas of a social and cultural setting for choice cut across our earlier distinction between (1) 'in-here' enablement and (2) 'out-there' possibility. They suggest that some of what is going 'out there' is imported into what is going on 'in here'. The culture we inhabit can be internalised as a habit-of-mind. It is, according to Pierre Bourdieu (1973), a dynamic of social stratification he calls 'habitus'. It means that people who set out to work do not do so in a social vacuum, their choices are connected to their upbringing. It means that there are some doctors who could have found more fulfilment in a supermarket, were it not for the expectations of their families. It also means that 'habitus' is unhappily consuming the lives of some supermarket checkout people. In both cases, so deep is that internalisation, they might say 'I chose this work'. But is that freedom?

This is not to say that freedom is unattainable; it is only to say that cultures-of-origin circumscribe choice, whether in leafy privilege or in rundown ghetto.

Careers work is supposed to help with this. Our programmes, information services, face-to-face work, programmed learning and community-linked learning, are designed to help people figure out what is going on and what they can do about it. They are for the enablement of choice.

But here is a final problem for nodders and murmurers. One of the earliest and most telling criticisms of attempts to enable choice is that, by concentrating attention on (1) how a person responds to opportunity, we divert attention from (2) the more significant forces that shape their availability. The charge is that we merely help people to accommodate their position in the pecking order (Cicourel and Kitsuse 1963; Musgrove and Taylor 1969; North 1972). If there is anything at all in this analysis, then we could be the enemies, not the allies, of liberation.

And so, don't nod and murmur too easily.

Ideas

Western cultures locate the capacity for choice inside the person. The word 'soul' once featured in this discourse. The phrase 'inner life' seems to stand in much the same position. There is something within us, it is thought, that is responsible, answerable and, when we kick over the traces, culpable. The idea of the freedom-of-the-will allows us to believe that, whatever is going on 'out there', we are still responsible.

Free though not free

Despite what the sceptics like Maurice North and Ken Roberts argue, this talking-up of inner life is not entirely nonsense. Psychotherapist Viktor Frankl's life in a concentration camp caused him to deeply reflect on the meaning of freedom. He comes close to a concept of a soul by concluding that 'Everything can be taken away from a person, but one thing; the last of the human freedoms – to choose one's own attitude in any given set of circumstances, to choose one's own way' (Frankl 1964: 65). Extreme conditions of entrapment reveal the possibility of choice. Psychologist Mihaly Csikszentmihalyi (2002) documents how people in confined conditions create inner freedom.

And so, while 'habitus' might inhibit some in the use of what little freedom they have, others with no freedom at all, find a way. Easy enough to put it down to 'character' (another of those vague terms). But Jonathon Rose (2001) surveys biographical documents which show how some working-class people beat the sociological odds, by nourishing their inner lives. All of this points to an inner readiness to act. A person must be internally free to realise external freedom. Despite the complaints of the sceptics, there is a clue here concerning where careers work must go in order to enable choice.

Not free to be free

Moving in that direction, clinical psychologist Gordon Allport (1955) argues that the process of working out what to do always increases tension; and it is this inner striving which makes us, as humans, what we are. But, he insists, in working on our freedom we must learn to deal with the walls we build around ourselves as well as those that others build around us. We can, he argues, be entrapped by our own instincts, impulses and drives. A person's freedom is deeply-embedded in her or his sense of self.

And so, like Frankl, Allport looks in two directions for freedom: and ability to deal with both 'out-there' and 'in-here' entrapment.

Purposeless freedom

Political philosopher Isaiah Berlin (1958) speaks of the two freedoms, but in other terms. There are, he shows, what might be called differences between 'freedom from...' and 'freedom to...' (pp.118–172).

'Freedom from...' is what most people mean by liberty, freedom from constraint. The most obvious constraints are physical, like those on Viktor Frankl. But there are also political and economic, like those indicated by Cicourel and Kitsuse and by Ken Roberts. And there are social constraints, like those suggested by Pierre Bourdieu. For all of us, in much of the time, freedom from such 'out-there' pressures is not a possibility.

'Freedom to...' suggests that we need a reason to be free, a purpose which freedom can serve. This not a freedom conceded, but won: not the absence of constraint, but the presence of purpose. It looks 'in here' for a basis for emancipation. It explains failure not by pointing to a position, but to inner life. Viktor Frankl speak of its strength; Ken Roberts worries about its vulnerability.

If Frankl and Allport have something important to say about freedom, we would need to re-anchor the mainspring of career development away from the skills of admission ('will they allow me?') and closer to the dynamics of motivation ('why would I?').

Scenarios

Sociologist David Riesman (1961) sets out four scenarios for articulating motivation. He sets them in a developing, and remarkably prescient, historical account.

Career traditions

Some careers would be what he calls 'tradition directed'. They belong to societies in which steadiness and predictability are valued. The lives of the parents tend to predict the lives of the children. Family, and other immediate cultural values, install in each a script for the roles that she or he is expected to occupy. Where things work that way, the children of the soil are likely to become farmers; doctors often turn out to be the offspring of medics; and military families spawn more uniforms. Working-class kids get working-class jobs; lasses get women's work; and children of migrant families get what's left. Ken Roberts (1977) uses the term 'anticipatory socialisation' to refer to the dynamics; it corresponds closely with what Pierre Bourdieu means by 'habitus'.

Career gyroscopes

Inner-directedness is, David Riesman (1961) says, appropriate to a 'frontier society'. Frontier societies (for example, in nineteenth-century America) are rapidly expanding, with lots of room for new ways of doing things. They require self-reliant, can-do and optimistic inner resources for moving on. He uses the imagery of a gyroscope which shows, in the midst of isolation, obstruction and uncertainty, which way is 'forward'. Because the roots of such an orientation are deeply 'in here', to fail to respond appropriately would be to risk feelings of guilt, a sense of not doing the right thing. That sense of deeply-respected inner values, as a basis of career development, is strongly represented in Anne Roe's (1956) account of motivation for career choice.

Career radar

David Riesman characterises recent historical conditions as calling upon a third orientation, 'other directedness'. It fits well to a society in which expansion is reaching its limits, and increasing crowdedness means that other people's view must be accommodated. To fail to find what is appropriate in such conditions is to risk shame, a sense of doing what is not alright with others. In such negotiations ready-made wisdom is not welcome, people seek a flexible response to what others are signalling, here and now. David Riesman uses the metaphor of a social radar, letting me know what will prove acceptable in each situation. A careful, well-networked, accommodating, tentative, and well-groomed person, with no strong ideology, can then do well. Sociologist Richard Sennett (1998) describes how an informed, experienced and disclosing voice comes into conflict with such attitudes at work, to the point where a career choice has to be reversed. Such a scenario has been said to depend on a cosmetic economy (Warhurst and Nickson 2001).

Losing career habits

David Riesman is not dismissive of tradition-, inner- and other-directedness. But he is clear that we can no longer afford habitually to take any one of these routes. Habit is out-of-kilter with prevailing conditions. Riesman doesn't use the term 'freedom' to characterise what we now need to cultivate, he uses 'autonomy'. Autonomy might be the better word for what it is that careers work is here to enable (Law 1992): freedom is 'out there'; autonomy is 'in here'.

According to David Riesman, an autonomous person can draw on an appreciation of tradition, inner life, and other people. But she or he creates, from that appreciation, a new basis for action. It means knowing who and what I am going to pay attention to, and why. It is about recognising links, but it also means breaking some, and making new ones. It does not describe a process of free-standing choice, in a social and psychological vacuum. Culture, self and other people feature in the achievement of this freedom.

The opposite of all this, says Riesman, is 'anomie': people do not act from any appreciation of fairness, attachment or inner life but in an impulsive, random or habitual manner.

This earlier literature brings us to an appreciation of the 'out-there' and 'in-here' processes of emancipation, and leaves us with a question about the difference between choice and (say) impulse. A contemporary literature can help us move on.

Evolution and freedom

The processes of freedom are probed by philosopher Daniel Dennett (2003). Dennett is close to a contemporary development in philosophy to which Richard Rorty (1999) has made significant contributions. Rorty, drawing on long-standing pragmatic thinking, argues that we do not learn in order to know 'the truth': as a species we survive because we learn in order to know what to do.

What-is-useful does not exclude what-is-true, 'true' is sometimes 'useful'. But, as a species, we need useful learning more than we need 'the truth'. This species-characteristic helps to explain much of the day-dreaming and boredom in too many of our classrooms.

Daniel Dennett develops the emancipatory possibilities of the thought. Like Rorty, he uses evolutionary science to introduce us to ourselves as a species; and he also makes extensive use of computer modelling.

What genes can do

Like other organisms, homo sapiens have made gains by degrees. And so, Dennett argues, we have not always been as free as we are now, 'freedom evolves'.

The key element in our freedom is complexity. Survival in changing environments means that we must differentiate the range of things we can do in response. Sexual reproduction is our means for achieving that complexity. By stages, we have evolved to perceive beyond the boundary of 'self', to communicate with each other, to anticipate the future, and to develop a mental map 'in here' of what is going on 'out there'. Biologist Richard Dawkins sees the evolutionary pay-off as a tool for working life, he characterises it in terms of a species-need to 'make a living'.

For us, the pay-off was, at first, 'gather or die'; later 'hunt or die'; and then 'co-operate or die'. It is now, says Daniel Dennett, 'think or die'.

Thinking means making a single, expanding and linked-up account of the way things are. That includes not only our account of the ways things are out there; we are also witnesses to our own participation in it.

Ideas of freedom hinge on the idea that nothing is inevitable; we can initiate change. We get that feeling of freedom by experiencing situations where we know that we must 'do it now, or lose the chance'. But Dennett's analysis needs no special location or faculty for this feeling. We feel free not because we are unconstrained, nor because we have something called 'free-will'. We feel free because we can learn what is going on, and can locate ourselves in that account, as able to do something about it.

So freedom is one of the things we do. We are free to be creative, to create cultures and to enter into contracted relationships. All have much to do with work.

This is not just speculation and computer games. Antonio Damasio (1999) has neurologically mapped much of what Dennett describes. His implications for careers work are in our literature (Law *et al.* 2002).

Looking for what works

Dennett's thinking cuts some philosophical corners: if we knew everything about everything, then we might be forced to conclude that this is the only universe which could result from our 'big bang'. How could we then, believe that we are free? Surely we would be part of a cosmic inevitability.

But the argument is theological: it can be conducted only in unverifiable terms, winding up with claims about, on the one hand, creation and, on the other, 'free will'. A pragmatist prefers to get on with what can be made to work: validity is usability. And, as we shall see, Dennett's ideas are like that. But they are not narrowly utilitarianism. He knows that trial-and-error is not our best shot at knowing how any complex thing pays off. Since we must use what we know in changing circumstances, we need to know both *that* it works and *how* it works. And, as species, we seek to know that for both use and pleasure.

But survival is at stake. Knowing where I am and what I can do about it, means being able to anticipate the consequences of my own actions. If I can't do that, I might well claim I'm free, but I won't last long. For the claim is as likely to support impulse as choice.

What memes can do

Daniel Dennett follows Richard Dawkins in his account of the evolution of ideas. Ideas that can reproduce themselves are called 'memes'; they are (this is a metaphor!) ideational genes. Like some of our genetically acquired characteristics, ideas can help us to see how things are and what can be done about them. They are passed from one individual to another and inter-generationally; and, if they are good enough, they are passed on again and again and again. If the metaphor holds, the DOTS analysis seems to have been a careers-work meme (Law and Watts 1977) and is further discussed below. Memes are not installed by the exchange of bodily fluids, but by communication: they are cultural phenomena.

The idea of memes is useful to Dennett's position on the importance of complexity. We internalise memes, for example as beliefs and values, so that they become part of how we know what to do. Neither Riesman nor Bourdieu would give Dennett a problem with that. Dennett sees the process as liberating. But Riesman and Bourdieu see that ideas that might once have been 'successful' may go on being retransmitted after they have become useless, even damaging. That would be a case of the survival of the not particularly fit. We will come back to the point.

But Dennett's general point is still useful. Freedom is being able to access and use the complexity of our own participation in what is going on and what we can do about it. Our instinctive, affective and cognitive organic natures equip us for that process. So, at least in some ways, do our cultures.

Thinking bigger

It means that freedom can be manifested in different ways: as the realisation of 'desire', as the implementation of 'rationality', but also as higher-order 'striving'. Everything depends on how much complexity we take on in seeing ourselves in the world. If we sense no more than instincts and associated feelings, then we have limited options. We can do better by putting our cerebral cortex into gear. But we can also install economic, social and cultural memes into that process. That expands the feeling of 'I can do something about this' to a point where we can talk about freedom.

It is an 'in-here' account that we make of our 'out-there' experience. In this respect, one of Dennett's images is particularly graphic. To exclude from my account much of what I could take into account would be, he says, to make my inner life 'smaller'. If I see myself as smaller, then what is 'out there' seems bigger, and beyond my control. Some superstitious beliefs actively encourage us to do this. They put the important things in our lives beyond our reach, and urge us to comply with what they require. The more we do that, the more we can avoid responsibility; because we see ourselves as small effects, in a big process over which we have little control. An extreme case is that of 'victim', a status Viktor Frankl flatly rejected. In order to see ourselves as causes rather than effects, we need a fuller account of what is going on and what can be done about it. The answer is, then, 'not in our stars but in ourselves', and we are no longer 'underlings'.

In Dennett's terms, this is to become 'bigger', to the point where one part of what we know can be in conflict with another. We might even take sides against some of our own motives. That struggle is, according to both Allport and Dennett, a marker for freedom.

The power of complexity

There is no shortage of causes and effects in Dennett's portrayal of freedom. But there is no determinism. His contention is that, although everything is caused, nothing is inevitable. The more we know about causes and effects, then the more we're able to change how they operate. It is because we have evolved to map and sequence this complexity, and to locate ourselves onto it, that we can do this. What, for simpler creatures and fatalists, might be inescapable is, for us, avoidable. Complexity is our handle on freedom.

Is careers work helpful about that?

Complexity as liberation

Good theory indicates key variables in career development. Six interacting sets of variables are set out in the table below. They are important because they offer a way of making Dennett's general position specific to careers work. The table sets out a framework for help, and the discussion suggests how greater complexity can enable learners for freedom.

Information

If a decision is not to be an impulse, people need information, about what is going on 'in here' and 'out there'. An analysis of this coverage is indicated in the table explaining the 'O', 'S', 'D' and 'T' in the DOTS analysis.

Such information features strongly in matching theory and its developments (Dawis 1994). It enables a person to say 'I am, or am not, suitable to

Table 4.1 Elements in career development and key words in their conceptualisation

Elements	*Key concepts*
information	opportunity/self/decision/transition
feelings	act or be still/approach or avoid defy or comply/hide or help
attachments	feedback/modelling/expectations impressions/support/contacts
culture	shared narratives/role-assignment insider-outsider-location
learning	sensing/sifting/focusing/understanding
purpose	survival/fulfilment/contribution

this work'. Relatively stable features of 'self' can be listed as 'traits and factors'. But that simplicity becomes more usefully complex where people can speak of experience ('I have done...'), abilities ('I can do...'), and motivations ('I seek to do...').

The importance of information is strongly emphasised by Ken Roberts' opportunity-structure theory. And that puts the emphasis on 'accurate', 'up-to-date' and 'neutral' information. Useful complexity would introduce more information about what people actually do in their work and, now more than ever, how things are changing.

Feelings

Career development entails risk, assertion and disclosure and frustration, evoking the emotions suggested in the table. To ignore affect in career is to ignore too much (Kidd 1998). And, so, Daniel Goleman (1996) wants us to be more emotionally intelligent.

We might also be able to make good use of a book about how to be intelligently emotional. What neurologist Antonio Damasio (2003) calls 'emotions' are immediate in their effects. They are instinctive, by-passing our information processing capacities with more basic commands, 'do something, and do it now!' Sometimes 'doing it' is better than 'thinking about it'. But instincts can also over-react, misdirect and panic, a triumph of simplicity over complexity.

But there is also complexity in affective life. The thesaurus of human feeling is more extensive and more subtly differentiated than the table can contain. That more complex process is called by Antonio Damasio (1999) the formation of 'the feeling of what happens' (pp.35–81). It infuses what he calls 'autobiographical consciousness' (see also Law 2003a).

Career thinking has, so far, paid more attention to sustained feelings than to transient emotions. The work of Anne Roe (1956) on career values, and Mark Savickas (1995) on life themes, infuse matching theory with more complex ideas about a distinctive, growing and sustained 'self' expressing needs and values.

Attachments

Emotions are often manifest when the learner's point of view comes into conflict with someone else's. But awareness of alternative points of view is by no means necessarily entrapping. In the nature of the case, career means action with, for, and in response to other people, and other points of view.

These other points of view are in family, peers, colleagues, customers and other social contacts. Like opportunity-structure theory, this account of community-interaction theory (Law 1981) looks 'out there' for explanations of what happens. But, unlike that other theory, it points to the impact of close-up encounters, where people are more likely to remember, trust and internalise other people's influence. The different forms of influence is suggested in the above table.

This thinking explicitly suggests the value of increasing the complexity of these encounters. Where people do not meet a wide range of other people, imaginable possibilities for one's self are correspondingly limited. The implications are for expanded and enriched social contact, new people bringing different feedback, other modelling, new expectations, and so on.

Culture

Group membership also means cultural roots in, for example, ethnicity, social class and religion. The beliefs and values of culture say what people should do, what should not be changed, who are 'insiders', and what is beyond the pale. They often touch on working life as they do in 'who should do what' stereotypes. Such beliefs and values are internalised; stories, music and icons become part of self (Law *et al.* 2002). A single and exclusive cultural perspective feels like God's own truth. Not liberating.

Social-reproduction theory (Willis 1977) was the first to document the impact of culture on career. It shows how working-class lads collude with their upbringing. Pragmatic-rational-choice theory (Hodkinson *et al.* 1996) expresses the same point, importing the concepts of 'habitus' and 'cultural capital'.

Habitually-engaged and culturally-rooted beliefs and values are a career disadvantage. The 'cosmetic economy' penalises bright but 'rough and ready' kids. And, as Warhurst and Nickson show, and Sennett illustrates, the 'nice but dim' can thrive in 'cosmetic' work cultures.

And so, where the culture of upbringing is narrow and exclusive, options will be limited. Being able to move on would then mean installing more cultural memes, adding to cultural capital. Both Riesman and Dennett have a point: memes can both entrap and liberate. But Dennett is right about this, greater complexity brings greater freedom.

Learning

Building an account of what is going on, from information, feelings, attachments, culture, relies on learning. A core proposition of career-learning theory (Law 1996) is that the process must be complex enough to enable change-of-mind, a pre-condition for free choice.

Part of the complexity stems from that fact that significant learning extends over periods of time from early upbringing. The theory therefore suggest a learning sequence. It is set out in the earlier table: sensing enough to go on, sifting things into useful order, focusing on what is significant, and understanding how things work. The end-point is understanding: knowing what causes give rise to what effects and, therefore, having a way of anticipating the effects of your own action. In career, future effects can only be spoken of as probabilities, career planning offers few guarantees. The journey to that end-point is a progression: faltering at any stage halts or distorts the whole. Symptoms of faltering include confusion, dependency, stereotyping and impulsiveness. All reduce freedom.

Anticipating the effects of my action is close to what the pragmatists mean by useful learning. But career-learning theory, along with most other career development theories, pays little attention to intuition in this process. It could suggest significant expansion in the help we offer.

Purpose

Career is purposeful behaviour, a major part of what we each mean to do with our lives. The implication is that people must be able to see the purpose for which career planning is useful.

Working can be said (see Law *et al.* 2002) to cluster around three centres: (1) making a living; (2) self-fulfilment, self-acknowledgement or self-realisation; and (3) outward looking, for bringing some new and valuable 'good' into the world. They are separated in the table presented, but they shade into each other; and most people's working lives move between them.

In career development thought it is hermeneutic theory (Collin and Young 1992) which has most to say about the importance of meaning and purpose in career. The theory explains career in terms of a person's interpretation of working life, the sense that people make of it for themselves.

Life themes express underlying, sustained, feeling-laden and often hard-to-express purposes. They may be rooted in early life, but persist in what people say and do about what is 'out there' and beckons them, and 'in here' and drives them.

This way of thinking can be applied to any aspect of life, spending, resting, loving and enjoying, as well as working. It can, then, help to explain how work dissatisfaction can be satisfied in other ways, as consumer, partner, parent and citizen. And criminality can feature in this calculation. Hermeneutics is one of the most useful tools for considering work–life balance. It is the most basic consideration in conceiving responsibility, 'do you mean to do this?' Purposefulness is at the heart of autonomé, deeper than liberté, a condition for egalité and the rejection of futilité.

About theory: the more ways a person has for framing what is going on, the more options she has for dealing with it. That is freedom. Careers work, therefore, needs a framework to accommodate all of what we know about how careers work. It argues against 'cherry picking' preferred theories; it argues for meta-theory. The table I have presented is a gesture in that direction.

Enabling freedom

Career is too frequently obstructed by physical, economic, social and cultural factors. That is why degrees of 'choice' are markers for degrees of wealth, well-connectedness and social sequestration. Most people have too-limited wealth and influence to deal with these obstructions: in Dennett's terms, we cannot always be as 'big' as we need to be. Where that is so, careers workers can, as mediator or advocate, help to get a better deal for learners.

But the primary task is to help people learn to manage their own lives. And, direct intervention may encourage people to be dependent, to stay 'small'. This chapter is, then, about enabling learning of what is going on, obstructions included, and to work out what to do about it.

At the heart of it is what Dennett calls 'enlargement', bigness. This is not a celebration of greater intelligence, but of the fuller use of whatever humanity I inherit and can acquire. This is not a place for mere academic knowledge. And, in these terms, there is no one incapable of becoming bigger.

Conclusions to this chapter can be set out quite simply:

1 Careers work can do little about what is going on 'out there'.
2 Careers work can work on the instinctive, feeling and rational processes which shape behaviour, and it can do it so that people are better enabled in knowing what to do.
3 Careers work can serve freedom more fully where people are enabled to reflect on their own participation in events, to learn from more than one set of contacts, and to internalise what is useful from more than one culture.
4 Careers work therefore requires complexity, because it is complexity which offers options, identifies causes and effects and enables autonomy.
5 Careers work must, then, be clearly and explicitly linked to purposes, so that people are reminded of their lives in our programmes, and of our programmes in their lives.

The practical implications of all of this are radical, and will not fit to conventionally organised careers work programmes (see Law 2003b).

It all shifts the marker for freedom away from wealth, well-connectedness and social sequestration, and towards thinkingness, understanding and insight. It changes the basis on which who-gets-to-do-what is determined, an equal opportunity issue. This is the policy issue closest to the heart of careers work, and too much neglected.

Bibliography

Allport, G. (1955) *Becoming*, New Haven: Yale University Press.

Berlin, I. (1958) *Essays on Liberty*, Oxford: Oxford University Press.

Bourdieu, P. (1973) 'Cultural reproduction and social reproduction', in R. Brown (ed.) *Knowledge, Education and Cultural Change*, London: Harper and Row.

Cicourel, A. and Kitsuse, J. (1963) *The Education Decision Makers*, New York: Bobbs-Merrill.

Csikszentmihalyi, M. (2002) *Flow*, London: Rider.

Collin, A. and Young, R. (1992) *Interpreting Career*, London: Praeger.

Damasio, A. (1999) *The Feeling of What Happens – Body, Emotion and the Making of Consciousness*, London: Heinemann.

Damasio, A. (2003) *Looking for Spinoza – Joy Sorrow and Feeling Brain*, London: Heinemann.

Davies, N. (1998) *Dark Heart*, London: Vintage.

Dawis, R. (1994) 'The theory of work adjustment as convergent theory', in M.L. and R. Lent (eds) *Convergence in Career Development Theories*, Palo Alto, CA: Consulting Psychologists Press Books.

Dennett, D. (2003) *Freedom Evolves*, London: Allen Lane.

Frankl, V. (1964) *Man's Search for Meaning*, London: Hodder and Stoughton.

Galbraith, J.K. (1992) *The Culture of Contentment*, London: Sinclair-Stevenson.

Goleman, D. (1996) *Emotional Intelligence*, London: Bloomsbury.

Hodkinson, P., Sparkes, A.C. and Hodkinson, H. (1996) *Triumphs and Tears – Young People, Markets and the Transition from School to Work*, London: David Fulton.

Kidd, J.M. (1998) 'Emotion: an absent presence in careers theory', *Journal of Vocational Behaviour*, 52: 275–288.

Law, B. (1981) 'Community interaction: a "mid-range" focus for theories of career development in young adults', *British Journal of Guidance and Counselling*, 9(2): 142–158.

—— (1992) 'Autonomy and learning about work', in A. Collin and R. Young (eds) *Interpreting Career*, London: Praeger.

—— (1996) 'A career learning theory', in A.G. Watts, B. Law, J. Killeen, J. Kidd and R. Hawthorne (eds) *Rethinking Careers Education and Guidance: Theory, Policy and Practice*, London: Routledge.

—— (2001) 'Connexions – mutant not monster', *Careers Guidance Today*, July–August: 33–36.

—— (2002) *How Do Careers Really Work?* Website: The Career-learning Network, free download – www.hihohiho.com.

—— (2003a) 'Guidance – too many lists and not enough stories', in A. Edwards (ed.) *Challenging Biographies – Relocating the Theory and Practice of Careers Work'*, Canterbury: Canterbury Christ Church University College.

—— (2003b) *Diagnosing Career-learning Needs.* Website: The Career-learning Network, free download – www.hihohiho.com.

Law, B. and Watts, A.G. (1977) *Schools, Careers and Community*, Westminster: Church House, 1977.

Law, B., Meijers, F. and Wijers, G. (2002) 'New perspectives on careers and iden-

tity in the contemporary world', *British Journal of Guidance and Counselling*, 30(4): 432–449.
Organisation for Economic Co-operation and Development (2003) 'Literacy skills for the world of tomorrow – further results from PISA', Organisation for Economic and Cultural Development. Website: www.pisa.oecd.org.
Musgrove, F and Taylor, P.H. (1969) *Society and the Teacher's Role*, London: Routledge and Kegan Paul.
North, M. (1972) *The Secular Priests*, London: George Allen and Unwin.
Riesman, D. (1961) *The Lonely Crowd*, London: Yale University Press.
Roberts, K. (1977) 'The social conditions consequences and limitations of careers guidance', *British Journal of Guidance and Counselling*, 5(1): 1–9.
—— (2003) *Class in Modern Britain*, London: Palgrave-Macmillan.
Roe, A. (1956) *The Psychology of Occupations*, New York: Wiley.
Rorty, R. (1999) *Philosophy and Social Hope*, London: Penguin.
Rose, J. (2001) *The Intellectual Life of the British Working Class*, London: Yale University Press.
Savickas, M. (1995) 'Constructivist counseling for career indecision', *The Career Development Quarterly*, 43: 363–375.
Sennett, R. (1998) *The Corrosion of Character – The Personal Consequences of Work in the New Capitalism*, London: W.W. Norton.
Warhurst, C. and Nickson, D. (2001) *Looking Good, Sounding Right*, London: The Industrial Society.
Willis, P. (1977) *Learning to Labour: How Working-Class Kids Get Working-Class Jobs*, Farnham: Saxon House.

Chapter 5

Cultural diversity and guidance: myth or reality?

Beatriz Malik and Teresa Aguado

Introduction

In today's technological societies, access to further education and labour opportunities depends largely on the attainment of academic credits and qualifications. Educational systems thus act as a selection mechanism from the moment they establish the type and amount of knowledge and skills students must master. The criteria used to evaluate this knowledge are of great importance, as they will determine the degree of acquisition of these skills and the qualifications required in order to access higher education, the world of work, and vocational education (Tomlinson 1994).

Economic globalisation, rapid advances in information and communications technology, and the move towards knowledge-based societies compel education systems to address equity issues. Differences in access to information and skills are rapidly increasing, and there is a generalised concern that this will further polarise rich and poor countries (Cavicchioni and Motivans 2001). However, the gap is not only growing between countries, but also between different groups within each country. It is thus imperative to address the issues underlying the sources of these disparities and inequalities.

Furthermore, as Irving and Malik contend in Chapter 1, education and guidance should not only educate students to ensure a steady supply of appropriately skilled workers, but should also prepare them to become active and critical citizens, able to question dominant paradigms and challenge inequitable practices. If social justice is to be achieved in the wider society, equity has first to be achieved in schools where many disparities originate and are embedded, and where students spend an important period of their lives.

This chapter will look at different ways in which compulsory schooling, supposedly aimed at providing basic quality education for all, is not adequately meeting the needs of many students, mostly those who come from culturally diverse groups, as well as those from economically disadvantaged settings. From a critical standpoint, we will analyse those factors largely responsible for inequalities within schools and which influence students' educational options and future career paths.

Career education and guidance practitioners must be able to identify discriminatory practices in order to deal with them effectively, working in collaboration with a wide range of other educational professionals. This chapter is structured into three sections. The first addresses the issue of equity and inequalities in educational systems. The second examines the sources of inequalities within schools, namely the dimensions of the school environment that relate to the informal curriculum. The final section emphasises the central role of guidance in the promotion of equity within schools, and the importance of collaborative working with teachers and other educational staff.

Education for all?

The primary goal of educational systems in democratic societies is to guarantee universal access to a worthwhile education, and provide opportunities for all students to achieve the necessary objectives. Institutional arrangements differ widely, but most 'industrialised' countries have established public education to give all children and youngsters equal access to, and opportunity in, education (Hutmacher 2001).

Comprehensive schooling for all has generally been embraced by modern democracies, where universal education is recognised as essential to universal suffrage, although there is an increasing shift back towards selective systems.[1] However, despite the rhetorical acceptance of this essential goal, on too many occasions school continues to limit the opportunities of those students who do not conform to the socio-cultural patterns that are valued and accepted in the official curriculum. This is particularly evident with reference to students, their families and communities who are seen to be culturally different and socially unequal. In contrast, school culture transmits specific socio-cultural values (those of the dominant group), excluding other cultural features that are not in accordance with its primary messages.

Equality of opportunities should be regarded as a real possibility of choice, which is in turn determined by the interaction between individual characteristics and social conditions. The way in which institutions manage these relations, in order to achieve educational results, determines students' real options and shapes their academic paths. Therefore, educational institutions play a fundamental role in ensuring that equality of opportunities becomes a reality for all (Aguado 2003), not only equality of access to education, but also of learning opportunities and outcomes.

'Education and educational systems lie at the heart of crucial tensions between formal civic and legal equality, on the one hand, and the inequality of real social conditions and positions on the other' (Hutmacher 2001: 5). Inequality is integral to the operation of schools, as they distribute goods unequally. For instance, throughout schooling students perform unequally in relation to prevailing standards; i.e. they receive unequal marks and rewards, obtain access to unequal tracks and curricula, achieve unequal knowledge and competencies, and attain unequal grades.

Inequalities in economic, cultural and social capital characterise the context of educational systems. The educational system is in many ways a microcosmic replica of the larger society, with its economic problems, social conflicts, and current events. Whether and how it can confront the needs and demands for competence in a complex, technical society and also continue to reach the diversity of youth in ways that are functional and appropriate for them (Axelson 1999) are major issues in today's globalised world. It is through education that most people hope to fulfil their aspirations for social and economic advancement, however many of them are left behind or alienated from a system that does not really respond positively to their needs.

> The provision of equal educational opportunities, or the development of unrecognized potential, continues to be a need unmet for many groups within the population, such as economically and educationally disadvantaged students, persons with physical disabilities, students with learning disabilities, culturally diverse students, preelementary children, urban youth, and women. Seemingly lost in the shuffle is the large array of average students whose problems, needs, and potential also go unrecognized [. . .]
>
> (Axelson 1999: 213)

Drawing on Bordieu's (1986) concept of cultural capital,[2] and assuming that schools and educational institutions operate as 'markets', Hutmacher (2001) suggests that the *embodied* form of students' cultural capital (habitus) plays a particularly important role, as the value of capital will vary with the markets in which it may be more or less advantageously used. We agree with Hutmacher in that:

> education systems are culturally not neutral, but privilege the standards of human excellence of dominant social groups and classes. Dispositions and attitudes (language and behaviour styles, work ethos, relationship to school, knowledge and learning, etc.), which students have acquired in different family and community environments, are therefore more or less akin to those valued at school, and are more or less rewarded.
>
> (Hutmacher 2001: 8)

The conversion of the embodied form of cultural capital into the institutionalised form depends not only on time and effort but also on the distance between the culture valued at school and students' habiti (Perrenoud 1984). Children from culturally diverse backgrounds generally bring to the school a set of behaviours and success expectations that are fostered both at home and in their communities. Regardless of cultural background, most families place a high value on education as an essential means to improve socio-economic status. These expectations, however, are often at odds with the realities of schools and the educational process (Lee 1995).

Cultural diversity in society is reflected in our school populations, but is seldom taken into account as an influential variable in the personal and social development of our students (Aguado *et al.* 2003). Although few teachers deliberately or consciously discriminate against students on the basis of their socio-cultural characteristics, it is true that in many cases their behaviour and ways of addressing children from diverse backgrounds is discriminating, even if unconsciously or unintentionally. Teachers hold pre-conceived notions and ideas concerning the behaviour patterns and degrees of ability of different 'categories' of children, and these stereotypes (with reference to social status, gender, nationality, ethnic group) influence not only teacher attitudes and behaviour, but also curriculum content, teaching styles, and assessment and evaluation procedures.

Incongruity often exists between what the teacher is accustomed to, or expects, and what may be the actual background of the students in a culturally diverse setting, since most teachers and other school personnel are trained in traditional, mainstream, middle-class cultural ways (Axelson 1999). At any rate, the educational system is not appropriately meeting the needs of culturally diverse students. In Spain, for example, school failure is very frequent among members of particular minority cultural and ethnic groups, such as Roma, or certain immigrant communities.

Lee's (2001) statement that schools in the United States have traditionally made little allowance for cultural diversity in educational practice can be applied to many other parts of the world, where cultural insensitivities inherent to the educational process tend not to validate the experiences of culturally diverse groups. In general, school success has been narrowly defined in terms of 'white', middle-class norms:

> Within such a framework, students whose cultural realities differ from these norms are often required to make important adjustments to ensure a measure of academic or social success. These adjustments become critical considering the lack of cultural awareness or cross-cultural sensitivity on the part of many educators.
>
> (Lee 2001: 259–260)

When conflicts arise, responsibility usually rests on the culturally different status of a student and its divergence from the educational norm. Little consideration is given to the notion that problems and challenges may in reality be reactive responses by many students to a system that tolerates little diversity (Lee 1995). Research has shown the importance of multicultural sensitivity and of using adequate strategies in the educational process based on principles of social justice (Aguado 2003).

It is thus clear that certain educational practices maintain, stress, and legitimise social inequalities for some students by not recognising and valuing their cultural differences (Aguado *et al.* 2003). Hence, many students are denied the possibility of achieving the same educational results as their peers from the majority culture. School promotes academic success for students in the dominant group, while presenting many barriers to students from non-dominant communities (Ogbu 1988). It is essential that students from diverse socio-cultural backgrounds be guaranteed real equality of opportunities and outcomes, ensuring that they are also developing their full potential, so that education acts as a fair, equitable and effective process for all.

Sources of inequality in schools

We have contended that schools contribute to inequalities in education and hinder future academic and career options, thus leading to the discrimination of some students through many of their practices. Is it possible to identify such practices? The answer to this question lies in the complex combination of variables shaping the school 'ethos' or school climate, which can be explicit (formal curriculum), and implicit (informal or 'hidden' curriculum). The informal curriculum, defined by Apple and Weiss (1983) as tacit teaching of norms and social and economic expectations, explains many of the inequalities and discrimination suffered by 'non-official' cultural groups in school contexts. The culture which school transmits and legitimates is embedded in several aspects of the informal curriculum (Kehoe 1984), regulating in a more or less covert way the activities and teaching practices that lead to unequal opportunities.

The attitudes of staff towards racial, ethnic and cultural diversity – the way it is dealt with in school, grouping practices (Oakes 1985; Banks 1994), testing practices and assessment, labelling practices, tracking of students, special classes, specific programs, such as compensatory education, or those for the gifted and talented – often contribute to ethnic and racial inequality within the school. Other important elements include teaching materials, teaching styles, organisation of time (schedules, time given to assignments) and space (how children are seated, etc.) within the classroom, interaction with the students, and the participation of both students and families in decisions made by the school concerning goals and norms (Aguado *et al.* 1999; Malik 2000; Aguado *et al.* 2003).

These schooling practices can be grouped into five main categories which, among others, contribute to, or even exacerbate, social inequalities (Oakes 1985; Aguado 2003), which are: classification or grouping; teaching methodology and the curriculum; organisation of time and space; participation; assessment and evaluation. These dimensions serve to create a climate of conformity within the school, and are the joint responsibility of principals, teachers, guidance practitioners,[3] the rest of the school staff, and the community (including the student's families). Assessment is especially crucial from the point of view of career education and guidance, as decisions derived from it too often result in the discrimination of students. Special attention should be given to assessment and evaluation processes, in order to ensure equity in education and to promote social justice. We will briefly explain these categories, discussing the latter more in depth.

Classification or grouping

Distributing students into 'homogeneous' groups of classes, areas, programmes or activities. The most harmful effects are alienation and marginalisation suffered by low-income students, those from socially disadvantaged backgrounds, and students from specific cultural groups. As a consequence of biased assessment and evaluation, these students are usually placed in lower ability classes, or special programs that lead to the separation of members of diverse groups.

The educational solution to individual differences and assistance given to 'non-traditional' students often includes compensatory and remedial procedures, bilingual/bicultural education, and other activities that tend to separate out individuals of culturally and socially different backgrounds (Axelson 1999). Efforts should be made to create a learning environment within the mainstream class where all children 'fit' and are given the opportunity to develop their potential. If separation occurs nonetheless, opportunities for interaction with the mainstream group should be ensured.

Teaching methodology/curriculum

Learning objectives, as well as teaching styles, techniques and methods are seldom flexible and therefore inadequate to respond to the cognitive/affective diversity of students. Differences in learning styles are not usually accounted for. Teaching should take into consideration the curriculum content and learning approaches that might be most appropriate and useful for diverse individuals.

Modification of the curriculum to encompass cultural diversity is rare.

Textbooks and other didactic materials do not reflect the social and cultural diversity present in the wider society. Stereotypes based on inaccurate knowledge and beliefs tend to be perpetuated, and perceptions of many cultural groups tend to be distorted or go unchallenged (Axelson 1999). Teachers and other professionals usually transmit the idea that learning and knowledge acquisition are static and linear, instead of a constructed and negotiated process; thus it is unlikely to provide or create the appropriate conditions to motivate all students to learn and think critically, in a significant way.

Organisation of time and space

Facilities to practice different sports or to engage in extracurricular activities, laboratories, study corners, or areas for informal gatherings are usually scarce. Schedules are not flexible and do not take into account the needs, routines or habits of minority group students. Teachers do not have enough time to plan different learning activities and to collaborate with colleagues, or they lack the necessary motivation and/or training related to these issues.

This dimension is also related to 'social organisation' in an educational context, which describes how teachers and students interact to fulfil their appropriate goals (Herring 1997). 'A central task of educational design is to make the organisation of teaching, learning, and performance compatible with the social structures in which students are most productive, engaged, and likely to learn' (Tharp 1989: 350). More often than not, social organization in schools corresponds to that of the dominant group, and does not take into account the social structures of other socio-cultural groups (e.g. competitive and individualistic oriented versus co-operative and collectively oriented environments).

Participation

This aspect refers to the role of students and their families in the elaboration of norms and rules regulating behaviour and discipline, as well as in other major decisions. Students from non-dominant cultural groups perceive that their traditions, languages and life experiences are excluded from school. Parental involvement in school activities is very scarce, particularly in the area of careers (Irving 2000), whilst links with the students' communities are rarely established. This is not strange considering that the contribution they make to the education of their children is seldom valued. Furthermore, as Lee (2001) suggests, not all parents perceive schools as welcoming environments, due to language differences or cultural customs which make schools alienating and intimidating, among other reasons.

Assessment and evaluation

Testing and other assessment techniques are not culturally adapted but present a high verbal component. They measure traits or aspects in which students from minority groups or from 'socially deprived' backgrounds usually score or perform lower. Students who do not conform to the 'norm', as defined by the dominant cultural group, are usually diagnosed with behaviour problems or learning disabilities. For instance, lack of competence in the official language of the school is considered a language 'deficit' and is often associated with a cognitive deficit (in general, language differences are viewed as deficits).

Assessment of students' abilities is too frequently based on a subjective appraisal of physical appearance, behaviour in relation to others, language, and a combination of social factors which include income, parents' educational level and family structure, number of siblings, and social services received (Jackson and Cosca 1974). Differences in cultural background are often perceived by school personnel in terms of deficiency or pathology (Axelson 1999: 226). This approach leads to limited solutions, restricted educational strategies, and labelling children according to alleged weaknesses based on their cultural group identity (Shade 1978). Presumptions of the innate intellectual inferiority of children from certain socio-cultural groups also continues to be held by many educators. The resultant negative effects of these oft repeated myths impacts on the support and 'treatment' such children receive.

Thus, many students from low-income families or those belonging to 'minority' cultural groups are ascribed to special education groups, compensatory classes or to lower educational streams than those reflecting their actual abilities, resulting in ongoing discriminatory educational treatment. Furthermore, this leads to an increase in the difference gap with the students of the dominant group, and acts to confirm expectations regarding the differences among groups (Samuda and Crawford 1986). Most frequently used tests, based on standardised or 'normalised' patterns, evaluate the outcomes or products, not the processes. They are used to assess and classify students, not to enhance the teaching and learning process.

Students who do not belong to the dominant cultural group are often diagnosed with learning disabilities, as previously mentioned, and are considered to have fewer possibilities of succeeding academically, expectations which many teachers frequently generalise and accept without question. Difficulties are attributed both to internal factors (deficits) and to the students' social environment, without considering the responsibility of the school, or questioning the assessment procedures or other practices which generate inequalities and low achievement of students from certain groups. As Lee (1995, 2001: 260) emphasises, 'obstacles to school success for young people from culturally diverse backgrounds are often perceived as student inadequacies rather than considered as originating with institutional insensitivity'.

It is now widely recognised that guidance theories and assessment techniques have been developed and standardised with reference to one group, namely white middle-class males, and underpinned by assumptions that are not valid across all cultures. Most tests and instruments are based on a mono-ethnic model. As Rollock and Terrell (1996) state, mainstream methods of assessment typically use 'standard' perspectives, instruments, and norms that are assumed to reflect universal truths about human nature. However, they do not really represent all people. Non-mainstream ethnic and cultural groups may not be understood appropriately if assessed according to those norms. Many students socialised within ethnic and cultural communities that often hold differing values to those of the majority group find the tests, and other aspects of the school, alien and intimidating. Thus they tend to perform poorly and are usually placed in low academic tracks, special education classes, or low-ability reading groups (Oakes 1985).

The use of these techniques or methods, without an awareness and understanding of their inherent bias, results in misjudgement of ability, behaviour, or other variables. It is therefore very important that guidance counsellors try to assess children in their own language, if different from the official one, and especially to be aware of the differences in cognitive processes, communication, learning styles, etc. (Aguado *et al.* 1999; Malik 2000).

> Counselors need to appraise the client as a cultural entity before any other assessment strategy is undertaken. Understanding the client as a cultural entity implies an understanding of the client's philosophy of life, beliefs, values, and assumptions in the context of his or her primary and secondary cultures and in the context of the larger social system ... Counselors need to use multisource, multilevel, and multimethod approaches to assess the capabilities, potentials, and limitations of the client.
>
> (Ibrahim and Arredondo 1986: 350)

This should be done without the placing of clients into predefined categories, e.g. Asian-Americans, Native Americans, Roma, Moroccans, Muslims, etc., as this can lead to assumptions that members from diverse communities will all share the same cultural patterns or worldviews. As we will contend at the end of this section, it is crucial to be aware of the distinctiveness of each person, obtaining information directly from them as to how this uniqueness is mediated and influenced by cultural variables, genuinely relevant to them (see Chapter 6 by Barker and Irving; and Barker and Irving 2003).

Regarding evaluation of students' learning, Aguado (2003) makes the following recommendations:

- Grades or marks should not be given to everything the student does. Essays, oral activities, work done in collaboration with peers should be appraised and supervised without a grade being awarded.
- Written assignments. Avoid putting a mark on the first drafts of essays or term papers. It should be done when the student is finally satisfied with his/her work.
- Criteria. Make the evaluation criteria clear from the beginning. Students should know from the start what is expected of them to obtain good grades. Discuss with them what makes a good assignment, and explain what would be considered unacceptable.
- Self-evaluation. As much as possible, students should be allowed to evaluate their own work according to the established criteria.
- Personal discussions. A few minutes should be spent with every child to discuss personally the tasks fulfilled and the outcomes. The most important purpose of evaluation is to assess and support their work and inform their development, not to judge their errors.
- Written communication with the parents. Inform them about their children's progress and activities. Use the family's language.
- Emphasise positive aspects. Focus attention on achievements, on what the student has accomplished, carried out, learned, improved, regardless of mistakes or gaps.

Other useful suggestions are identified by Axelson (1999), both in the evaluation of students and in the promotion of positive intergroup relations:

- Introduce new norms of intelligence and achievement by emphasising multiple intellectual abilities in addition to reading, writing, and computing skills. Logic, problem solving, creativity, expression of ideas, leadership, and cooperation are other areas in which students can take pride.
- Work against the self-fulfilling prophecy that minority children will fail and work for the success of *all* children.
- Keep children mixed in as many activities as possible.
- When children are segregated into bilingual or other programs, allow for activities in which different children can mix, work, or interact together.

Maintaining high expectations and standards of excellence for every student is essential. In today's world, all students should be able to read, write, speak, listen and think critically, and to use these skills to promote fairness and inclusion (OISE 2002). An inclusive curriculum should help students understand that all people and all cultures are interrelated and interdependent, part of the emerging global community.

The role of guidance in the promotion of school equity and social justice

As we pointed out in the previous section when examining different dimensions of the school environment, guidance practitioners play an important role in the promotion of equity in schools, helping teachers and other staff to identify and eliminate the sources of inequalities in the informal curriculum. School counsellors can work towards the enhancement of educational settings, applying the same commitments to the guidance and counselling process with students and in their consultative services to teachers (Axelson 1999), assisting them in the individualisation of the educational process by making more apparent the distinctiveness of each person. Some strategies have already been discussed in relation to each of the dimensions of the informal curriculum.

Collaboration between school counsellors and teachers is essential to meet the educational needs of all students. Teachers are in daily contact with their students and are therefore in a better position to observe them. Unlike teachers, counsellors are trained in developmental issues alongside a range of other competencies necessary in delivering guidance interventions. Thus, through collaborative partnerships, school counsellors and teachers can 'generate appropriate strategies to ensure culturally compatible classrooms and school environments' (Herring 1997: 204), as outlined in the following strategies:

- Experiment with varied grouping arrangements to encourage social cooperation (e.g. 'study buddies').
- Provide multiple approaches to teaching to accommodate diverse learning styles (verbal, visual and auditory materials, projects, collaborative work).
- Teach classroom procedures and norms directly, even things that are usually taken for granted (e.g. how to get the teacher's attention).
- Recognise the meaning of different behaviours for the students (e.g. how do they feel when they are corrected).
- Stress meaning in teaching (ensure meaningful learning, e.g. making sure students understand what they read, relating abstract concepts to everyday experiences).
- Know the customs, beliefs, and values of students (e.g. analysing different traditions for common themes; discussing different ways in which knowledge is constructed).
- Help students identify stereotypes and racist or sexist messages (analysing curriculum materials, news from the media, etc.).

Besides the general interventions to eliminate bias and discrimination within the informal curriculum, cultural diversity must be effectively addressed in the provision of comprehensive school counselling programs. Guidance initiatives, and education in general, should be based on two essential premises as stated by Lee (2001: 259): '(1) All young people can learn and want to learn; and (2) cultural differences are real and cannot be ignored'. Three concepts underscore the importance of promoting cultural diversity in school counselling interventions: access, equity, and educational justice. All students, regardless of their cultural background and heritage, deserve access to a quality education. Denying this right to any child implies a grave educational injustice. School counsellors need a different perspective from which to operate if they are to ensure that students from culturally diverse backgrounds have access to services that promote optimal academic, career, and personal-social development (Baruth and Manning 2000).

Some research studies have found that students from diverse cultural backgrounds who attain academic success usually display the following characteristics, not traditionally associated with school success, but relevant to their educational achievement (Rosenthal and Jakobson 1968; Nieto 1992; Aguado 2003):

1 Positive self-concept, both at individual level as well as related to their identity within a specific cultural group.
2 Understanding of, and ability to deal with, racism.
3 Realistic self-assessment. They are aware of their own abilities and limitations.
4 Intrinsic motivation on the part of the student.
5 A family that values and encourages educational achievement. There is generally an adult person who has, or has had, a strong influence and acts as a role model.
6 A feeling or sense of belonging to the group.
7 Demonstrates critical thinking.
8 Links with the community of origin, and participates in extracurricular activities. Experience in leadership.
9 Wide array of competencies and interests, beyond the purely academic.

The preceding characteristics can be enhanced through guidance interventions. Counsellors should be able to help students from a variety of cultural backgrounds develop healthy self-concepts and learn to respect cultural diversity, while setting educational, career, and personal–social goals, both through individual and group counselling, as well as large group guidance interventions. Other chapters in this book address specific issues related to career education and guidance in diverse settings. Here we will only consider some distinct functions which, in this regard, 'emerge for culturally effective counsellors' (Lee 2001: 259):

- Promoting the development of positive self-identities among students. This could be accomplished by conducting self-awareness groups that emphasise self-appreciation through a validation of cultural heritage. It is also useful to use culturally specific curriculum materials to cultivate self-pride from a number of cultural perspectives (see Kincheloe and Steinberg's objections to this in Chapter 13 by Reid). These activities should be carried out with all students, not only those from minority groups.
- Facilitating the development of positive interpersonal relations among students from diverse cultural backgrounds. Opportunities should be provided for students to engage in group interactions and to explore cultural variations as a way to develop mutual respect and understanding.
- Promoting the development of positive attitudes towards academic achievement among all students. Guidance activities should focus on inherent cultural potential by incorporating educational experiences of influential people from a variety of backgrounds.
- Facilitating academic achievement through the development of academic skills and competencies necessary for school success. Guidance activities should be planned in areas such as academic planning, study skills, and time management. These workshops can ensure that all young people have an opportunity to develop the skills to achieve, given differences in learning styles.
- Facilitating career exploration and decision-making processes. Issues of career interest and choice are complex and challenging dimensions in the development of young people. Career role models from a variety of cultural backgrounds can be invited to schools to share with students their perceptions and experiences in the working world. Internships and cooperative experiences with culturally diverse businesses and professionals could also be developed.

It is clear that a fundamental aspect of any guidance approach is to understand the cultural realities of children. Nevertheless, it is very important to avoid the use of culture as a pretext to label and to classify students, which would lead to further discrimination. 'Counselors who approach their clients with an attitude that there is individual diversity within groups of people will be more successful than counselors who tend to lump individuals into labeled categories that have been defined by outside spectators' (Axelson 1999: 220). All individuals from one group do not necessarily share the same beliefs or customs. It is necessary to take into account the students' cultural worldview, but bearing in mind the distinctiveness of each child. Information should be obtained directly from the children themselves and their families, in relation to their group of reference, and to what is genuinely relevant and significant for them.

Conclusions

Schools transmit an 'official' culture, derived from the notion of a homogeneous and mono-cultural society, adopting the values, norms and world-views of the majority or dominant group. These are seldom in accordance with the cultural patterns of different groups, which are largely disregarded and excluded. The dominant paradigms and inequitable practices present in society are reproduced in educational systems, and inequalities thus arise within schools. The notion of school success should also be questioned.

As Lee (2001: 261) points out, 'appropriate educational processes require that schools move beyond the myth of a monolithic society to the reality of cultural diversity'. Guidance practitioners must be aware of this diversity, and learn to address it effectively. They must also identify those school practices that are at the root of inequalities, blocking the way for many children. In collaboration with teachers, strategies should be developed to promote an inclusive curriculum, free of bias and discrimination, ensuring that all children benefit fully from educational opportunities. This is essential in the promotion of equity, educational justice, and social justice, along with other social and economic factors, which are addressed elsewhere in this book.

Notes

1 Many school systems which had endorsed the principles of comprehensive education are taking a step backwards, adopting again a selective system. This is the case in Spain, where a major educational reform is currently taking place *Ley de Educación* (LOCE) (MECD 2003), placing a strong emphasis on individual determination (the 'culture of effort') and fostering tracking of students at an early age. Certain categories of students are identified and ascribed to specific programs: disabled, immigrants, and gifted children.

2 Bordieu (1986) analyses material and/or symbolic resources (which are at the heart of inequalities) as a configuration of three major forms of capital (economic, cultural and social) that individuals and groups can mobilise:

- *Economic capital* refers to the amount of material resources, mainly income and wealth (determining access to basic assets as well as to goods more directly useful at school).
- *Cultural capital* which encompasses three forms: the *embodied* form, consisting of durable competencies and dispositions of mind and body *habitus* – learned and embodied by individuals through lengthy experience and interaction with a given social environment (family, community, school, etc.) and that predispose their future interactions and strategies; the *objectified* form of cultural goods (books, art works, other productions); and the *institutionalised* form referring to academic credits and qualifications.

  - *Social capital* is embodied in the networks of social relations among individuals and groups.

3 Throughout the chapter we mean guidance practitioners in *schools*. We also refer to them as 'school counsellors', especially when quoting authors from the North-American context.

Bibliography

Aguado, T. (2003) *Pedagogía Intercultural*, Madrid: McGraw-Hill.

Aguado, T., Ballesteros, B. and Malik, B. (2003) 'Cultural diversity and school equity: a model to evaluate and develop educational practices in multicultural education contexts', *Equity and Excellence in Education*, 36(1): 50–63.

Aguado, T., Gil, J.A., Jimenez-Frias, R., Sacristán, A., Malik, B., Sánchez, M.F. and Ballesteros, B. (1999) *Diversidad Cultural e Igualdad Escolar: Un modelo para el diagnóstico y desarrollo de actuaciones educativas en contextos escolares multiculturales*, Madrid: MEC.

Apple, M. and Weiss, S. (eds) (1983) *Ideology and Practice in Schooling*, Philadelphia: Temple University Press.

Axelson, J.A. (1999) *Counseling and Development in a Multicultural Society*, 3rd edn, Monterey: Brooks/Cole.

Banks, J.A. (1994) *Multiethnic Education: Theory and Practice*, 3rd edn, Boston: Allyn and Bacon.

Barker, V. and Irving, B.A. (2003) 'Challenging educators; culture specific careers programmes: a human rights imperative', paper presented at UNESCO Conference on Intercultural Education, Jyvaskyla, Finland, June.

Baruth, L.G. and Manning, L.M. (2000) 'A call for multicultural counseling in middle schools', *Clearing House*, 73: 243–246.

Bordieu, P. (1986) 'The forms of capital', in J.E. Richardson (ed.) *Handbook of Theory of Research for the Sociology of Education*, Westport: Greenwood Press.

Cavicchioni, V. and Motivans, A. (2001) 'Monitoring educational disparities in less developed countries', in W. Hutmacher, D. Cochrane and N. Bottani (eds) *In Pursuit of Equity in Education: Using International Indicators to Compare Equity Policies*, Dordrecht: Kluwer Academic Publishers.

Herring, R.D. (1997) *Multicultural Counseling in Schools: A Synergetic Approach*, Alexandria: American Counseling Association.

Hutmacher, W. (2001) 'Introduction', in W. Hutmacher, D. Cochrane, and N. Bottani (eds) *In Pursuit of Equity in Education: Using International Indicators to Compare Equity Policies*, Dordrecht: Kluwer Academic Publishers.

Ibrahim, F.A. and Arredondo, P.M. (1986) 'Ethical standards for cross-cultural counseling: counselor preparation, practice', assessment, and research, *Journal of Counseling and Development*, 64: 349–352.

Irving, B.A. (2000) 'Reaching out to parents: a rationale for the development of inclusive approaches within career education and guidance', in Institute of Career Guidance (ed.) *Careers Guidance. Constructing the Future: Global Perspectives*, Stourbridge, ICG.

Jackson, G. and Cosca, C. (1974) 'The inequality of educational opportunities in the South West: an observational study of ethnically mixed classrooms', *American Educational Research Journal*, 11(3): 219–229.

Kehoe, J.W. (1984) *A Handbook for Enhancing the Multicultural Climate of the School*, Vancouver: University of British Columbia Press.

Lee, C.C. (ed.) (1995) *Counseling for Diversity: A Guide for School Counselors and Related Professionals*, Boston: Allyn & Bacon.

—— (2001) 'Culturally responsive school counselors and programs: addressing the needs of all students', *Professional School Counseling*, 4(4): 257–261.

Ministerio de Educación, Cultura y Deporte, MECD (2003) *LEY ORGÁNICA 10/2002, de 23 de diciembre, de Calidad de la Educación* (LOCE). Ministerio de Educación, Cultura y Deporte (MECD): Boletín Oficial del Estado (BOE) núm. 307 de 24/12/2002. Available on 'PDF' format at http://www.mecd.es/leycalidad/index.htm (last visited: 15 December 2003).

Malik, B. (2000) 'Intercultural competencies and strategies in guidance: tools for intervention in schools', in Proceedings of IAEVG Conference: *Guidance for Education, Career and Employment. New Challenges*, Berlin. Available online on PDF format (accessed 20 September 2003): http://www.arbeitsamt.de/laa_bb/international/InhaltKongressF/F64Malik.

Nieto, S. (1992) *Affirming Diversity: The Socio-political Context of Multicultural Education*, New York: Teachers College Press.

Oakes, J. (1985) *Keeping Track: How Schools Structure Inequality*, New Haven: Yale University Press.

Ogbu, J.U. (1988) 'Class stratification, racial stratification, and schooling', in L. Weiss (ed.) *Class Race and Gender in American Education*, New York: State University of New York Press.

Ontario Institute for the Study of Education (2002) *Inclusive Curriculum 2002: Strategies and Resources to Support K-8 Curriculum Development.* Available on HTML and PDF: http://www.oise.utoronto.ca/~cwse/inclusive/ (last accessed 20 September 2003).

Perrenoud, P.H. (1984) *La Fabrication de l'Excellence Scolaire,* Geneva: Droz.

Rollock, D. and Terrell, M.D. (1996) 'Multicultural issues in assessment: toward an inclusive model', in J. DeLucia-Waack (ed.) *Multicultural Counseling Competencies: Implications for Training and Practice*, Alexandria, VA: Association for Counselor Education and Supervision.

Rosenthal, R. and Jakobson, W. (1968) *Pygmalion in the Classroom: Teacher Expectations and Pupils Intellectual Performance*, New York: Holt, Rinehart and Winston.

Samuda, R. and Crawford, M. (1986) *Testing, Assessment, Counseling and Placement of Ethnic Minority Students: Current Methods in Ontario*, Ontario: Ministry of Education.

Shade, B.J. (1978) 'Socio-psychological characteristics of achieving Black children', *Negro Educational Review*, 29: 80–86.

Tharp, R.G. (1989) 'Psychocultural variables and constraints: effects on teaching and learning in schools', *American Psychologist*, 44, 349–359.

Tomlinson, S. (1994) 'Achievement, assessment and the school effect', in J. Lynch, C. Modgil and S. Modgil (eds) *Cultural Diversity and the Schools*, IV, London: The Palmer Press.

Chapter 6

Career education for Muslim girls

Meeting culture at the crossroads

Vivienne Barker and Barrie A. Irving

Introduction

This chapter critically explores ways in which gender, culture and ethnicity can impact on young people's choice in relation to career and opportunity. Historically, national career education frameworks, curriculum objectives and learning outcomes have been developed within a predominantly individualistic and ethnocentric ethos. In recent years however, concern with the social exclusion of certain groups of young people has led the government to refocus its attention. The Department for Education and Skills (DfES) now acknowledges that schools should provide greater differentiation in the development of programmes for young people, that are responsive to both individual *and* 'group' career learning needs. The authors discuss how the political drive to tackle social exclusion is of particular relevance to Muslim girls, and they critically reflect on key issues that emerged in their development of a career education pack for this group. They suggest that an inclusive ethos towards career education *can* cater for difference and need not be divisive, whereas assimilationist and integrationist approaches run the risk of perpetuating cultural dominance and the imposition of an ethnocentric curriculum and associated values. Moreover, it is argued that the lessons learnt in England can also be translated to other contexts and countries.

Muslim girls: cultured choices

The terms ethnicity and culture are context dependent, yet often used interchangeably. This has a tendency to mask, or at times confuse, key issues that may emerge in discussion concerning career, opportunity, 'race' and gender, and how these influence notions of choice. Whilst ethnicity can be seen to relate to a person's birthplace and/or historical place of origin, '(C)ulture is . . . a system of beliefs and practices in terms of which a group of human beings understand, regulate and structure their individual and collective lives' (Parekh 2000: 143). For Muslims, religion is the organising principle that is central to the establishment of culturally derived norms and conventions, and thus utilised to guide the behaviour and practices of its members. How different Muslim communities interpret Islam leads to variations in practice and behaviour that are considered to be acceptable. Yet whilst diversity is apparent, both between and within Muslim communities, they all still adhere to a belief in a single Islamic faith and the importance of a collective and communal sense of being.

'Islam therefore is premised on the development of a confident sense of self yet within a supportive collective culture, built upon religious tenets' (Parker-Jenkins *et al.* forthcoming). Whilst each individual develops and displays their own unique characteristics it is the sense of belonging to a faith-based community that exerts significant influence, and therefore is of primary importance when considering the position of Muslim girls. We would agree with Harris *et al.* that, '(S)tudents live out their school careers in a continual interaction with their family, community, peers and teachers' (1993: 12). This is of particular significance for Muslim girls who engage in a continuous process of shaping and reshaping their identity and sense of self as they interact with a range of, at times contradictory and conflicting, worlds. However, for many this still occurs within an Islamic context that reflects the central importance of family, community and culture (Parker-Jenkins 1995; Puri 1995; Irving *et al.* 2003).

For Muslims, discrimination can be experienced not only on the basis of their 'race', gender and/or social class, but also as a result of the religious beliefs they hold. When considered alongside a rising tide of Islamaphobia and anti-Muslim feeling (Runnymede Trust 1997; Parker-Jenkins *et al.* 1998), this is of significant importance when exploring how discrimination is interpreted and understood. The position of women within Islam presents a complex and at times contradictory picture to many western eyes. The popular portrayal of the Muslim girl as a victim of outright male oppression, resulting in a denial of choice and opportunity, serves to perpetuate beliefs in some quarters that Muslim girls need to be 'liberated' from their communities. For others, their lack of insight and understanding of Muslim communities and their practices leads to a sense of distance, whereby Muslim girls are 'left alone'. Bradley observes that:

> The international revival of Islam has opened up a positive identity and source of pride for Muslim women, as opposed to being the stigmatized 'Other' in the playground. Thus many women willingly embrace Islamic dress styles, such as wearing of headscarf or veil.
>
> (1996: 108)

In many respects dress codes act as visible signifiers of the Muslim girls' 'difference' to those of mainstream western society. However, the public wearing of the hijab 'has become an embodiment of what is perceived, by some, as symbolic of both anti-western and anti-feminism views' (Benn and Jawad 2003: xiii). It has led to a number of controversies in countries such as France and Turkey that have enshrined secularism in their constitutions. Yet for many Muslim girls, this external display is a positive cultural act, through which they are asserting their sense of identity as members of cohesive, and distinct, communities. Moreover, Muslim girls may also feel more liberated within their culture due to the lack of commercial and sexual pressure exerted on western women.

In many western countries there has been a belief that the provision of equal opportunities, enabling each individual to compete from the same starting point, will result in a just distribution of economic rewards. However, efforts to equalise access to opportunities all too often results in attempts to treat each individual in the same way, thereby assuming that all have the same needs and, more specifically, desire success in the labour market. Human value and worth are thus linked to economic activity and productive output, giving little recognition to those who choose alternative pathways due to culture, religion or necessity. If an inclusive multicultural society is to come about, built upon a belief in social justice *and* human rights, then it will be important to go beyond such notions of simple equality (Irving *et al.* 2000; Barker and Irving 2003). The acceptance of a dominant culture's mores should not be a precondition of full citizenship rights as this serves to marginalise those who are 'different', whilst reinforcing a monocultural world-view. It also denies the contribution that minority cultures might make to the development of a vibrant and meaningful nation. As Young observes,

> oppressed groups have distinct cultures, experiences and perspectives on social life with humanly positive meaning, some of which may even be superior to the culture and perspectives of mainstream society. The rejection and devaluation of one's culture and perspective should not be a condition of full participation in social life.
>
> (1990: 166)

The cultural differences and sense of mistrust experienced by Muslims is exacerbated through degrees of ignorance about Islam, which is still regarded as alien by many in the (predominantly Christian) west. Allied to this are fears that the indigenous cultures of European nations are being overshadowed and devalued. Ultimately this impacts on concepts of nationality, nationalism and citizenship, as identity becomes tied to issues concerning 'who belongs' and 'who does not' (Solomos 1993). This has a resonance for the British situation which, unless it is addressed, could result in ongoing discrimination against minority groups and heightened inter-cultural and inter-community tensions. Positive action is required therefore to redefine multiculturalism and create an inclusive society comprised of a diverse '...community of citizens and a community of communities' (Parekh 2000: 140). Through constructive and meaningful dialogue, which engages with the views of both white and non-white communities, *all* may begin to feel valued (Alibhai-Brown 1999) and develop a sense of belief and belonging.

When considering the position of Muslim girls in relation to their post-16 choices, it is important to acknowledge the ways in which multi-layered social identities can play a determining factor in decisions made, alongside cultural affiliation. There has, however, been much criticism of teachers' attitudes towards Muslim girls. It is reported in the literature that, all too often, they do not have high enough expectations of Muslim girls' abilities (Parker-Jenkins *et al.* 1997) and/or assume that they will only have limited aspirations due to the perceived constraining impact of their culture (Mirza 1992; Brah 1994; Ghouri 1997). Cultural positioning, and the sense of role and duty, clearly impacts on the lives of many Muslim girls, and may influence decisions taken about future options. Arthur notes that,

> Although an individual may wish to pursue available choices, there may be severe and long-lasting consequences for going against the expectations of significant others in one's culture of origin. For example, values of religion, ethnicity or notions of appropriate gender roles may determine style of dress, food, social activities, occupational selection and choice of friends and marital partners.
>
> (2002: 11)

It is important to keep this in mind when exploring ways in which schools can contribute both to the opening up and restriction of opportunities for Muslim girls. However, the belief that Muslim girls are simply subject to the whims and/or expectations of the family, and have no choice or input into decisions about their future when they complete their compulsory period of schooling, is open to question (Basit 1996). The influence of the family for ethnic minority pupils is well documented (NIACE 1997; Robinson 2002) along with issues related to cultural practices (Parker-Jenkins *et al.* 1997) and should not be overlooked or taken lightly. Recent research in England reports that Muslim girls do exert a sense of agency with regards to decisions about their post-school choices (Archer 2002).

Whilst Arthur (2002) provides a helpful insight into a range of issues that could be encountered by Muslim girls during their time at school, there is also the risk that her observations may be interpreted by some teachers and careers professionals in a negative way, further feeding into restrictive and stereotypical images. Such images, observes Archer (2002),

> have further contributed to stereotypes of young Muslim women as heavily oppressed, suffering from 'wasted potential' and prevented

> from continuing in education/employment because they are expected and/or 'forced' into arranged marriages on account of authoritarian, 'alien' cultural norms and practices.
>
> (p.361)

If such stereotypical and limiting perceptions of Muslim girls are to be addressed, the challenge for educational institutions, educators in general, and career educators in particular, are evident. Responding positively to issues of culture, 'race', religion and diversity will begin to open up opportunities that many may have had denied in the past. Recognising the interplay between school, community, family and pupils, and how this impacts on post-16 choices, will help to raise awareness of the multiplicity of pathways and possibilities. Whilst it may not be able to defeat the endemic racism in the labour market, or remove other forms of discrimination on the basis of social class, gender and (dis)ability, it may go some way to reducing its impact (Irving and Barker 2004).

Career education: reflecting a multicultural reality?

Career education in England has historically been a contested concept (Harris 1999). Its definition has varied with changing political, social and economic agendas and ideologies. As Barnes *et al.* (2002) note, in the 1990s the function of career education and guidance was to contribute to the development of a skilled workforce able to compete in a global economy by preparing young people for lifelong learning and employability. The economic benefits of career education and guidance that predominated at that time continue to exert influence, and sits comfortably alongside the educational and social inclusion policies instigated by New Labour since 1997. This is evident in the non-statutory National Framework 11–19 for Careers Education and Guidance in England (2003) which aimed to give schools, colleges and work-based training organisations a tool to improve the quality of career learning opportunities for young people. In this document, government Ministers describe career education as an essential component of the education policy for 14–19 year olds that will provide more individually-tailored learning programmes to better meet the aspirations of young people, and to help them achieve their full potential. Further, career education is presented as a means for enabling young people to '...make the right choices about their education and prepare them properly for working life' (2003: 2). *Career* therefore appears to be interpreted as a working life in the labour market. However some confusion is evident as the National Framework is also described as a guide to improve career education and guidance provision '...to better prepare young people for the opportunities, responsibilities and experiences of adult life' (2003: 5). This suggests a wider, socially and culturally inclusive construction of career. This should encourage career educators to consider with young people, parents and local communities, issues of relevance in preparation for a changing and dynamic variety of roles and functions assumed throughout adult life (for example homemaker, citizen, learner, volunteer, carer) as well as paid worker. Such a move would recognise and attribute value and worth to *all* young people, including those for whom entry to the labour market may not be feasible, or a desired goal in the foreseeable future. Yet the Framework document does not expand on this earlier stated aim in the learning outcomes. Instead it is reduced in scope to a narrow definition of career education, wherein young people are helped, '...to develop the knowledge and skills they need to make successful choices, manage transitions in learning and move into work' (2003: 6).

The Framework draws on the DOTS analysis (Law and Watts 1977) which has widely influenced career education programmes in Britain since its introduction as a tool for reviewing and identifying specific learning aims for career education and guidance. It covers the areas of self, opportunity awareness, decision and transition learning, which have been translated into the following three broad aims (SCAA 1995):

- Self development – understanding themselves and the influences on them.
- Career exploration – investigate opportunities in learning and work.
- Career management – make and adjust plans to manage change and transition.

These aims are supported in the Framework at Key Stages 3 and 4 and post-16 (i.e. ages 11–19) by recommended learning outcomes. In addition, lesson plans and guidance on programme development provide additional support through the web based Careers Education Support Programme (CESP). The learning outcomes for students include a consideration of how to combat stereotyping, tackle discrimination and promote equal opportunities, and have respect for diversity. This appears to concur with a policy agenda identified by Ruff (2001) in which, '(T)he social/cultural imperative for careers education and guidance is to promote the goals of social inclusion, social justice, equal opportunities and community citizenship' (in Gothard *et al.* 2001: 103).

As Ruff (in Gothard *et al.* 2001) notes, community ownership and a recognition of the value of individual and cultural differences is central to this social–cultural imperative. Therefore this learning objective needs to be mirrored in schools' career education policies and actively put into practice if young people are to not only learn *about* equality and diversity, but also *experience* a socially just approach through the career education programme they follow. This could involve the provision of differentiated programmes which recognise and address the different needs of different groups.

In the Framework document it is also recognised that there may be a need to modify and adapt it to meet particular needs of young people, although these are not specified. Further, it is suggested that reference is made to a section in the document which provides 'particular advice on using it when planning programmes for individuals with special educational needs or learning difficulties and/or disabilities, and in non-mainstream provision such as pupil referral units and young offender's institutions' (Department for Education and Skills 2003: 9). Thus, the Framework is presented as supporting a generic approach, with scope for the differentiation of programmes for those who fall within the government's definition of pupils 'at risk' of, or experiencing, social exclusion. However, others may also experience social exclusion due to their occupancy of one or more traditional sites of discrimination (religion/gender/ 'race'/culture) and might also benefit from differentiated provision.

A culturally sensitive approach to career education necessarily involves addressing the distinctive needs of particular groups of students through the design of focused programme content; involving parents, families and local communities i.e. those who have an active commitment to, and social–cultural investment in, its success; and through a culturally sensitive approach in its delivery. These issues are at the core of Ruff's assertion:

> Provision needs to help individuals develop the skills and knowledge to access and make best use of the opportunities open to them, according to their own needs and desires, but within a positive context of recognition and regard for the aspirations and concerns of the students, family, culture and community.
>
> (in Gothard *et al.* 2001: 103–104)

Research by Parker-Jenkins *et al.* (1999) found that career education in English state-funded schools has tended to be based on universally applicable programmes, which reflect western values by, for example, focusing on individual responsibility for career exploration and management. In this research few opportunities were identified that would enable Muslim girls to address the collective, cultural–religious aspects of their lives in relation to career.

The National Framework (DfES 2003) makes no explicit reference to addressing differences in culture, ethnicity or religion through career education programmes, nor is there any indication of this in the learning outcomes. It is essentially a culturally neutral set of guidelines and recommendations which makes no statement that recognises socially constructed cultural differences, the diversity of cultural backgrounds of students and differing career issues concerning them. This is not to assume, however, that culturally specific programmes would not be acceptable or encouraged by those bodies responsible for career education, work-related learning accreditation, and quality standards in England (i.e. the Qualification Curriculum Authority, Office for Standards in Education, and the Adult Learning Inspectorate). Indeed, with the drive towards the introduction of formal assessment schemes (QCA 2003) leading to, for example, a Certificate in Career Planning based on units assessed as pass or fail through submission of a portfolio, it will be an imperative that course specifications are relevant to all young people and therefore that programme developers have access to appropriate materials. CESP has been established by the DfES to disseminate resources and exemplars of good practice in career education, and therefore the initiative to develop culturally specific programmes for inclusion appears to lie with career educators.

If career education is to meet the diverse needs of multi-ethnic clients, we suggest that there is a place for differentiated programmes that enable students from specific groups to articulate, share and address culturally derived career-related issues and concerns. This may be particularly relevant for students, for example Muslim girls, who have a common basis of understanding developed through a shared experience of everyday living, influenced by a particular and identifiable set of principles and practices transmitted by parents, family and community.

In Law's (2001) expansion of the DOTS analysis, to consider the 'how?' and 'why?' as well as the 'what?' of career learning, he points to the importance both of seeing the learner in a social world, and taking cognisance of the values and responsibilities that contextualise the decisions and problems they face. As he notes:

> The issue is relevance – which would require that 'classroom' learning remind learners of their lives and their lives remind them of their 'classroom'. A relevant outcome would, therefore need to be more than can be verified by tests; it would need to show that it can be used in life... The transfer is to life – as parent, consumer and citizen as well as worker.
>
> (2001: 22)

Therefore, there arises the issue of how to ensure that career education programmes are not remote from the real, lived experiences of young people that are played out within, and for some at the boundaries between, cultures.

Law's (2001) view of enabling people to think about career by setting action in a social context, considering the different roles identified with and adopted, and showing the interdependence between these, has particular relevance for career education in a multicultural society where roles may be interpreted and valued from different cultural perspectives. It also gives overt recognition to a holistic approach to careers work which does not compartmentalise people's lives for the purposes of career education into work–learning and non-work–learning nor, as a result, run the risk of problematising students within their own communities and cultures.

The concept of developing career programmes that are focused on particular cultural groups is not unique to Britain. In New Zealand, programmes are in the process of development for use with Maori and Pasifika secondary school students (Reid and Atiga 2002). Within these cultures and communities, understanding of career and opportunity differ from western traditions of self-promotion and the importance placed on individual choice in isolation of wider considerations.

One step forward: developing career education for Muslim girls

Muslim girls inhabit a world in which they are bound together by a common faith founded on certain basic and commonly held principles and beliefs that influence many or all aspects of their lives. Further, the interdependent and interacting identity aspects of gender, culture and religion can work positively by contributing to the richness of their experience, but also presents challenges when living in a western society where those who are regarded as 'different' by a majority group may be openly challenged, and subject to unfair discrimination. As outlined earlier, key issues concerning perceptions of self in relation to 'Muslimness' (including choice of dress, observance of prayer, social interactions with a wider community, single-sex education and unaccompanied travel); the position of women within Islam; and engaging in education and work in a western society where certain behaviours, attitudes and values may be eschewed by some Muslim parents and communities; can present many Muslim girls with specific dilemmas when considering their futures.

In our discussions with Muslim career advisers working with Muslim girls in mainstream and faith-based schools a need was expressed for the development of career education resources designed to address the above issues with students during their final three years of compulsory education. We therefore initiated a project to design a Muslim girls' careers education pack (Irving *et al.* 2002) that would enhance an already established career education provision or act as a basis for a new programme, depending on local needs. Muslim and non-Muslim professionals have been involved at all stages in the design, writing and evaluation of the pack, through the auspices of a working group comprised of career advisers, educationalists and academics. Advice and views of Muslim parents, headteachers, a Muslim scholar and representatives from a range of communities also informed the project.

Muslim girls do not form a single homogeneous group, yet are bound by a common belief system and their gender. Therefore the working group considered it to be impractical to devise a careers programme that would be of equal value for Muslim girls and families who fully adopt a western lifestyle, and those who choose to follow an orthodox interpretation of Islam. As such, the pack is designed primarily for use with those for whom the 'Muslim issues' identified earlier are likely to be real and relevant. The pack includes a careers framework, lesson plans and materials for years 9–11, together with a 'Careers Guide for Muslim Parents and Family Members' which addresses questions concerning choosing options in year 9; work experience; completing and continuing in education; and training and employment opportunities after 16.

An early evaluation of the pack conducted in 2003 with teachers and career advisers across England, indicated that it has provided a vehicle for enabling Muslim girls to share and consider career-related issues from a Muslim viewpoint. For example, case studies of Muslim girls portrayed in a variety of situations stimulated discussion of possible skills and culturally appropriate strategies for engaging parents and family members in conversations about career-related decisions. The girls' enthusiasm and interest was described by teachers as arising from the opportunity to talk openly together about their culture and Islam:

> The session ... enabled the girls to share amongst us an insight into their futures, considering their cultural/family/personal values and the Islamic influence...
>
> (Head of Year)

Whilst many Muslim and non-Muslim schools have welcomed the pack, both practical and conceptual issues have been raised by teachers and career advisers working in multicultural settings. A few Muslim and non-Muslim career educators expressed anxiety that non-Muslim teachers would lack sufficient knowledge and personal experience of Islam to effectively deliver the lessons. Concern was voiced that inappropriate responses by these teachers during lessons, based on inaccurate and stereotyped views of Muslims, could negate any potential benefits. This may apply in some instances, however we suggest that if there is a commitment by teachers to address the specific career education needs of Muslim girls, then the question is how to provide effective support for them to acquire further knowledge, understanding and insight into Islam and the lives of Muslim girls. This may involve a variety of methods, including direct contact with Muslim communities and other members of staff e.g. religious studies teachers, and other professionals who can provide specific knowledge.

Some multicultural schools that chose not to participate in the project expressed resistance to the notion of differentiated provision as this was interpreted as potentially divisive and 'at odds' with an inclusive ethos, whereby all provisions within the school are available to every student. Further, some schools in which Muslim girls are in a minority anticipated that differentiated provision would result in Muslim girls feeling singled out, whereas others may feel left out.

Although further research is needed in this area, these preliminary findings indicate that there may be tensions for some career educators who subscribe to an equal opportunities policy that advocates this 'inclusive' ethos, whilst also recognising value in culturally sensitive and differentiated careers provision. Some also indicated that it would be politically inexpedient to use the pack as parents and the local community may be resistant to a socially just agenda in which minority groups are seen to receive different support and resourcing which is not also available to members of the dominant culture. A parallel can be drawn with the establishment of a Maori meeting place (whare) in a predominantly white European (Pakeha) secondary girls school in New Zealand. Resistance was expressed by some sections of the school who interpreted the initiative as divisive or providing 'special treatment', and by some local Maori who saw the development as an empty gesture, offering no challenge to the cultural dominance of the Pakeha colonisers. Concern was expressed that the introduction of multiculturalism was an attempt by the state to 'divide and rule', as there is also competition between ethnic minority groups for resources and recognition. As Smith (1993: 74) recounts, 'The life of a whare in the school will always be problematic simply because it represents a different world-view ... [that] celebrates and validates cultural difference.'

We suggest that if career education is not to be misrepresented as culturally divisive within multicultural schools, a core programme needs to provide sessions whereby all students can explore and consider their own culture, and those of others. Issues of equality might also be explored, for example discrimination and stereotyping (including self-stereotyping), 'race', religion and gender in relation to career. This does not preclude the value of providing opportunities (which may be optional sessions) in which students can share and examine particular interpretations of work, life roles, and career-related issues associated with, and transmitted by, the cultural–religious group with which they identify.

If parents, students, teachers and local communities are to support and value a socially just educational agenda they will *all* need to be informed and involved. Therefore the underlying rationale must be clearly communicated, transparent and open to debate, with initiatives taken to demonstrate that all students are equally valued, regardless of whether they receive the same provision.

Changing perceptions and challenging practice: lessons for us all?

Culture and identity are inextricably intertwined. Commenting on the situation in New Zealand, Wilson provides a helpful warning of how things might be: '. . . unless the dominant culture . . . engages with the issue of cultural rights . . . we are likely to experience increasing conflict as various "minority cultures" compete for recognition and dominance' (2000: 14–15). Movement towards a more complex critical–recognitive social justice approach (see Chapter 2 by Irving) that encompasses collective rights, engages with complex cultural practices, encourages critical dialogue and debate (Irving and Marris 2002), and respects difference and diversity, will help provide a collective sense of belonging and active engagement. Giving legitimacy to the voices and concerns of *all* citizens, along with an open acceptance and acknowledgement of diverse ways of being, will serve to reconstruct an inclusive society that accommodates the interests of all. Moreover, given that cultural identity is never static but subject to shifts over time in response to local and world events, continued engagement and ongoing dialogue will help to transcend cultural differences and perspectives on life.

The development of career education materials that are gender specific, culturally sensitive, and community focused will serve to ensure that the best interests of Muslim girls are both protected and progressed. As Parker-Jenkins *et al.* (concerning faith-based schooling) propose:

> what is being argued for here is a right for *all* ethnic groups to be equal *and* different, to participate in the majority world, but not at the expense of their own collective sense of being, as reflected in their cultural and/or religious affiliations.
>
> (forthcoming 2004)

By recognising and understanding the particular experiences of Muslim girls as individuals, as members of religious communities, and citizens of a nation that actively embraces cultural diversity and difference, it may then be possible to identify, and begin to meet their career needs. With regards to educational policy and practice, active responses to difference and diversity will need to be embedded and reflected in proposed actions and outcomes if it is to actively promote social justice for all.

Bibliography

Alibhai-Brown, J. (1999) *True Colours: Public Attitudes to Multiculturalism and the Role of the Government*, London: IPPR.

Archer, L. (2002) 'Change, culture and tradition: British Muslim pupils talk about Muslim girls' post-16 "choices"', *Race, Ethnicity and Education*, 5(4): 359–376.

Arthur, N. (2002) 'Preparing students for a world of work in cross-cultural transition', *Australian Journal of Career Development*, 11(1): 9–13.

Barker, V. and Irving, B.A. (2003) 'Challenging educators. Culture specific careers programmes: a human rights imperative', paper presented at UNESCO Conference on Intercultural Education, Jyvaskyla, Finland, June.

Barnes, A., Donoghue, J. and Sadler, J. (2002) 'Improving careers education: an analysis of recent research and inspection findings', *Career Research and Development*, 7(7): 15.

Basit, T.A. (1996) 'I'd hate to be just a housewife: career aspirations of British Muslim girls', *British Journal of Guidance and Counselling*, 24(2): 227–242.

Benn, T. and Jawad, H. (2003) 'Muslim women in the United Kingdom and beyond: setting the scene', in H. Jawad and T. Benn (eds) *Muslim Women in the United Kingdom and Beyond: Experiences and Images*, Leiden: Brill.

Bradley, H. (1996) *Fractured Identities: Changing Patterns of Inequality*, Cambridge: Polity Press.

Brah, A. (1994) '"Race" and "Culture" in the gendering of labour markets: South Asian young Muslim women and the labour market', in H. Afshah and M. Maynard (eds) *The Dynamics of 'Race' and 'Gender': Some Feminist Interventions*, London: Taylor and Francis.

Department for Education and Skills (2003) *Careers Education and Guidance in England: A National Framework 11–19*, London: DfES.

Ghouri, N. (1997) 'No single voice from Asian girls', *Times Educational Supplement*, 24 October: 15.

Gothard, B., Mignot, P., Offer, M. and Ruff, M. (2001) *Careers Guidance in Context*, London: Sage.

Harris, S. (1999) *Careers Education: Contesting Policy and Practice*, London: Paul Chapman.

Harris, S., Nixon, J. and Rudduck, J. (1993) 'School work, homework and gender', *Gender and Education*, 5(1): 3–15.

Irving, B.A. and Marris, L. (2002) 'A context for connexions', in Institute of Career Guidance (ed.) *Constructing the Future. Social Inclusion: Policy and Practice*, Stourbridge: Institute of Career Guidance.

Irving, B.A. and Barker, V. (2004) 'Career education for Muslim girls: developing culturally sensitive provision', *Australian Journal of Career Development*, 13(1): 42–49.

Irving, B.A., Barker, V., Jones, S. and Woolmer, D. (2002) *Muslim Girls' Careers Education Pack*, Reading: The Centre for British Teachers.

Irving, B A., Barker, V., Parker-Jenkins, M. and Hartas, D. (2000) 'In pursuit of social justice: career guidance provision for Muslim girls in England', *Revista Española De Orientación Y Psicopedagogia*, 11(20): 175–186.

Irving, B A., Barker, V., Parker-Jenkins, M. and Hartas, D. (2003) 'Choice and opportunity: supporting young Muslim women's career aspirations', in H. Jawad and T. Benn (eds) *Muslim Women in the United Kingdom and Beyond: Experiences and Images*, Leiden: Brill.

Law, B. (2001) *New Thinking for Connexions and Citizenship*, Derby: The Centre for Guidance Studies.

Law, B. and Watts, A.G. (1977) *Schools, Careers and Community*, London: Church Information Office.

Mirza, H.S. (1992) *Young, Female and Black*, London: Routledge.

National Institute for Adult and Continuing Education (1997) *Learning to Live in a Multi-Cultural Society: Home-School Liaison*, Leicester: NIACE.

Parekh, B. (2000) *Rethinking Multiculturalism: Cultural Diversity and Political Theory*, Basingstoke: Macmillan Press.

Parker-Jenkins, M. (1995) *Children of Islam: A Teachers Guide to Meeting the Needs of Muslim Pupils*, Stoke on Trent: Trentham.

Parker-Jenkins, M., Haw, K. and Irving, B.A. (1998) 'Bringing Muslim schools into the mainstream', *Discernment*, New Series, 4(3): 34–38.

Parker-Jenkins, M., Hartas, D. and Irving, B.A. (forthcoming 2004) *In Good Faith: Schools, Religion and Public Funding*, Aldershot: Ashgate.

Parker-Jenkins, M., Hartas, D., Irving, B.A. and Barker, V. (1999) *The Careers Service and Young Muslim Women*, Sheffield: Department for Education and Employment.

Parker-Jenkins, M., Haw, K., Irving, B.A. and Khan, S. (1997) 'Trying twice as hard to succeed: perceptions of Muslim women in Britain', paper presented to the British Educational Research Association, University of York, September.

Puri, S.R. (1995) 'Working with parents in a multicultural secondary school', in J. Bastiani (ed.) *Home-School Work in Multicultural Settings*, London: David Fulton.

Qualifications and Curriculum Authority (2003) 'Using new qualifications to support careers education in schools and colleges.' Online. Available HTTP: http://www.qca.org.uk/14-19/11-16-schools/s4-4-1-using-new-qu.htm (accessed 29 July 2003).

Reid, L. and Atiga, L. (2002) 'Culture-specific career programmes for Maori and Pasifika secondary school students', paper presented at New Zealand Careers Services/rapuara conference on the Heightened Role of Career Planning in Knowledge Societies, Wellington, November.

Robinson, S. (2002) 'Influences on the career decision-making of ethnic minority pupils at Key Stage 4 – implications for careers education and guidance in a multi-ethnic school', *Careers Education and Guidance*, February: 2–5.

Runnymede Trust (1997) *Islamaphobia, its Features and Dangers, a Consultative Paper*, London: Runnymede Trust.

SCAA (1995) *Looking Forward: Careers Education and Guidance in the Curriculum*, London: Schools Curriculum Assessment Authority.

Smith, L.T. (1993) 'Getting out from down under: Maori women, education and the struggle for Mana Wahine', in M. Arnot and K. Weiler (eds) *Feminism and Social Justice in Education*, London: Falmer.

Solomos, J. (1993) *Race and Racism in Britain*, 2nd edn, Basingstoke: Macmillan Press.

Wilson, M. (2000) 'Cultural rights: definitions and contexts', in M. Wilson and P. Hunt (eds) *Culture, Rights and Human Rights: Perspectives from the South Pacific*, Wellington: Huia Publishers.

Young, I. (1990) *Justice and the Politics of Difference*, Princeton: Princeton University Press.

Chapter 7

(En)gendering socially just approaches to career guidance

Wendy Patton and Mary McMahon

Introduction

The levels and patterns of women's participation in the workforce have undergone substantial change over the last forty years, with women now constituting a significant presence in the workforce in most western countries. For example, in the United States (Fitzgerald and Harmon 2001) and in Australia (Australian Bureau of Statistics 2002), women constitute more than one half of the paid workforce. This demographic change represents a situation that is far removed from that when Osipow (1975: 3) proffered his analysis that '(T)he ... basic assumption was that men had careers and women (did) not'. This view is reflected in a comment on the state of vocational psychology made by Tyler (1967: 62) which highlights the inadequacy of much thinking in relation to women's career development; 'Much of what we know about the stages through which an individual passes as *he* prepares to find *his* place in the world of work might appropriately be labelled the vocational development of white middle class males' (original italics). While the literature generally remains in conflict on the nature and development of women's careers, the previous two decades has seen a significant increase in theoretical and empirical work. This chapter will explore current definitions and present a brief background on issues relevant to understanding women's career behaviour. It will explore theoretical and empirical work which strives to assert a socially just place for women in the career literature and within the world of work. Finally it will discuss implications of the status of our knowledge on career practice.

Meaning of career for women

In describing career for women, early theorists (e.g. Psathas 1968; Zytowski 1969) focused on the link between sex role and occupational role, and emphasised the role of marriage, motherhood and homemaking. Similarly, during this period, interest inventories still came in separate versions for women and men, generally reflected fewer options for women, and those that were offered were mainly sex-stereotyped. Subsequent work has clearly shown that the meaning of work is as potent for women as it is for men. Astin's (1984) sociopsychological model was one of the first major attempts to propose a comprehensive theory to explain the career development of women and men, with Astin maintaining that 'work motivation is the same for men and women, but they make different choices because their early socialization experiences and structural opportunities are different' (Astin 1984: 118). Work by a number of authors (e.g. Betz and Fitzgerald 1987; Betz 1993; Cook 1993) has more fully confirmed the notion that female aspiration 'was not absent or deficient, but blocked' (Fitzgerald and Harmon 2001: 218).

The broad and radical changes in the workforce generally have prompted changes in our understanding of the meaning of career in individuals' lives. Parallel to the increasing focus on women's career behaviour is the increasing reconceptualisation of the notion of career. The literature is consistent in emphasising that the nature of future careers will be increasingly non-linear, indeed that a combination of a number of positions, projects and roles, or of jobs, may constitute a career (Hall 1996). In this context, a career relates to the meaning an individual gives to this pattern of work and non-work opportunities. Herr (1992) emphasises that careers need to be construed as the creations of individuals; the word career can no longer be regarded as synonymous with job or occupation. Individuals need to 'regard themselves as being self-employed' (Collin and Watts 1996: 391), as they are expected to 'manage their own career' (Savickas 1997: 256).

These current views about career are similar to the world of work experience of many women. Traditional definitions of career assumed male hierarchical career patterns, chosen during post adolescence and remaining continuous and static throughout life. Females' careers were expected to be chosen as a temporary measure, until entering the full-time 'career' of motherhood and homemaking. Rather, many women's career patterns can be conceptualised as a range of working positions interspersed with periods of childcare. Women's vocational behaviour is arguably more complex than that of men as it is frequently characterised by child-care responsibilities resulting in different employment patterns (Bimrose 2001). The most common employment arrangement in families is for both parents to be working (in Australia in 2000, 63 per cent of couple families with dependent children had both partners employed, Australian Bureau of Statistics 2002). Most men were working full-time and their employment rate was less affected by the presence of children than women's, indicating that for most families, men were still the primary financial provider. From a woman's perspective, a career then could resemble the development of a 'tessellated' structure whereby a number of interconnected networks of life experience move the individual in and through self-actualisation. Other 'careers' such as motherhood, paid full-time and part-time employment, and voluntary work, are then eligible to be included in the structure since these too provide opportunities for self-growth and may be viewed as potentially meaningful lifecareer experiences.

Gallos (1989: 125) insists that women's notions of career are a rejection of male notions, that a career is not a

> lock-step linear progression of attainments directed by a focus on 'the top'; not a job sequence aimed at upward mobility and success at all costs; not job complacency, fear of professional success or low needs of achievement; not simply a mechanical issue of learning how to juggle marriage, children and women.

Recent research by Hallett and Gilbert (1997) studied university women's perception of their future patterns of work and family life and found that college-educated women did not see themselves as having to choose between career and a family. They assumed both are possible and not all wanted to integrate work and family in the same way. Crompton and Harris (1998: 123) also proposed an alternative framework for explaining women's career patterns which allows the possibility of women 'desiring both "employment" and "family" careers', with their work commitment varying according both to the stage reached in their lifestyle and context, emphasising that women's orientations to employment and family life were complex and variable (Crompton and Harris 1998). Overall, it would seem then, that the traditional linear developmental and hierarchical conception of career in the vocational literature is not adequate to explain women's perceptions of, and experiences of, their working life. It can be seen that the concept of 'career' varies for women depending on their life context. New perspectives and construction of a career theory that takes into consideration life experiences and broader context are needed.

Women's career development: theoretical understanding

While the previous two decades have seen a significant increase in theoretical and empirical work, criticisms remain about the failure of much career development theory to adequately account for the lives of women. Fitzgerald and Crites' pivotal 1980 paper was instrumental in outlining issues for research and theory building, prompting reconceptualisations from traditional theorists (e.g. Holland 1985; Super 1990) who subsequently attempted to include applications to women within their theories.

Despite substantial activity during these two decades, there remains considerable theoretical uncertainty.

One of the earliest theoretical models was that proffered by Farmer (1976; 1985) who proposed that background characteristics and personal variables interact to foster achievement and career motivation. Background variables (gender, race, social class, school location, age) interact with personal psychological variables (self-esteem, values, homemaking attitude and commitment, success attributions) and environmental variables (societal attitude to women working, support from teachers and parents). These variables in turn are hypothesised to influence three motivational factors: level of aspirations, mastery strivings, and career commitment. Research testing this model has generally supported the salience of background factors such as gender-based attitudes, support, and commitment to career and family in career aspirations and choices (e.g. Farmer 1985). While career commitment increased from 1980–1990, based on the supportiveness of the environment, Farmer *et al.* (1993) noted that women may reject more demanding careers because of the perceived role conflict. This adjustment of aspirations is similar to the notion of 'satisficing' discussed by Fitzgerald and Weitzman (1992).

Gottfredson's (1981; 1996) theoretical view focused on processes of circumscription and compromise relevant to women and men, and proposed that self-concept (being composed of gender, social class, intelligence, interests and values) interacts with occupational images (sex type, prestige, and field of work) to determine an individual's occupational preferences. Together with perceptions of job accessibility which incorporate perceptions of opportunities and barriers, a range of acceptable alternatives is formulated. Her model highlights the relevance of sex-role socialisation of women and men, whereby individuals make decisions based on sex type of occupations and perceptions of opportunities and barriers. Gender type, for example, influences career choice because individuals narrow their perceived appropriate occupational alternatives based on societal notions of gender appropriate careers.

Astin's (1984) model discussed previously incorporates four major constructs: motivation, work expectations, sex-role socialisation, and the structure of opportunity. She proposed that an individual's motivation for work behaviour is related to the need for survival, pleasure and the making of a societal contribution. Career choices, therefore, are related to accessibility of various occupations, and the expectation of the individual that these three needs will be met. She acknowledges that these expectations are related to early gendered socialisation, and the structure of opportunity, each of which interact with each other. Factors incorporated within the structure of opportunity include distribution of jobs, sex typing of jobs, discrimination, job requirements, the economy, family structure, and reproductive technology.

Other theoretical models include the work of Betz, Fitzgerald, Fassinger, and Hackett. Hackett and Betz (1981: 326) recognised that women's socialisation mediates the cognitive processes which are crucial in career decision-making: '(Women) lack strong expectations of personal efficacy in relationship to many career-related behaviours and thus fail to fully realise their capabilities and talents in career pursuits'. Betz and Fitzgerald (1987) identified four sets of factors which influence women's career choices. The factors, deemed to be particularly crucial in promoting realism of career choice, included individual variables (self-concept, ability, liberated sex role values); background variables (parental support, parents' education level and occupational status, work experience); educational variables (women's schools, higher education, continuation in mathematics); and adult life style variables (timing of marriage, number of children). Fassinger (1985; 1990) tested the Betz and Fitzgerald model and proposed several refinements. Her 1985 study found ability, achievement orientation, and feminist orientation to be independent variables influencing family and career orientation, and career choice, leading to a revision of the original model. In her 1990 study, higher ability levels interacting with aspects of personal agency (e.g. instrumentality and self-efficacy) and sex-role attitudes, specifically a feminist orientation, influenced career orientation and career choice.

Forrest and Mikolaitis (1986: 76) proposed the integration of a 'relational component of identity' into existing career theories, defining this concept as 'a guiding principle, although not necessarily a consciously organised one, that influences heavily one's perceptions and actions toward self and others'. They noted that 'women reflect their sense of identity primarily in terms of their connection to others'; men on the other hand describe their sense of self by 'differentiating themselves from others in terms of abilities and attributes' (Forrest and Mikolaitis 1986: 80).

While there has been considerable development in theoretical work on the career behaviour of women, the construction of a unified picture remains difficult. The field remains complex, disparate and developmental, with existing theorists continuing to incorporate women's issues into their frameworks or rejecting the value of doing so, and individual differences models addressing different dimensions. The frameworks discussed in this section have highlighted the importance of relevant background factors in women's career behaviour. Similarly, they have addressed in different ways the importance of socialisation processes. While internal traits and attitudes have also been shown to be important in women's career-related behaviour, the interaction of these with processes of socialisation has not been adequately addressed. For example, if relational identity is socially constructed, can it be incorporated within a male identity? How do women learn gender role attitudes which are career positive, family positive, or amenable to a balance of both with minimal conflict?

These questions have begun to be answered by the sociocognitive approaches of Hackett and Betz (1981), Lent and Hackett (1994), and Lent *et al.* (1996, 2002). These approaches have the capacity to address the intricacy of internal socialisation processes through the inclusion of cognition in their models. In addition, they incorporate contextual issues into their explanations. Finally, they address another problem with existing work, that is the static nature of current descriptions and explanations. Hackett and Lent (1992: 439) discussed this succinctly when they reminded us that:

> social changes impact social roles generally, and women's roles in particular. These shifts may shorten the shelf life of past research findings; they also highlight the need for researchers to attend to current social realities and their interaction with career development processes.

More recently, the development of the Systems Theory Framework (Patton and McMahon 1999) has enabled a coherence to be given to the myriad of influences on the career development of all individuals. In addition, this theoretical framework emphasises the central role of the individual and not the theory in the career development process. The potential for this theoretical framework in enhancing the usefulness of all theory in relation to women's career behaviour is yet to be fully determined.

Issues in women's careers

As discussed previously, post-Second World War has seen what has been referred to as 'a quiet revolution in women's participation in the paid workplace' (White *et al.* 1992: 1). This increased workforce participation has emphasised the importance of career for women. However, while the number of women in the workforce has increased, the nature of their participation continues to differ from that of men. Women's employment is more likely to be part-time, and concentrated in a smaller number of occupational categories. In addition, women tend to enter and remain in low-paying, low-status positions. These differences are suggestive of structural opportunity differences operating in concert with gender differences.

In 1974, Hansen detailed what she perceived as limitations in relation to women's career development. These included societal trends and changing life patterns, and obstacles to the career development of women, such as sex-role socialisation, role conflicts about marriage and work, focus on marriage, lack of work orientation, sexism and sex discrimination. In a positive prophecy, she suggested that a focus on women 'perhaps . . . will not be necessary in another 12 or 15 years' (Hansen 1974: 1). Twenty years on, Eccles (1994) commented on the ongoing differentiation between women and men in occupations and the continued underrepresentation of women in high status occupational fields. She commented that 'Many factors, ranging from outright discrimination to the processes associated with gender role socialization, contribute to these gendered patterns of educational and occupational choices' (Eccles 1994: 585). Despite developments in the field of career development theory during the past twenty to twenty-five years, there is only minimal change in the career experiences of most women.

In their 1995 review, Fitzgerald *et al.* identified concepts which had been labelled as unique to women's career development as 'pre-theoretical developments' (Fitzgerald *et al.* 1995: 68). These concepts included career versus homemaking orientation, career salience, traditionality of choice, and career patterns based on the relationship between work and family in women's lives. While more recent conceptualisations have moved on from the either-or classification of home or career, women's traditional roles continue to be important in career choice and adjustment issues. This movement away from a dichotomous classification has prompted a voluminous work on multiple roles, and an attendant discussion on role conflict. Despite changes in women's roles, research cited by Fitzgerald *et al.* (1995: 73) continues to show an inverse relationship between being married and number of children with every known criterion of career involvement and achievement, and that 'this continues to be the main difference between women's career development and that of men'.

More recently, Fitzgerald and Harmon (2001: 208) reviewed a seminal work edited by Samuel Osipow in 1975 entitled *Emerging Woman: Career Analysis and Outcomes*, and proposed 'a postmodern extension of his ideas'. Fitzgerald and Harmon assert that various aspects identified in earlier literature as relevant to women's career behaviour are no longer relevant. They discuss individual factors, societal factors, and individual–social factors. For example, while they recognised the continuing importance of interest, abilities, attitudes–values, and career self-efficacy, they de-emphasise the importance of occupational stereotyping and argue that while pockets remain, occupational segregation (at least in western countries) is more an issue of level than field. In relation to societal influences, these authors emphasise the increase in importance of the media, the economy, and technology and its advances, and a decrease in the relevance of the church. They suggest that the reciprocal individual–social factor, including such variables as race, ethnicity, sexual orientation and social class, are now far more acknowledged as important influences in women's career behaviour. Fitzgerald and Harmon also assert that fear of success and formal discrimination are no longer meaningful descriptors, however role conflict and geographical restrictions continue as salient issues. In essence, Fitzgerald and Harmon (2001: 219) suggest that issues of equality in the world of work are more important in the twenty-first century than issues of entrance, maintaining that 'women may have formal access to careers traditionally closed to them, but once in the job they face numerous barriers to achieving success and satisfaction'. Specifically these barriers include issues of inequality in pay and opportunity in the workplace, issues of harassment, and the reality that women are still perceived to be the primary caregiver for young children, and increasingly for the elderly, what Fitzgerald and Harmon (2001: 215) assert is 'one of the most intransigent conditions affecting women's career development; that is the dramatic increase in their work participation implies that they are now expected to cope simultaneously with two full-time jobs'.

Implications for practice

We have emphasised the enormous body of work of theorists and researchers in describing the complexity of career decision-making and adjustment issues for women, particularly during the previous two decades. This work is an example of the social justice efforts of individuals who attempt to advocate for a greater understanding of these issues. Approaches designed to engender socially just outcomes for women's career exploration and behaviour also include individual counselling and programme development.

The aim of career guidance is ultimately to meet the career decision-making needs of clients. This can only be achieved if their real needs are understood, and when theories which meet criteria such as comprehensiveness, clarity, predictive value and guidance for practice are available. For years, career practice has been influenced by theories which assume that the career behaviour and development of women is the same as that of men, or career preparation activities have focused on males on the basis that women's foray into the world of work would be a short-lived gap filler between school, marriage and full-time homemaking. To be effective across the full range of clients, career theory and practice must take account of diversity in all its forms, including class, ethnicity, age, sexual orientation, and gender, and acknowledge the contexts in which clients live their lives. O'Brien (2001) emphasises that to actively practice according to social justice principles, practitioners need to understand the unique and dynamic interrelationship between intrapersonal influences, and interpersonal and environmental influences.

> Thus, career counselors, in individual work with clients, can be agents of social change by conceptualizing clients holistically, using more integrated models of career counselling, being cognizant of multicultural issues, identifying environmental barriers, and using non-traditional interventions.
>
> (O'Brien 2001: 68)

In describing their theories, a number of theorists have made specific suggestions with respect to practice. Gottfredson (1996) argues that her theory of 'circumscription and compromise' has implications at the level of individual work and at the level of the organisation through career education/career development programs (Bimrose 2001). Work with individual clients should encourage both 'exploration and constructive realism' (Gottfredson 1996: 227). This implies thorough and methodical discussions with clients about why some compromises are more acceptable or accessible than others. Career practitioners working within this framework would explore career ideas that have been ruled out by clients, as well as their preferred options. Gottfredson (1996: 20) suggests that career education programs should span ages 6 to 14+ and deal explicitly and developmentally with ways in which individuals restrict (circumscribe) their career choices. Such programs would also need to be sensitive to the dimensions of self and occupations along which circumscription and compromise take place (e.g. sex, social class, ability, and vocational interests).

Betz and Hackett (1997: 383) assert that; 'Meta-analyses and reviews of 15 years of research . . . strongly support the role of career self-efficacy as a predictor of educational and career preferences, academic performance, and persistence in the pursuit of desired career options'. Taking this key idea that career self-efficacy is a reliable predictor of career behaviour, Brown (1990) argues that the theory has considerable practical potential for broadening options in career practice with women. For example, the practitioner could help the client build on her successful experiences to develop self-confidence in areas where she has poor perceptions of her ability. Alternatively the practitioner could arrange for work shadowing experiences with successful representatives of groups not normally successful in a particular area.

The theoretical framework developed by Patton and McMahon (1999) discussed previously also offers some specific suggestions in relation to practice. In identifying influences in career development as they are relevant to each individual, the opportunity is provided for each woman to tell the story of her own individual career journey. Individuals are able to determine relevant themes and dominant stories and their sense-making of these can be facilitated through a process with the career counsellor acting as facilitator.

Brooks and Forrest (1994) outline some implications of applying a feminist underpinning to career practice with women. Two stages are identified as necessary to practice within this framework: pre-assessment and assessment. The pre-assessment stage refers to the preparation of practitioners, which would involve their becoming familiar with research on the complex interactions between gender, race, social class and career development. The authors also identify a need for practitioners to gain an accurate knowledge of discrimination in education and in the workplace.

The second stage, assessment, involves working with clients and focuses on how gender-role socialisation has been experienced. This could involve gathering contextual data on the culture of family origin and the client's perception of society's gender expectations. Additionally, this approach aims to help clients develop a political awareness of the ways the social structure has moulded and limited them, and advocates that an equal relationship between client and practitioner be established and maintained (Bimrose 2001).

Fitzgerald and Harmon (2001) urge career practitioners not to make the mistake of focusing on only one career outcome as the right choice for young women's careers. They acknowledge that much previous work focused on facilitating access to careers that were previously closed to women. Instead they propose that the career decision-making process emphasise that

> any choice that is realistic and satisfying for the individual is a good one ... [and that practitioners] may be best encouraged to support a process of discovery that encourages young women to explore themselves and their options in a lifelong search for challenge and satisfaction on whatever level they may find them.
>
> (Fitzgerald and Harmon 2001: 214)

In addition to social justice aims underpinning support at the individual and programme level, it is important to focus on the role of career practitioner as a social justice advocate at the institutional level. For example, Fitzgerald and Harmon (2001) assert that a major set of organisational and institutional barriers in the career behaviour of women is the lack of child care, at an employer level and at the level of national policy. They emphasise that the consequences of maternal employment should more appropriately be reframed as the consequences of inadequate childcare resources.

Conclusion

The challenges of describing, understanding and facilitating women's career behaviour are neither static nor immune from rapid changes occurring in the world of work. Within this broad context, there is widespread agreement that individuals need to be much more than passive recipients of a life–career process. Rather they will need to be proactive life–career managers in order to be responsive to their own changing needs and changes in the nature and structure of paid employment including the proliferation of short-term contract work, casual work, contingent work and a decrease in full-time permanent work, the irrefutable influence of globalisation and lifelong learning requirements. Thus, emerging definitions of career and career development are reflective of a proactive, individual centred, lifespan, life–career management process where individuals are active in responding and adapting to change and in creating, constructing, designing, and identifying paid employment opportunities, life and learning experiences that will enable them to create satisfying lives.

Patton (2001: 14) described career development as 'the process of managing learning and work over the lifespan'. The challenge is for all individuals to play a greater role in constructing their own career development, in both the access of ongoing learning opportunities, and in their representation in the world of work. Savickas (1999) suggests that in preparing for such a dynamic working life, individuals need to constantly 'look ahead' and 'look around'. Amundson *et al.* (2002: 27) further this notion in discussing 'a continuing tension between leveraging past experience and positioning for future opportunity'. In line with other writers, they emphasise the imperative that individuals need to learn to actively engage with environments of change. Therefore, individuals increasingly need to focus on learning the skills which will assist them in taking responsibility for the direction and evolution of their own careers. Developing skills that enhance current performance and equip for the next employment experience is an important underpinning of this focus.

These principles emphasising the skills required of the new worker suggest that individuals need to be more involved in their career than ever before. Fitzgerald and Harmon (2001: 226) suggest that again such demands are an additional contextual issue for women who are managing a current job or project, in addition to assuming the role of primary caregiver for children and probably for the elderly in an ageing society; 'how free can she be to prepare herself for the inevitable changes today's world will require?' While the dynamic changes in the world of work offer exciting opportunities, these authors assert that 'the individual who has the most freedom to do so will have the most fun … but in the majority of cases, will not be female' (Fitzgerald and Harmon 2001: 226).

As advocates for social justice, and for all women (Blustein 2001), we must do all we can to enhance the opportunities for women to participate as full and equal members of society. As such we need to continue our efforts as theoreticians, as researchers, as practitioners, and as policy makers in the development of individual, programme, institutional and policy interventions. We can all make a difference.

Bibliography

Amundson, N., Parker, P. and Arthur, M. (2002) 'Merging two worlds: linking occupational and organisational career counselling', *Australian Journal of Career Development*, 11: 26–35.

Astin, H.S. (1984) 'The meaning of work in women's lives: a sociopsychological model of career choice and work behavior', *The Counseling Psychologist*, 12: 117–126.

Australian Bureau of Statistics (2002) *Australia Now: Australian Social Trends 2001*, Canberra: ABS.

Betz, N. (1993) 'Women's career development', in F. Denmark and M. Paludi (eds) *Psychology of Women: A Handbook of Issues and Theories*, Westport, CT: Greenwood Press.

Betz, N.E. and Fitzgerald, L.F. (1987) *The Career Psychology of Women*, Orlando, FL: Academic Press.

Betz, N.E. and Hackett, G. (1997) 'Applications of self-efficacy theory to the career assessment of women', *Journal of Career Assessment*, 5: 383–402.

Bimrose, J. (2001) 'Girls and women: challenges for careers guidance practice', *British Journal of Guidance and Counselling*, 29: 79–94.

Blustein, D. (2001) 'Extending the reach of vocational psychology: toward an inclusive and integrative psychology of working', *Journal of Vocational Behavior*, 59: 171–182.

Brooks, L. and Forrest, L. (1994) 'Feminism and career counseling', in W.B. Walsh and S.H. Osipow (eds) *Career Counseling for Women*, Hillsdale, NJ: Erlbaum.

Brown, D. (1990) 'Summary, comparison, and critique of the major theories', in D. Brown and L. Brooks (eds) *Career Choice and Development: Applying Contemporary Theories to Practice*, 2nd edn, San Francisco, CA: Jossey-Bass.

Collin, A. and Watts, A.G. (1996) 'The death and transfiguration of career – and of career guidance?', *British Journal of Guidance and Counselling*, 24: 385–398.

Cook, E. (1993) 'The gendered context of life: implications for women's and men's career life plans', *The Career Development Quarterly*, 41: 227–237.

Crompton, R. and Harris, F. (1998) 'Explaining women's employment patterns', *British Journal of Sociology*, 49: 118–136.

Eccles, J.S. (1994) 'Understanding women's educational and occupational choices', *Psychology of Women Quarterly*, 18: 585–609.

Farmer, H.S. (1976) 'What inhibits achievement and career motivation in women', *The Counseling Psychologist*, 6: 12–14.

Farmer, H.S. (1985) 'Model of career and achievement motivation for women and men', *Journal of Counseling Psychology*, 32: 363–390.

Farmer, H.S., Wardrop, J.S., Andersen, M.Z. and Risinger, F. (1993) 'Understanding women's career choices', paper presented at the Annual Meeting of American Psychological Association, Toronto, Canada, August.

Fassinger, R.E. (1985) 'A causal model of college women's career choice', *Journal of Vocational Behavior*, 27: 123–153.

—— (1990) 'Causal models of career choice in two samples of college women', *Journal of Vocational Behavior*, 36: 225–248.

Fitzgerald, L.F. and Crites, J.O. (1980) 'Toward a career psychology of women: what do we know? What do we need to know?', *Journal of Counseling Psychology*, 27: 44–62.

Fitzgerald, L. and Harmon, L. (2001) 'Women's career development: a postmodern update', in F.T.L. Leong and A. Barak (eds) *Contemporary Models in Vocational Psychology*, Mahwah: Erlbaum.

Fitzgerald, L.F. and Weitzman, L. (1992) 'Women's career development: theory and practice from a feminist perspective', in Z. Leibowitz and D. Lea (eds) *Adult Career Development: Concepts, Issues and Practices*, Alexandria, VA: National Career Development Association.

Fitzgerald, L.F., Fassinger, R.E. and Betz, N.E. (1995) 'Theoretical advances in the study of women's career development', in W.B. Walsh and S.H. Osipow (eds) *Handbook of Vocational Psychology*, 2nd edn, Mahwah, NJ: Erlbaum.

Forrest, L. and Mikolaitis, N. (1986) 'The relational component of identity: an expansion of career development theory', *The Career Development Quarterly*, 35: 76–88.

Gallos, J.V. (1989) 'Exploring women's development: implications for career theory, practice and research', in M.B. Arthur, D.T. Hall and B.S. Lawrence (eds) *Handbook of Career Theory*, Cambridge: Cambridge University Press.

Gottfredson, L.S. (1981) 'Circumscription and compromise: a developmental theory of occupational aspirations', *Journal of Counseling Psychology*, 28: 545–579.

Gottfredson, L.S. (1996) 'Gottfredson's theory of circumscription and compromise', in D. Brown and L. Brooks (eds) *Career Choice and Development*, 3rd edn, San Francisco, CA: Jossey-Bass.

Hackett, G. and Betz, N. (1981) 'A self-efficacy approach to the career development of women', *Journal of Vocational Behavior*, 18: 326–339.

Hackett, G. and Lent, R.W. (1992) 'Theoretical advances and current inquiry in career psychology', in S.D. Brown and R.W. Lent (eds) *Handbook of Counseling Psychology*, New York: John Wiley and Sons.

Hall, D.T. (ed.) (1996) *The Career is Dead – Long Live the Career: A Relational Approach to Careers*, San Francisco, CA: Jossey-Bass.

Hallet, M.B. and Gilbert, L.A. (1997) 'Variables differentiating university women considering role-sharing and conventional dual-career marriages', *Journal of Vocational Behavior*, 50: 308–322.

Hansen, L.S. (1974) 'Counseling and career (self) development of women', *Focus on Guidance*, 7: 1–11, 14, 15.

Herr, E.L. (1992) 'Emerging trends in career counselling', *International Journal for the Advancement of Counselling*, 15: 255–288.

Holland, J.L. (1985) *Making Vocational Choices: A Theory of Vocational Personalities and Work Environments*, Englewood Cliffs, NJ: Prentice Hall.

Lent, R.W. and Hackett, G. (1994) 'Sociocognitive mechanisms of personal agency in career development: pantheoretical aspects', in M.L. Savickas and R.W. Lent (eds) *Convergence in Career Development Theories*, Palo Alto, CA: CPP Books.

Lent, R.W., Brown, S.D. and Hackett, G. (1996) 'Career development from a sociocognitive perspective', in D. Brown and L. Brooks (eds) *Career Choice and Development*, 3rd edn, San Francisco, CA: Jossey-Bass.

Lent, R.W., Brown, S.D. and Hackett, G. (2002) 'Social cognitive career theory', in D. Brown and associates (eds) *Career Choice and Development*, 4th edn, San Francisco, CA: Jossey-Bass.

O'Brien, K.M. (2001) 'The legacy of Parsons: career counselors and vocational psychologists as agents of social change', *The Career Development Quarterly*, 50: 66–76.

Osipow, S.H. (1975) 'The relevance of theories of career development to special groups: problems, needed data and implications', in J.S. Picou and R.E. Campbell (eds) *Career Behavior of Special Groups*, Westerville: Merrill.

Patton, W. (2001) 'Career education: what we know, what we need to know', *Australian Journal of Career Development*, 10: 13–19.

Patton, W. and McMahon, M. (1999) *Career Development and Systems Theory: A New Relationship*, Pacific Grove, CA: Brooks/Cole.

Psathas, G. (1968) 'Toward a theory of occupational choice for women', *Sociology and Social Research*, 52: 253–268.

Savickas, M.L. (1997) 'Career adaptability: an integrative construct for life-span, life-space theory', *The Career Development Quarterly*, 45: 247–259.

—— (1999) 'The transition from school to work: a developmental perspective', *The Career Development Quarterly*, 47: 326–336.

Super, D.E. (1990) 'A life-span, life-space approach to career development', in D. Brown and L. Brooks (eds) *Career Choice and Development: Applying Contemporary Theories to Practice*, 2nd edn, San Francisco, CA: Jossey-Bass.

Tyler, L. (1967) 'The encounter with poverty: its effect on vocational psychology', *Rehabilitation Psychology Bulletin*, 11: 61–70.

White, B., Cox, C. and Cooper, C. (1992) *Women's Career Development: A Study of High Fliers*, Oxford: Blackwell.

Zytowski, D.G. (1969) 'Toward a theory of career development for women', *Personnel and Guidance Journal*, 47: 660–664.

Chapter 8

Women, work and career development

Equal employment opportunity or employment equity?

Maria Humphries and Suzette Dyer

Introduction

Women

- Make up half of the world's population
- Do two thirds of the world's work
- Produce, process, and market over three-fifths of the world's food
- Represent three-fifths of the world's illiterate
- Receive one-tenth of the world's income
- Own less than one per cent of the world's property
- Hold less than 14 per cent of parliamentary seats world wide[1]

Motivated by statistics such as these, our specific (but not exclusive) concern is to contribute, through our research, writing and teaching, to the wellbeing of women and their dependants. Part of this concern is expressed through our focus on the career aspirations of women, and their outcomes in practice. For over a decade we have participated in discussions of career theory as a way of understanding and influencing discourses of justice in our own country (Aotearoa/NewZealand[2]) and in the international community's engagement with the rapid globalisation of western corporate capitalism. Our interest in the relative influence of women and men to determine their own and collective wellbeing has drawn us to the diagnostic work and liberatory aspirations of critical theorists in the organisational disciplines.

In keeping with the critical perspective of this book, the requirement to address the exploitative tendencies of the predominating global economic system is assumed. In this chapter we discuss the contemporary political emphasis on human rights approaches to inequality and we outline research and policy focused on the gendered and gendering aspects of society associated with such inequality. The challenges arising from these concerns have their most visible manifestation in the discourses of Equal Employment Opportunities (EEO) and Affirmative Action (AA). Career endeavours are one site where we see such discourses in practice. Our focus in this chapter is on the lives of women and on the organisational mechanisms and metaphors that influence, motivate, or circumscribe their lives.

We begin this chapter with a brief outline of our understanding of the context and processes that influence women's career experiences in western countries. We provide an overview of the position of women in employment in Aotearoa/New Zealand and we review efforts to bring the position of women in employment in this country more in line with that of men. We conclude the chapter by encouraging researchers to contribute to the necessary task of ensuring that equal opportunities are an actionable right in the achievement of career aspirations and outcomes for all women. We see this achievement as a necessary, but not sufficient condition for justice. We urge this task must coincide with an associated focus on the overall wellbeing of all people, in and out of employment, and in keeping with wise stewardship of the earth that sustains us.

The context of women's careers

The form of corporate capitalism known as neo-liberalism or free market capitalism (and sometimes referred to less specifically as 'globalisation') has been criticised for its devastating effects especially on the lives of the poor (Stiglitz 2002; Hertz 2001; Kelsey 1999) and on the environment that sustains human life (Shiva 1993; 2003). Such capitalism could not function, if not for the systematic participation of numerous trustworthy functionaries, people like ourselves, merely attempting to fulfil our career aspirations within the context of the given game (Dyer and Humphries 2002). In principle, the gender of these functionaries is irrelevant. In keeping with the technical selection capacities now available to the system, sexism, racism, or any other form of systemic discrimination is counterproductive in the search for the best-fit-for-purpose at the lowest price (Humphries and Grice 1995). Discrimination does not make economic sense. Based on this analysis alone anti-discrimination legislation, policies, and practices are consistent with 'best practice' discourses in any organisational settings.

Increasingly, compulsory market participation of all people has generated interest in the life issues that might prevent some people from gaining access to jobs or achieving retention and promotion in employment. In this regard, along with the myriad of anti-discrimination and equal employment opportunity mechanisms, there has been a concurrent expansion of the very notion of 'career'. The career concept has been invested with a meaning encompassing more that just paid employment to take account of the many commitments and interests people have beyond their employment (Greenhaus *et al.* 2000; Arthur *et al.* 1999; Hall and Associates 1996).

This expansion of the meaning of career has opened a raft of possible considerations that are of interest to people who juggle responsibilities as parents, care-takers of others, or who contribute to human and environmental well-being through a variety of voluntary activity.

While the concept 'career' is indeed under pressure to extend beyond the consideration of paid employment it would be fair to say that most people, when asked about their career, speak about their jobs. Such an intuitive connection makes sense. Human wellbeing is increasingly defined by our relationship to markets. Market opportunities and outcomes determine our income, our access to services, and our opportunities for leisure. Such market outcomes within and among countries are very uneven but women are typically represented as:

- earning less than men (often for the same or similar job);
- congregated in patterns of vertical and horizontal segregation; and
- predominantly responsible for family, domestic, emotional, and community work.

Why, then, given the significant resources associated with gender equalisation, do these outcomes persist? We suggest that, against conscious attempts to achieve gender equity, the interests of capitalist and patriarchal ideologies combine and contest in new ways to counteract any progress towards a more egalitarian society. The concept of individual responsibility, along with a lexicon of social fabrications constituting the ethos of social Darwinism, for example, underpins the ideological edifice of neo-liberalism. Each one of us, women and men, are now responsible to create and maintain a career in this context. However, the competitive individualism associated with the neo-liberal agenda that seeks maximum profits for lowest cost, according to critical theorists, leads to exploitation and minimisation of protection of vulnerable people and the natural environment. Under this regime, some women will indeed be able to attain improved career opportunities but increased peripheralisation will be the outcome for many more (Calas and Smircich 1993). As many as fifty thousand women and children per year, for example, are taken into the United States to be forced into slavery and prostitution, bonded sweatshops and domestic servitude (McCormick and Herron Zamora 2000).[3]

Whether a form of capitalism underpinned by strong national and international commitments to universal human rights and stringent adherence to environmental stewardship can curtail the exploitative tendencies of unfettered market modalities is still an open question. To assess this question, we require a climate of vigilance against the complacency generated through the daily assault on our critical faculties by the economic mandate that 'growth is good'. We urge analysis of our institutional compliance with the 'techniques of efficiency' that are believed to produce this growth.

Job losses, downward pressure on incomes and conditions of service, withdrawal of state services (or universal entitlements) for basic health, education, clean water, and other basic necessities for human existence are still the order of the day. From a critical perspective, emerging 'careers discourses' that harness 'individual responsibility' for employment (and therefore life) outcomes to the achievement of technical efficiency servicing the maximisation of profit (or economic growth) as its primary purpose, might be read as a component of an overall discourse of compliance, assimilation or domestication. Consistent with the transformational aspirations of critical theorists however, we seek not merely to analyse but to contribute to transformation towards justice. We remain open to the possibility that the creation of a society respecting and ensuring wellbeing for all may be achievable. To this end we would support an elaborated definition of careers, properly underpinned with life-enhancing human rights, universal access to sustainable livelihoods, and encased by social institutions supportive of human responsibilities and interests beyond employment. Aotearoa/New Zealand is one country committing itself to this approach to social justice and human wellbeing. Thus, this country may again attract the attention of the world, not for its achievement of the most rapid and extensive liberalisation of its economy as it did during the 1980s and 1990s (Kelsey 1999), but for its achievement of a just and sustainable society for all people. In the next section we describe how attention is being given to this broad agenda in the area of equal employment opportunity and gender.

Women, work, and careers in Aotearoa/New Zealand

At the opening of the twenty-first century in Aotearoa/New Zealand, a number of the most influential and prestigious institutional positions were held by women.[4] Many more women have achieved management positions and entered forms of employment traditionally associated with men. It would appear from this that career opportunities for women in this country abound. Does the experience here indicate a significant change in the gendered arrangements of socio-economic circumstances of women in this country? These high profile examples, while very worthy of celebration in their own right, do not reassure us, as feminist researchers and teachers, that gender equality is close to achievement. Moreover, we would also argue that even if, under the present economic regime in this country and the world more generally, women and men were achieving demonstrably similar career outcomes, in the context of widening gaps between rich and poor and the economic and social alienation of those who cannot or will not comply with the system, our particular concept of equity may still be unmet (Humphries and Grice 1995).

In Aotearoa/New Zealand, the pattern and the pressures of employment for women are consistent with those articulated in the western international literature. Women's earnings have been most optimistically estimated at approximately 85 per cent of male incomes. This statistical representation is, however, overly simplistic and distractingly optimistic. The New Zealand Income Survey (2003), for example, reports that the average weekly income from wages and salaries indicates men earn $674 per week and women $410 (Statistics New Zealand 2003). In the government's report to the United Nations, increasing participation of women in the labour force is documented but it is noted that women earned 78 per cent of ordinary-time weekly earnings compared with men (The Ministry of Women's Affairs 2002).

Attempts to address seemingly intractable gender disparities have generated studies of occupational choice and outcomes of women and men. These have consistently demonstrated persistent horizontal and vertical gendered segregation in employment here as elsewhere. In Chapter 7 of this book Patton and McMahon provide a comprehensive review of much of this literature. Making sense of such persistent gendered disparity becomes more complex when other human characteristics are included in the categorisation. Ethnicity, age, and many other dimensions of human identity are significantly associated with access to, and outcomes of, employment. In Aotearoa/New Zealand, statistics indicate that for Maori and Pacific Island women the employment uptake and outcomes gaps are much greater than the averaged statistic. On the whole, these disparities of outcomes are deemed undesirable and attempts to address them have taken many forms. Below we outline several ways in which equity in employment and career opportunities for women are being attended to in Aotearoa/New Zealand.

Redressing gendered disparity in Aotearoa/New Zealand

As a founding member of the International Labour Organisation, Aotearoa/New Zealand has been an active citizen in the articulation of human rights instruments in the international context. We ratified the Convention Against Slave Trading and Slavery in 1927, and as part of the unanimous adaptation of the Universal Declaration of Human Rights in 1948, the government of Aotearoa/New Zealand joins with other signatories to declare commitment to

> the inherent dignity and the equal and inalienable rights of all members of the human family [as] the foundation of freedom, justice and peace in the world ... [reaffirming] faith in fundamental human

> rights, in the dignity and worth of the human person and in the equal rights of men and women.
>
> (The United Nations 2004)

In ratifying this Declaration, all subsequent governments of this country are committed to providing the conditions for

> free choice of employment, to just and favourable conditions of work and to protection against unemployment ... to equal pay for equal work ... to just and favourable remuneration ensuring ... an existence worthy of human dignity, and supplemented, if necessary by other social protections ... to form and to join trade unions (Article 23); ... to rest and leisure, including reasonable limitation of working hours and periodic holidays with pay (Article 24): ... to a standard of living adequate for health and wellbeing ... including food, clothing, housing, and medical care and necessary social services ... Motherhood and childhood are entitled to special care and assistance (Article 25).
>
> (The United Nations 2004)

These aspirations generated further commitment at the United Nations Beijing Platform for Action in 1995 (United Nations 1996). Immediately after the Beijing Conference, the Ministry of Women's Affairs identified six crosscutting themes of the Platform which could be addressed by the government. These require that attention be given to:

- mainstreaming a gender perspective in the development of all policies and programmes
- women's unremunerated work
- the gender pay gap
- the need for more and better data collection about all aspects of women's lives
- the Platform's recommendations which are relevant to Maori women and girls [as indigenous people]
- enhancing women's role in decision-making [including through a government commitment to 'gender balance' on all government-appointed committees, boards and other relevant official bodies].

(Ministry of Women's Affairs 2002: 9)

Since then, the government has produced a series of action plans to construct a set of strategies which are intended to develop and strengthen the promotion and protection of human rights (Ministry of Women's Affairs 2002).

In the specific focus on gender, the government of the day reports back to the United Nations under the Convention on the Elimination of All Forms of Discrimination Against Women (CEDAW) for progress on the commitments made for the redress of issues affecting women in this country. Government generated reports are commented on by Non-Governmental Organisations (NGOs). These organisations draw upon the same statistical material and have an opportunity to argue that actual progress is not quite as optimistic as government reports might indicate. While there are various possible interpretations of the statistical indicators in this country, and there is disagreement on how such inequalities (or their representation in the statistical pictures) are manufactured, on the whole, there is a strongly articulated commitment to equalising career participation and outcomes. Perceptions about what influences inequality has been the subject of much research, some of which is reviewed in the section below.

Gender research

The persistence of gender inequality has generated all manner of analysis associated with what might be considered gendered and gendering institutions and practices. This research, for example, has pointed to the articulation of language that excludes women or diminishes their worth. Also under scrutiny are organisational structures that inhibit the freedom of women to take up employment or other activities beyond the constraints of continued allocation of primary responsibility for home, family, and community; religious practices that embed patriarchal values and so on. Researchers have documented and challenged educational developments that not only channel girls and boys differently but also treat them differently in gendered and gendering ways of being, from subtle differences in teacher communication patterns to the differentiated allocation of physical space. Disparate participation, resourcing and recognition in sport, or sexualised representation of women in music and in popular culture more generally, variations in health investments and outcomes, and differential outcomes for retirement resourcing continue to be examined and challenged for their gendered and gendering effects. The differences documented have been claimed as expressions of a hierarchical value system of male (or the masculine) over female (or the feminine) (Du Plessis 1998; Kedgley and Varnham 1993; Olsson 1992).

Our research over the years has focused largely on the careers of women at a time of radical economic and organisational restructuring in this country (Gatenby and Humphries 1992; 1996; 1999a; 1999b; 2000a; 2000b; Humphries and Gatenby 1994; 1999). Over a twelve-year period, for example, we conducted a longitudinal, participative career development study with women graduates from a ‘Women and Management’ course (Gatenby and Humphries 1992). Our participants indicated that despite their qualification, and despite their dedication to balancing their career and family commitments, the gender issues these women faced were much the same as those expressed in the literature reporting the experiences of women's careers in the decades before them.

In our research we have paid attention also to attempts to flatten organisational structures and to recreate a workforce based on core and peripheral demarcations facilitated through the achievement of a more 'flexible' workforce (Dyer and Humphries 2002). The long established call from women for access to better career opportunities and outcomes ironically provided a useful lexicon for the achievement of such flexibility. Women had long been calling for more participation in employment, and more flexibility in the hours and processes of employment. Women were promoted, and promoted themselves, as having those characteristics deemed attractive to employers of flattened organisational structures that depend on multi-tasking, teamwork and low union participation. For women of Maori and Pacific descent, much was made of their culturally specific capacity to work in teams and to show concern for the wellbeing of their group (Dyer and Humphries 2002). This restructuring of work, for which women were specifically recruited, was also a period in which the overall conditions of workers in this country was undermined, downward pressure on pay and conditions of service was exerted, and poverty for some was exacerbated (Humphries 1998). This outcome was not what we had in mind as we, as teachers and researchers, became involved in supporting the enhanced career aspirations and outcomes for women in this country. Thus elaborated, conditions in Aotearoa/New Zealand fall demonstrably short of the aspiration for gender equality articulated in the Declaration of Human Rights. This gap between aspiration and outcome has remained of concern to liberal as well as more radically inclined thinkers and has driven the policy and legislative changes discussed in the sections below.

Achieving equality

Significant legislative changes that have sought to address employment disparities in Aotearoa/New Zealand began with the Government Service Equal Pay Act 1960 and the Equal Pay Act 1972. These two Acts, aimed at public and private sector employees respectively, provided the mandate for women to be paid the same rate of pay as men for performing the same job. However, over the subsequent decades it was recognised that the disparities of outcomes lay not only with the unequal pay for men and women doing the same jobs. Studies of horizontal and vertical segregation of genders indicated that women's employment was concentrated in industries and occupations that attracted lower average wages than the industries and occupations dominated by men. The Employment Equity Act 1990 was designed to redress this aspect of pay inequity by providing the mechanisms to compare those jobs and industries in which women were concentrated with those where men predominated, and to reassess the ways these jobs were valued (Humphries and Gatenby 1994). The mantra became 'equal pay for jobs of equal worth' (Hyman 1994: 83–89).

Today there are still arguments about the nature, causes and effects of this persistent gender gap. Some suggest women take up lower paying, lower status jobs than men because women have a comparatively underdeveloped sense of career commitment. Others argue that women's career ideas include a prioritisation of the careers aspirations of their partners, or that they believe that their family and social responsibilities preclude commitment to demanding (and high paying) jobs. There are those who believe the gap continues because some employers believe women are worth less, are less career focused and less reliable than men, or that jobs done predominantly by women are valued less *because* they are done by women. There is plenty of empirical evidence to suggest that all these are possible influences on the gendered career outcomes in western societies.

It is important to note that at the same time as the work underpinning the Employment Equity Act was undertaken in this country, consecutive governments of the day were committing themselves to increasing a free trade agenda known here as 'Rogernomics' and 'Ruthenasia'. These were economic directives increasingly driving socio-political policy under the leadership first of Roger Douglas, as the Finance Minister of a Labour government, and then Ruth Richardson, as the Finance Minister for a subsequent National (Conservative) government (Kelsey 1999).[5] An absolute anathema to these directives was any form of market intervention. 'The market' according to this dogma, would be the arbiter of justice. Accordingly, the Employment Equity Act was repealed to allow the Employment Contracts Act (1991) to take its place. This Act intended to liberalise the labour market in keeping with the overall philosophy of neo-liberalism (Humphries and Gatenby 1994).

The outcome of this era has now been well documented. While few people were better off, many were net losers. Losses were not equally shared across the sectors. 'Most were in the wholesale, retail, and hotel industries, those represented by the distribution unions and the SWU (Service Workers Union) and those in which most workers are minorities, women, youth and part-timers' (Dannin 1997: 188). Contrary to the advocates of the free market, critics portrayed the economic policy as a flawed dogma, a playing field, purportedly level but one which levelled women (Bunkle 1993). Gender equality, as a desirable but not yet achieved goal, was recognised by both the advocates for, and critics of, the liberalisation agenda. The strategy of the liberals, however, was to supplant legislative pressures with educational approaches to social change. The most prominent of the educational focus was the establishment of the Equal Employment Opportunities Trust set up to move employers from an awareness and acceptance of Equal Employment Opportunities (EEO) to action through partnership, research, information and action (EEO Trust Deed 2004).

The current situation for women in employment in Aotearoa/New Zealand has received a mixed report card. Certainly official figures indicate that the market sector has marginally closed the gap between male and female ordinary earnings. However, these improvements may also be explainable by a decrease in the rates of pay for work done by men, rather than due to increases in the pay rates of women. It would appear that forty years of legislation, policy, and educational attempts to achieve employment equality between women and men here have not made an appreciable difference. We can, of course, only speculate what the outcomes might have been without such pressures.

Compared with men, women in this country today still congregate in a limited number of occupations. In almost all occupations women hold a predominant number of the lower paid, lower status jobs, even in occupations dominated by women. The current Labour government has recognised that the headlong leap into economic neo-liberalism taken by its predecessors in the early 1980s has left much to be desired in terms of the differentiated allocation of privilege and hardship for a country purporting parallel commitment to the indivisibility and equality of human rights and the democratic rights to wellbeing for all citizens. The Employment Contracts Act (1991) has been replaced with the Employment Relations Act (2000) which defines discrimination as when employers treat individuals differently in terms of employment, conditions of work, fringe benefits, or opportunities for training, promotion and transfer. Discriminations such as these, however, are notoriously difficult to prove (Gatenby and Humphries 2000b). Certainly, we are not short of evidence to suggest such discrimination is part of everyday social and organisational life in this country. This new Act does not refer to remuneration as a form of discrimination and does not directly provide the legal mechanisms for women to demand equality of pay. New strategies for pay equity between men and women, and between ethnic groups that make up this country's population, will need to be driven from other initiatives. Stronger interdepartmental links between legislation, policy, and organisational practice are being undertaken. Pertinent to this chapter is the commitment by the current government to a 'whole of government approach' to improving social outcomes, particularly for those most marginalised under the current economic circumstances.

Attempts at a 'whole of government approach' to addressing a variety of marginalisations in this country include a strengthening of the human rights commitments made in our association with the United Nations. In keeping with this book's focus on issues of career management and development, of interest is the government's Career Services *rapuara*. Career

Services *rapuara* is mandated to assist with the achievement of economic and social outcomes through the provision of career information, support and guidance (Oakes and von Dadelszen 1999; Oakes *et al.* 2001). The organisation articulates the most up to date career concepts, information, and various programmes of support in keeping with the issues of justice and wellbeing for all. It specifically acknowledges that career planning on the part of individuals must be coupled with a reasonable standard of income that ensures economic and social success for all New Zealanders. In keeping with this mandate, a number of its key services are directed towards the needs of the most disenfranchised in this country. Commitment to equal employment opportunities is highly visible in both their documentation and in their practice. Moreover, as a government service, it has a specific mandate to work with other government agencies to progress the 'whole of government' approach to achieve enhanced wellbeing for all citizens. What is perhaps less clear, and makes Aotearoa/New Zealand of ongoing interest to the international community, is whether these policy directives together with strengthened commitment to human rights agendas and EEO mechanisms can redress the out-fall of the free market economic policies simultaneously pursued. The invigoration of the Human Rights approach by the recent appointment of an EEO Commissioner (from January 2003) seems a useful contribution. However, we remain concerned about the limitations of neo-liberal approaches to equity. From more radical points of view, such directions are likely to result in the assimilation of gender to render other inequalities gender-neutral, leaving poverty and exploitation (perhaps also gender-neutral) explained as the fair outcome of individual choices made by rational beings. Whether a concerted effort to embed a human rights approach to the elimination of exploitation and slavery and the achievement of fair wages and conditions of service may be achieved, requires vigilance and creative action.

Employment equality, career equity, and wellbeing

As the twenty-first century gets under way, 'the market' is still deemed to be the most important vehicle for achieving human aspirations in this country. In this chapter we have concerned ourselves with the institutional pressures evident in human rights, legislative, and careers discourses that link wellbeing for women with the achievement of employment equality with men. This is perhaps too simplistic a position and overly sympathetic to the concepts and fabrications associated with western market ideologies. Whose interest do such ideologies serve? In the view of Joseph Stiglitz (2002), Nobel Laureate and former Chief Economist at the World Bank, the current form of globalisation serves very selective interests and has devastating effects especially on the lives of the poor (p.xiv). He argues for the strong hand of government in setting and maintaining standards of ethical capitalist practice in order to lift the standards of living for all. More radical critics of capitalism remain concerned about the fundamental exploitative directives of capitalism that will seek to minimise costs, and is not too fussy about which groups of vulnerable people come within reach of this exploitation. There are many more such potential groups, although a number of women in the west may expect to be part of the relatively secured labour force with the opportunities and risks this brings them.

Equal opportunities discourses and human rights approaches to human wellbeing have been argued in this chapter to be central to the liberal project of globalisation of economic liberalism. More radical theorists believe that equalising the participation of women within the economic and political system that now exists merely exchanges the demographic characteristics of the favoured few in power. This system will continue to control the destiny of a majority of people, a proportion of whom will be relegated to the periphery of society to remain alienated and bereft of the life-sustaining opportunities needed for human thriving (Calas and Smircich 1993; Humphries and Grice 1994). Of those so alienated, the majority will be women and their children. The careers of many currently consist of work associated with survival in poverty, scavenging, prostitution, and many other forms of dehumanising activities. While the work focused on female career experiences is necessary it is not sufficient for the achievement of justice and wellbeing for women, men and all those who depend on them. Increased global competition, the devaluing of work as it becomes feminised, and the emphasis on the achievement equality between women and men is leading to increased competition among all people for access to increasingly insecure employment within flattened organisational structures, and in a climate of work intensification (Dyer and Humphries 2002; Bradley 1999). Will the strengthening of human rights approaches to wellbeing, together with the contemporary career metaphors, diminish exploitation? It seems that in Aotearoa/New Zealand we have pinned our hopes on this. We urge critical theorists to continue their vigilance and, where unconvinced by the observable trends in this market mechanism for a decent future, be proposing and promoting alternative possibilities for consideration.

Notes

1 Ministry of Women's Affairs Fifth Report to UN CEDAW: www.mwa.govt.nz ISBN 0-478-25206-4.

2 The convention of naming this country with two names signals the aspirations of many indigenous people of this land. Sovereign tribes collectively known as Maori, and some later settlers in this country (known as Pakeha or Tauiwi) seek to establish Maori as (for some) 'sovereign' or (for others) 'partners' in the rule of this land. Claims to sovereignty may be based on The Declaration of

Independence (1835) or The Treaty of Waitangi (1840). For those Maori who reject these legal fictions altogether, their very existence here as people of the land (Tangata Whenua) is all the 'authority' they need to assert direction over their own lives.

3 *The New Internationalist* (Vol. 337 Aug. 2001) uses United Nations information to draw a complex picture of contemporary slavery, trafficking in women, men, children, and other forms of bondage. http://www.newint.org.

4 These positions have included two Governors General, two Prime Ministers and Leaders of the Opposition, the Chief High Court Judge, the Attorney General, the Leader of the Trade Union Movement, the Chief Executive of one of our biggest commercial enterprises, the President of the Tertiary Union to name just a few.

5 Loosely defined as local versions of Thatcherism in the UK and Reaganism in the US.

Bibliography

Arthur, M.B., Inkson, K. and Pringle, J. (1999) *The New Careers*, Sage: London.

Bradley, H. (1999) *Gender and Power in the Workplace; Analysing the Impact of Economic Change*, London: Macmillan Press.

Bunkle, P. (1993) 'How the level playing field levels women', in S. Kedgley and M. Varnham (eds) *Heading Nowhere in a Navy Blue Suit*, Wellington: Daphne Brasell Associates Co Ltd.

Calas, M. and Smircich, L. (1993) 'Dangerous Liaisons; the "Feminine" meets "Globalization"', *Business Horizons*, March–April, 71–81.

Dannin, E. (1997) *Working Free: The Origins and the Impacts of New Zealand's Employment Contracts Act*, Auckland: Auckland University Press.

Du Plessis, R. (ed.) (1998) *Feminist Thought in Aotearoa New Zealand*, New York: Oxford University Press.

Dyer, S. and Humphries, M. (2002) 'Normalising workplace change through contemporary career discourse', *The Australian e-Journal for the Advancement of Mental Health.*

EEO Trust Deed (2004) Online. Available HTTP. http://www.eeotrust.org.nz (accessed 5 February 2004).

Gatenby, B. and Humphries, M.T. (1992) 'Save it for women in management', in *The Gender Factor*, Palmerston North: Dunmore Press.

Gatenby, B. and Humphries, M.T. (1996) 'Feminist commitments in organizational communication: participatory action research as feminist praxis', *Australian Journal of Communication*, 23(2): 73–88.

Gatenby, B. and Humphries, M.T. (1999a) 'Exploring gender, management education and careers: speaking in the silences', *Gender and Education*, 11(3): 281–294.

Gatenby, B. and Humphries, M.T. (1999b) 'Doing gender: role models, mentors and networks', *International Review of Women and Leadership*, 5(1): 12–29.

Gatenby, B. and Humphries, M.T. (2000a) 'Feminist participatory action research: methodological and ethical issues', *Women's Studies International Forum.* 23(1): 89–105.

Gatenby, B. and Humphries, M.T. (2000b) 'The more things change, the more they stay the same: reconstructing gender through women's careers', *Australian Journal of Career Development*, 9(1): 45–53.

Greenhaus, J.H., Callanan, G.A. and Godshalk, V.M. (2000) *Career Management*, London: The Dryden Press.

Hall, D.T. and Associates (1996) *The Career is Dead: Long Live the Career: A Relational Approach to Careers*, San Francisco, CA: Jossey-Bass.

Hertz, N. (2001) *The Silent Takeover: Global Capitalism and the Death of Democracy*, London: Random House.

Humphries, M.T. (1998) 'For the common good? New Zealanders comply with quality standards', *Organisation Science*, 9(6): 737–749.

Humphries, M.T. and Gatenby, B. (1994) 'Employment equity', in J. Deeks and P. Enderwick (eds) *Business and Society*, Auckland: Longman Paul.

Humphries, M.T. and Gatenby, B. (1999) 'Defining careers', *International Career Journal*, January, http://www.icg-uk.org/icg/ICG2.HTM.

Humphries, M.T. and Grice, S. (1994) 'Management of diversity: a modern tale of assimilation?', in P. Boxall (ed.) *The Challenge of Human Resource Management: Directions and Debates in New Zealand*, Auckland: Longman Paul.

Humphries, M.T. and Grice, S. (1995) 'Equal employment opportunity and the management of diversity: a global discourse of assimilation?', *Journal of Organizational Change Management*, 8(5): 17–33.

Hyman, P. (1994) *Women and Economics: A New Zealand Feminist Perspective*, Wellington: Bridget Williams Books.

Kedgley, S. and Varnham, M. (eds) (1993) *Heading Nowhere in a Navy Blue Suit*, Wellington: Daphne Brasell Associates Co Ltd.

Kelsey, J. (1999) *Reclaiming the Future: New Zealand and the Global Economy*, Wellington: Bridget Williams Books.

McCormick, E. and Herron Zamoroa, J. (2000) 'Slave trade still alive in U.S. *San Francisco Examiner*', Sunday, 13 February, 2000. Online. Available HTTP. http://www.cs.cmu.edu/People/spok/serials/sfexaminer.html (accessed 4 February 2004).

Ministry of Women's Affairs (2002) *The Status of Women in New Zealand*, The Ministry of Women's Affairs: Wellington.

Oakes, L. and von Dadelszen, J. (1999) The New Zealand Policy Framework for Career Information and Guidance Paper. Presented at the International Symposium Career Development and Public Policy: International Collaboration for National Action, May 1999, Ottawa, Canada.

Oakes, L., von Dadelszen, J. and Barker, P. (2001) New Zealand Country Paper. Presented at the International Symposium on Career Development and Public Policy, March 5–6, Vancouver, British Colombia, Canada.

Olsson, S. (1992) (ed.) *The Gender Factor: Women in New Zealand Organisations*, Palmerston North: Dunmore Press.

Shiva, V. (1993) 'Reductionism and regeneration: a crisis in science', in M. Mies (ed.) *Ecofeminism*, London: Zed Books.

Shiva, V. (2003) 'Food rights, free trade and fascism', in M.J. Gibney (ed.) *Globalising Rights*, Oxford: Oxford University Press.

Statistics New Zealand (2003) New Zealand income survey, table one: average weekly income for all people. Online. Available HTTP.http://www.stats.govt.ns (accessed 4 February 2004).

Stiglitz, J. (2002) *Globalization and its Discontents*, London: Allan Lane.

United Nations Declaration on Human Rights (2004) Online. Available HTTP. http://www.un.org/overview/rights.htlm (accessed 4 February 2004).

United Nations (1996) *Platform for Action: Fourth Conference on Women Beijing, China 4–15 September, 1995*, United Nations: New York.

Chapter 9

The career education curriculum and students with disabilities

Paul Pagliano

Introduction

Prior to 1975 most students with disabilities attended segregated special schools. Thirty years later the majority are included in their local community school learning alongside their same age peers. The essential difference between integration (the term used to describe the original goal of placing students with disabilities with their peers for the purposes of education) and inclusion (the term currently in use) is that with integration, the school asks; 'Can we provide for the needs of this student?' With inclusion, the school asks; 'How will we provide for the needs of this student?' (Foreman 1996: 12). With integration, a school may feel unable to adapt their practices to meet the needs of some disabled students, leading to their exclusion. However, where a policy of inclusion is in place, a whole-school approach is instituted to ensure that the particular needs of all disabled students are appropriately accommodated and always met.

Career education emerged in the late 1960s as a 'phenomenon' that 'took root in many parts of the world almost simultaneously'. Those nations involved all experienced 'particular levels of industrialization, occupational specialization and diversity', that required them to, 'shift their educational content . . . to accommodate these conditions' (Herr and Cramer 1996: 34–35). Bogged down in the logistics of provision, it then lost momentum in the 1980s during the 'back-to-basics' educational movement. Emphasis reverted to the traditional core subjects (Isaacson and Brown 2000: 234) and career education came to be regarded as supererogatory.

Ongoing attempts to revitalise career education by making it a more integral part of the school curriculum have met with varied degrees of success. In many school systems career education is still regarded as an add-on activity. However, enthusiasm is not dormant. McCowan and McKenzie (1997: 3) listed the four rationales associated with 'the resurgence of interest in career education' in the 1990s as:

- economic rationale – career education has a significant contribution to make to the development of a competent society that facilitates the

development of an appropriately placed and skilled workforce which, in turn, enhances productivity and international competitiveness;
- social justice rationale – career education can help promote equity for socially and economically disadvantaged students, including those with disabilities, and prepare all students to be full participants in society generally;
- student development rationale – career education facilitates the psycho-social aspects of overall development as students grow from a position of dependence to that of becoming responsible independent adults; and
- workforce rationale – career education assists students in dealing with the multiple pathways which are emerging and orientating them towards areas of structural growth and demand.

There is still much to achieve in all four of the above areas, particularly for students with disabilities. Since 1975 there has been the ongoing de-institutionalisation of adult services for adults with disabilities. Nowadays by far the majority of adults with disabilities live and work in regular communities. However, whatever equity measures one uses to assess employment and quality of life (equality of opportunity, representation or outcome), people with disabilities 'are almost universally at the bottom rung of the socio-economic ladder' (Schriner 2001: 645). Less than one third are employed compared with more than two thirds of the general population. Those that are employed often have low earnings and, despite protective legislation, are more vulnerable to job discrimination (Kennedy and Olney 2001). Only one in three identify themselves as very satisfied with life in general compared to sixty one per cent of the non-disabled population (Harris and Associates 1998). Clearly, to date, people with disabilities have not been adequately served by career education.

The career education curriculum

The career education curriculum refers to a course of study designed to prepare students for life after school. It starts prior to kindergarten and extends beyond secondary education. To be effective, the programme must be forward looking, simultaneously serve the needs of the local community and show cognisance of developments in the wider world.

In the past definitions of career tended to focus on one's occupation. However, recent changes to society, and to the work environment, have resulted in the focus being expanded to comprise, in addition to occupation, 'pre-vocational and post-vocational concerns as well as integration of work with other roles: family, community, leisure' (Herr and Cramer 1996: 32). This 'new' interpretation 'potentially means everyone has a career' (Arnold and Jackson 1997: 429) even those who are not in active employment. It refers to all roles a person plays throughout one's life (Wolffe 2000).

> At a personal level it is about our well being and quality of life. For employers, it is about harnessing and developing the potential of all their employees. For society, it raises issues about the importance of social cohesion and what the consequences will be if some groups are excluded from having careers in any meaningful sense. It has profound implications for our education and training systems, and represents a major challenge to providers of career guidance.
>
> (Arnold and Jackson 1997: 429)

Career education therefore involves learning about work, leisure and life-skills (Pagliano 2000).

This wider remit highlights the interconnection between career and personal education, and reinforces the push for career education to become more integrated in the core curriculum. Indeed Herr (1997) insists that 'career and personal counselling must fuse' (p.81). The traditional narrow description of career education, which Isaacson and Brown (2000: 12) give as:

> a systematic attempt to influence the career development of students and adults through various types of educational strategies including providing occupational information, infusing career-related concepts into the academic curriculum, taking field trips to businesses and industries, having guest speakers representing various occupations talk about their jobs, offering classes devoted to the study of careers, establishing career internships and apprenticeships, and setting up laboratories that stimulate career experiences

therefore needs to be expanded to incorporate:

- a joint emphasis on personal and career development (student development rationale);
- a focus on the task of preparing students for a time when they leave school (economic and workforce rationale);
- the promotion of equity (social justice rationale).

The implications of such changes are profound. The curriculum needs to be sensitive to the diverse individual life-needs of all students. Unless the school system adopts a career education curriculum that is both forward looking and integrated, students who are disadvantaged, particularly those with disabilities, will not receive a career education that is appropriate to their needs.

> The danger is that our traditional schools and colleges will lag behind, designed by people from a world that used to be, for a world that will

> be no more, rather like our armies, which were always well trained for the last war.
>
> (Handy 1997: 228)

There is little doubt that there are grave concerns as to the effectiveness of the traditional narrow-focus career education curriculum. As McMahon (1997) concludes, for a large number of students 'the influence of school on their career development is unintentional', even 'minimal' (p.132). After his study at one secondary school in Queensland, Australia, Vick (1996) observed:

> Across the board the students claimed that they learned very little about the world of work at school . . . the social background of those interviewed [middle class] suggests the urgency of the problem . . . if students from these families are poorly prepared, it is likely that the majority are even more seriously ill-equipped.
>
> (pp.10–15)

Student participation in a career education curriculum generally seems to depend more on which school the student attends than on personal need. Despite ongoing recommendations that 'career education be embedded in the curriculum' (McMahon 1997: 132), in some schools career education is left off the curriculum altogether. Often there is insufficient 'time, training, personnel resources, materials resources' (Turnbull *et al.* 1999: 116). Such fortuity makes it even more likely that students who are disadvantaged will fall between the cracks.

Students with disabilities

The World Health Organisation has defined the terms impairment, disability and handicap. *Impairment* is a 'loss or abnormality of psychological, or anatomical structure or functions'. *Disability* is 'any restriction or lack of ability (resulting from impairment) to perform an activity in the manner or within the range considered normal for a human being'. *Handicap* is 'a disadvantage for an individual resulting from impairment or disability, that limits or prevents fulfilment of a role that is normal for that individual' (Ashman and Elkins 1998: 11). Understanding the differentiation of these terms is important as impairment and disability will only result in handicap in adverse social circumstances. For example, a student who is blind has a visual 'impairment' because of loss of vision (function). This impairment makes it impossible for the student to visually read print (hence there is a restriction) so the student has a print 'disability'. Not being able to read print becomes a 'handicap' when the individual tries to independently shop in the print-organised supermarket (hence the individual is prevented, or at least hindered, from fulfilment of a role that is considered normal). However, if the supermarket had both Braille and print signs, then this individual would not be handicapped. Handicap therefore is not only a consequence of impairment, it is also a reflection of attitudinal limitations imposed on the individual by society. This means that career education has the dual role of preparing the individual with a disability for life after school. It also has a role in helping to break down potential barriers, of helping to confront negative attitudes to disability.

Much of the literature on the career education curriculum for students with disabilities is either written by experts in career development with minimal, even token information about students with disabilities or by experts in a particular disability field with less sophisticated insights into career education. Both approaches are problematic because they fail to adequately synthesise the two areas. This synthesis is an essential prerequisite to achieving second-generation inclusion in education.

> Whereas first-generation inclusion was additive (in the sense that resources and students with disabilities were added to the general curriculum), second-generation inclusion is generative in the sense that it requires the overhaul of the entire educational enterprise. The extent of this reform calls for all educators to teach to the diversity that now occurs in schools, rather than teaching to a homogenized group of relatively similar students. Second-generation inclusion expects school-wide reform, teacher renewal, intensive support for students, and a retreat from education based on labels.
>
> (Turnbull *et al.* 1999: 116)

The 'retreat from education based on labels' (Turnbull *et al.* 1999: 116) involves the adoption of a non-categorical approach. This is an attempt to break down many of the attitudinal limitations that lead to handicap. Labelling tends to obscure individual differences because the very process of classifying directs one's gaze in a fixed direction. For students with disabilities this means

> their individual identities are often lost under the label and they become known primarily by the label ... This can result in lowered self-esteem and expectations by teachers, parents, and the students themselves. Sometimes, a label becomes a self-fulfilling prophecy whereby a student fulfils only the lower expectations implied by the label.
>
> (Wood and Lazzari 1997: 23)

As McKnight (1995) reminds us:

> We know that if one surrounds any individual with messages and experiences that are always saying to them, what is important about you is what is wrong with you, that will have a powerful, depressing, disillusioning and degrading effect upon that person.
>
> (p.4)

A non-categorical approach seeks to break the student out of this spiral of negativity (Wolfensberger 1972) by redirecting the gaze in more positive ways. This involves emphasising student achievement not ability deficit; positioning students in active rather than passive ways; employing respectful, enabling and hopeful language; using individual first terminology with more generic descriptors (e.g., 'student with a disability' not 'disabled student'); and separating the student from the behaviour (e.g., 'the student has a problem behaviour' not 'the student is a behaviour problem'). Special education becomes more of a service where the emphasis is on the 'development of better means of meeting the learning needs of children who are different' (Deno 1970, cited in Turnbull *et al.* 1999: 14) and less of a separate placement. The assumption is that the mainstream curriculum is the first and best option.

The goal of second-generation inclusion in education is to help students with disabilities achieve greater independence, productivity and community integration once they leave school. Unfortunately, despite major changes in the structure of education, many students with disabilities 'face rather dismal prospects after leaving school' with '(T)he competitive employment of students with disabilities' lagging 'significantly behind the employment rate for peers' (Turnbull *et al.* 1999: 11). One major reason for this is the increased pressure attributed to globalisation.

Looking forward – globalisation

Globalisation refers to the ongoing movement towards the world becoming a single market place. If we, as educators, are to make more accurate predictions about what type of career education is going to be the most appropriate to student needs as adults, we must examine globalisation from a range of different perspectives. These include questioning the impact of globalisation on the workforce in general and on people with disabilities in particular to, not only identify possible future trends, but also devise ways to help students with disabilities 'positively navigate this changing' terrain (Szymanski and Vancollins 2003: 14).

Rapid developments in technology, communication and transport, as well as the blurring of international boundaries, have combined to intensify competition and engineer a shift from industrial manufacturing to service provision. This, in turn, has created a widening diversity of career patterns but with increased emphasis on improving efficiency and effectiveness, particularly at the individual level. The impact of globalisation, therefore, has meant that, for many, work is now less predictable, more fragmented, requires greater flexibility, increased personal initiative, and the ongoing acquisition of credentials.

Hutton (1996) talks about emerging workforce divisions, such as core and peripheral workers, where the capable reap great rewards while the less able are centrifugally tossed into uncertain, often marginalised regimes built on crumbling social and political safety nets. 'These changes', Szymanski and Vancollins (2003) suggest, 'may be particularly challenging for some people with disabilities' (p.14). They target five areas of concern where people with disabilities may be seriously handicapped.

Job insecurity and changing labour market

Mergers, downsizing and the move towards employing temporary workers means that people with disabilities are especially vulnerable to ongoing job insecurity, with many regularly slipping in and out of work. Not only is this going to negatively impact on personal psychological wellbeing, there will be increased competition for compensation packages and other stepping stones to further employment.

The challenge of technology

Even though technology will help many people with disabilities, there will be ongoing problems associated with ensuring accessibility and affordability. Unless protective legislation is introduced, adaptive technology is likely to lag behind innovative developments and be much more expensive than mainstream technology.

Special challenges for people with cognitive disabilities

People with intellectual and learning disabilities are going to be increasingly disadvantaged because the majority of new careers are going to be in the fast-paced, knowledge-dependent, service industries.

Challenging policies

Increasing competitiveness will result in people from many different disadvantaged groups becoming rivals for limited social justice funding. Furthermore industries, established to assist, may foster unnecessary dependence in order to retain government funding.

Stress and the work environment

In the future there are likely to be increased levels of workplace stress which, when added to the already considerable stress of having a disability, may mean that paid employment becomes a less attractive option.

Colley (2000) charges that 'it is immoral to continue to portray the effects of globalisation as either acceptable or inevitable [because to] do so draws [career] guidance into collusion with a process of social control'. This 'particular triumphalist discourse of globalisation', she argues, 'dominates concepts of vocational realism' (p.11) to such an extent that it becomes 'hegemonic' (p.14). She recommends that we start by becoming 'more realistic ourselves about inadequacies in the way we have served the most disadvantaged' (p.25).

The move towards a single world market has increased emphasis on competition, efficiency and effectiveness at individual, national and international levels, privileging the able and marginalising these who are disabled. Colley (2000) questions whether this is acceptable. She challenges us to find more 'proper' pathways (Handy 1997: 205). 'In the interests of democracy and social justice, we can legitimately see [career] guidance as a process for shaping the world of work rather than simply reflecting one view of it' (Colley 2000: 25).

Predictions suggest that future job shortages will occur more in the skilled areas while unskilled and low skilled jobs will continue to move off shore to developing countries.

The overhaul of the entire educational enterprise

The call for career education to be embedded in the regular curriculum and the move towards greater inclusion for students with disabilities, both require an overhaul of the entire education enterprise guided by social justice.

Social justice involves the fundamental principle of taking the standpoint of the least advantaged to inform and implement educational strategies that are in their best interests (Connell 1990). Rawls (1971) argued that most individuals believe justice requires impartiality. Therefore discrimination on the grounds of negative or positive attitudes towards particular people is unacceptable. A problem of distributive justice in education is evidenced by the fact that students from disadvantaged backgrounds including those with disabilities are getting the worst deal from education and from life (Connell 1990). Education in the form of credentials (qualifications) plays a powerful role in determining social order because these credentials have become the prerequisites for professional employment. As the amount of education necessary to obtain these credentials expands, education as a social asset increases and the gap between the 'haves' and the 'have nots' becomes even more accentuated. This then threatens our form of democracy, which is based on the assumption of equal rights.

All three complementary curricula logics designed to promote equality in education apply to both the career education curriculum and to students with disabilities (Connell 1990).

The *compensatory* curriculum involves the addition of extra human and material resources. Unless additional funding is made available to ensure that teachers receive specialist training in career education to cater for students with disabilities and to provide for the purchase of relevant specialist materials, these human and material resources will not be forthcoming.

An *oppositional* curriculum rejects the logic of the mainstream and develops a separate curriculum specifically for the needs of particular students. Unless a career education curriculum is specifically designed to 'really suit' (Connell 1990: 10) particular special needs, the specialist know-how and resources will not be at the cutting edge of development and over time will disappear altogether.

A *counter-hegemonic* curriculum involves an attempt to generalise the point of view of those with special needs in order to reconstruct the system as a whole (for example, a panel of adults with disabilities could be invited to advise on the design of the career education curriculum). Unless the hegemony of a curriculum is continually challenged, the able-privileged will continue to be advantaged at the expense of those who are less able.

These three curricula logics help ensure that social justice is not just add-on but 'fundamental to what good education is about' (Connell 1990: 10). For Giorcelli (1993), a good education, which is synonymous with a good career education, is one that

> is successful in teaching all of its students the essential learnings and skills they need to know or to be able to apply. If the focus of the school is on *quality* and *equity*, the outcome indicators selected to demonstrate student achievement should reflect with accuracy the curriculum being taught, and the outcome results should be examined in such a way that educators can be certain that no major subset of the student population is left behind.
>
> (p.85)

Teaching to accommodate the diversity that now occurs in schools necessitates the introduction of a fourth curricula logic, the *differentiated curriculum*. Whereas in the past the curriculum tended to be fixed and inflexible, the new curriculum must be differentiated (Farmer 1994). This allows the teacher to modify content, process and product to match learning tasks with individual student learning needs. The differentiated curriculum is based on the establishment of a student centred learning environment, where the emphasis is on student interests, input, and developing independence. Teaching therefore begins with the identification of student achievements. For capable students it involves deleting already mastered material and introducing new material earlier (acceleration) or at greater depth (enrichment). For less able students it involves more opportunity for consolidation. Content can be made more concrete or abstract. Process can be moved from factual to higher-level thinking and product can be modified to make stronger links with the real world.

Second-generation inclusion is based on an assumption of inclusion for all students. Alternative placement only becomes an option once the regular system has proven to be inadequate. Intensive support for individual students, over and above that provided by the differentiated curriculum, is organised using the individualised education program (IEP). The IEP guides the provision of additional services and facilitates collaboration. The IEP contains

- a statement of the student's current educational achievement levels;
- the annual educational goals, including short-term instructional objectives;
- a statement detailing educational services to be provided and the extent to which each child will participate in regular programs;
- the anticipated date for the start of these services and the expected duration of the services;
- the appropriate objective criteria and evaluation procedures, with at least an annual review to determine if the instructional objectives have been met.

(Ashman and Elkins 1998: 23)

The IEP has two adaptations: the Individualised Family Services Plan (ISFP), used with children from birth through to age two to assist with early intervention, and the Individual Transition Plan (ITP) for students from age 14 through to age 18. The ITP

> must include a statement of the linkages and/or responsibilities that various agencies such as employment services, vocational rehabilitation, and the school system will assume in order to move the individual smoothly from school to living and working in the community.... [It] must also include a statement of transition service needs beginning at age 14. This part of the adolescent's ITP focuses on the curriculum and courses of study that are intended to enhance the student's postschool success. Simply stated, an ITP is an annually updated instrument of coordination and cooperation. It is a working document that identifies the range of services, resources, supports, and activities that each student may require during the transition process.
>
> (Garguilo 2003: 34–35)

Students with disabilities require career education even more than their 'able' peers because their disabilities reduce both their ability and opportunity to learn particular essential concepts for independent, productive and integrated community adult life. For example, a student who is educationally blind will not gain the same wealth of incidental career-related experiences available to those who are sighted. The student will miss the opportunity to visually observe people at work, in the home, in the community or in the visual media. Furthermore this student is unlikely to encounter role models who are blind.

Students with disabilities need to be taught to be critically aware of pertinent issues so that they may not only recognise inequality and discrimination but also have the self-advocacy skills to do something about them. This begins with the inclusive career education curriculum and the provision of additional services specifically for the student with a disability.

Developing an inclusive career education curriculum

Nowadays most students with disabilities primarily engage in the regular curriculum. There is a considerable body of literature to inform regular curriculum design (Herr and Cramer 1996; McCowan and McKenzie 1997; McMahon 1997). Additional services for students with disabilities are provided through the IEP and ITP, which are linked into the regular program through the differentiated curriculum.

Benz *et al.* (2000) identified a number of key components that contributed to improved outcomes for students with disabilities. These included:

- Focused secondary and transition services on the two goals of school completion and postschool preparation.
- Promotion of curricular relevance and student self-determination through student-centred planning and individualised services.
- Expanding the use of collaborative service delivery programs as a mechanism for delivering transition services.
- Extending secondary reform efforts to include career development, applied learning in the community, and transition planning as a central part of the regular education curriculum for all students.

Additional services are discussed using an updated redesign of Marland's (1974) eight elements of career education (cited in Isaacson and Brown 2000).

Self-awareness

Often students with disabilities need to be explicitly taught self-awareness as a stepping-stone to achieving skills of self-determination.

Students become self-determined achievers when they:

- Become aware of their own needs, interests, and abilities.
- Learn self-direction by setting their own goals and developing their own plan.
- Gain self-confidence by increasing their skills and abilities to perform important tasks well.
- Become more self-reliant by learning to initiate 'risky actions' on their own.
- Increase their self-esteem by achieving intermediate successes in their talent areas.
- Take responsibility for positive and negative results by evaluating themselves objectively and then deciding what to adjust to improve next time.

(Mithaug 1991: xviii)

Education awareness

Students who experience difficulties making connections between education and life roles learn best by being actively engaged in real life learning activities, such as an orientation and mobility lesson in a bank. These students need to be explicitly exposed to a wide variety of work, leisure and life skill roles so that they might choose those that suit their lifestyle. Handy (1990: 146) used the word 'portfolio' to describe:

> how different bits of work in our life fit together to form a balanced whole.... There are five main categories of work for the portfolio: wage work and fee work, which are both forms of paid work; homework; gift work; and study work; which are all free work.

Similar portfolios could be used to develop leisure and life skills as well.

Skill awareness and beginning competence

Some students with disabilities experience difficulties understanding how humans are able to extend their behaviour. Such students may benefit from making connections with adults in the community with similar disabilities to the student, and being explicitly helped to recognise the ways those adults have developed competence.

Career awareness

Some students with disabilities benefit from being explicitly taught about the total spectrum of careers. This also involves learning about the spectrum of careers that might be suitable for students with particular disabilities, and then identifying adults with similar disabilities and finding out about their career choices. Students with disabilities need help to explore suitable careers, they need to be explicitly taught how to prepare for these careers and they also need to be actively involved in career placement (work experience).

Economic awareness

Students with disabilities need to be explicitly taught about the processes of production, distribution and consumption with particular focus on learning to become independent. Independent living skills relate to both personal management (eating, grooming, hygiene, clothing, medical, money, time) and home management (food, diet, cleaning, repairs, measurement, shopping, gardening).

Employability skills

Effective social and communication skills are essential for integration into society, developing worthwhile personal relationships and finding and maintaining employment. Integration involves a hierarchical progression that starts with physical presence, independent functioning, social engagement, personal relationships, becoming a valued team member and finally taking part in decision making at a group level.

Decision making skill

This involves the student being able to use information in rational ways to reach decisions. They link back to self-determination and are fundamental to what an appropriate education is all about. Life skills are as important as academic skills. Being independent enhances self-esteem and feelings of self-worth. Lower levels of dependence promote higher self-esteem.

Critical awareness

This involves critical literacy. It teaches students ways to examine 'texts to question the attitudes, values and beliefs that lie beneath the surface'. Critical literacy enables students with disabilities to 'uncover social inequities and injustices' and help them become 'agents of social change' (About English – Critical Literacy 2002).

These issues are germane to the general school population too, but particularly so to those with disabilities.

Conclusion

In this chapter I have argued that the universal adoption of the new expanded definition of the careers education curriculum is essential if the needs of all students are to be met in the twenty-first century. The curriculum incorporates leisure and life skills as well as work. It fulfils economic, social justice, student development and workforce rationales. Furthermore there must be adequate commitment by education authorities to its delivery to ensure that this curriculum is central to the core work of schools from early childhood to post-secondary education.

In the post-school world students with disabilities have historically tended to be disadvantaged physically, psychologically, economically and socially. These disadvantages are going to be made even more challenging and complex by the progressive impact of globalisation. Authors like Colley (2000) advocate for a much more deliberate interventionist approach. One such approach is the development of an inclusive career education curriculum, founded on social justice principles. Eight key elements of this curriculum are self-awareness, education awareness, skill awareness and beginning competence, career awareness, economic awareness, employability skills, decision-making skills, and critical awareness.

Bibliography

About English – Critical Literacy (2002) *English Learning Area*, HTTP: <http://www.discover.tased.edu.au/english/critlit.htm#whatis> (accessed 15 August 2003).

Arnold, J. and Jackson, C. (1997) 'The new career: issues and challenges', *British Journal of Guidance and Counselling*, 25: 427–433.

Ashman, A. and Elkins, J. (1998) 'Learning opportunities for all children', in A. Ashman and J. Elkins (eds) *Educating Children with Special Needs*, 3rd edn, Sydney: Pearson.

Benz, M.R., Lindstrom, L. and Yovanoff, P. (2000) 'Improving graduation and employment outcomes of students with disabilities: predictive factors and student perspectives', *Exceptional Children*, 66: 509–521.

Colley, H. (2000) 'Deconstructing "realism" in career planning: how globalisation impacts on vocational guidance', in Institute of Career Guidance (ed.) *Career Guidance: Constructing the Future, a Global Perspective*, Stourbridge: Institute of Career Guidance.

Connell, R. (1990) 'Curriculum and social justice: why is education and social justice an issue?', *Queensland Teachers Union Professional Magazine*, 8(3): 7–11.

Farmer, D. (1994) *Meeting the Needs of Gifted Students in the Regular Classroom*, Strathfield: NSWAGTC.

Foreman, P. (1996) 'Disability, integration and inclusion: introductory concepts', in P. Foreman (ed.) *Integration and Inclusion in Action*, Sydney, Australia: Harcourt Brace.

Garguilo, R.M. (2003) *Special Education in Contemporary Society: An Introduction to Exceptionality*, Belmont: Wadsworth/Thomson Learning.

Giorcelli, L. (1993) 'Creating a counter-hegemonic school: a model for the education of children with disabilities', in *Social Justice, Equity and Dilemmas of Disability in Education*, Brisbane: Department of Education.

Handy, C. (1990) *The Age of Unreason*, London: Arrow Books.

—— (1997) *The Hungry Spirit*, London: Hutchinson.

Harris, L. and Associates (1998) *National Organization on Disabilities/Harris Survey of Americans with Disabilities*, New York: Author.

Herr, E.L. (1997) 'A personal view – career counselling: a process in process', *British Journal of Guidance and Counselling*, 25: 81–93.

Herr, E.L. and Cramer, S.H. (1996) *Career Guidance and Counseling Through the Lifespan: Systematic Approaches*, 5th edn, New York: Harper Collins.

Hutton, W. (1996) *The State We're In*, London: Vintage.

Isaacson, L.E. and Brown, D. (2000) *Career Information, Career Counseling, and Career Development*, 7th edn, Boston: Allyn & Bacon.

Kennedy, J. and Olney, M. (2001) 'Job discrimination in the post-ADA era: estimates from the 1994 and 1995 national interview surveys', *Rehabilitation Counseling Bulletin*, 45: 24–31.

McCowan, C. and McKenzie, M. (1997) *The Guide to Career Education*, North Sydney: New Hobsons Press.

McKnight, J. (1995) *The Careless Society: Community and Its Counterfeits*, New York: Basic Books.

McMahon, M. (1997) 'Career education', in W. Patton and M. McMahon (eds) *Career Development in Practice: A Systems Theory Perspective*, North Sydney: New Hobsons Press.

Mithaug, D. (1991) *Self-Determined Kids: Raising Satisfied and Successful Children*, New York: Macmillan.

Pagliano, P.J. (2000) 'Careers guidance preparation: (re)constructing the future', in Institute of Career Guidance (ed.) *Career Guidance. Constructing the Future: A Global Perspective*, Stourbridge: Institute of Career Guidance.

Rawls, J. (1971) *A Theory of Justice*, Cambridge: Harvard University Press.

Schriner, K. (2001) 'A disability studies perspective on employment issues and policies for disabled people', in G.L. Albrecht, K.D. Seelman and M. Bury (eds) *Handbook of Disability Studies*, Thousand Oaks: Sage.

Szymanski, E.M. and Vancollins, J. (2003) 'Career development of people with disabilities: some new and not-so-new challenges', *Australian Journal of Career Development*, 12: 9–16.

Turnbull, A., Turnbull, R., Shank, M. and Leal, D. (1999) *Exceptional Lives: Special Education in Today's Schools*, 2nd edn, Upper Saddle River: Merrill.

Vick, M. (1996) 'Fumbling in the dark? School students' knowledge of work as a basis for subject selection', *Australian Journal of Career Development*, 5(3): 11–15.

Wolffe, K. (2000) 'Career education', in A.J. Koenig and M.C. Holbrook (eds) *Foundations of Education*, 2nd edn, vol. II, New York: AFB Press.

Wolfensberger, W. (1972) *The Principle of Normalization in Human Services*, Toronto: National Institute on Mental Retardation.

Wood, J. and Lazzari, A.M. (1997) *Exceeding the Boundaries: Understanding Exceptional Lives*, Forth Worth: Harcourt Brace.

Chapter 10

Social class, opportunity structures and career guidance

Ken Roberts

Introduction

Any social justice agenda is bound to engage with social class. Career guidance will inevitably seek to tackle class in so far as it aims to confront and challenge injustices. Indeed, this book's aim is to position career guidance within anti-discrimination and anti-disadvantage agendas. The book seeks to infuse guidance with empowering and emancipatory ideologies. These are noble objectives. However, the following passages will query whether career guidance is actually capable of engaging successfully in these confrontations and challenges. Maybe the true strengths of guidance lie elsewhere. This is despite the daily workloads of career advisers reminding them how heavily class-dependent young people's life chances remain. Up to now educational reform has failed to inject greater fluidity into the class structure, not just in Britain but in all other modern societies. Life chances today are just as dependent on social class origins as at the beginning of the twentieth century. Nowadays in Britain around four-fifths of children from the top social class (higher level managers and professionals) enter university compared with around one in six from non-skilled manual homes. This particular class gap has actually widened over time (see Roberts 2001). Maybe career advisers would like to respond to this challenge, but it is not self-evident that they possess the capability.

This chapter will confirm that the opportunity structures which surround young people remain heavily class-dependent. It will argue that these same opportunity structures govern what career guidance can realistically hope to achieve. It will explain why class blindness is normally required of the guidance profession not just by its political paymaster but also, nowadays, by young people's own preferred ways of thinking about their circumstances and life chances. Thus class is destined to remain a troublesome topic for career advisers: one which some feel their pursuit of justice requires them to address but which, as a matter of fact, they are professionally incapacitated from tackling.

What is class?

Let us set aside what journalists, politicians and the proverbial man or woman in the street mean by class and confine ourselves to the stipulative definitions offered by sociologists. Anyone acquainted with sociology will know that the discipline has different, competing definitions of class. Marxist, Weberian and functionalist sociologists define class in rather different ways but there are some important common denominators. We all agree that classes have an economic base and that the best way of 'classifying' individuals is via their occupations. We also agree that classes of occupations are the main strata in modern societies, which, in this respect, differ from slave, caste and estate societies, and that before we can begin to analyse the role that class plays in people's lives we need to devise or adopt a class scheme. It is impossible even to begin to think coherently about class without conjecturing a scheme, however simple, maybe just distinguishing higher and lower, or middle and working classes, though no sociologists believe that the class structure can be portrayed so simply yet realistically.

One of the first class schemes to be used in large-scale social research was devised in Britain in 1911 by the Registrar General's office (at that time the central government department which collated statistical information about the population). Amazingly, this class scheme has continued to be used right up to the present-day with the sole change (introduced in 1921) of a sub-division of class 3 (see box, page 132). Similar class schemes have been devised and used extensively in most other countries. In 1911 the British government was particularly interested in variations in rates of mortality. It wanted to identify the sections of the population that were most vulnerable. Specifying precisely who was at risk was rightly regarded as the first step towards identifying the causes then finding a cure. Needless to say, since 1911 we have found that the Registrar General's class scheme predicts many other things apart from rates of morbidity and mortality such as fertility, unemployment, church attendance, criminal convictions and criminal victimisation, children's educational attainments, sport participation, and so on. In fact there has proved to be precious little that is not class-related to some extent in Britain or in any other country.

It was claimed originally that the Registrar General's social classes grouped together occupations of similar social standing, and this remained the scheme's official rationale until 1981 when, prompted by the UK government of the day, there was a sudden change of mind and it was claimed that the classes represented skill levels. Now although they often used it, sociologists were never truly comfortable with the Registrar General's class scheme. From time to time alternatives were proposed but none displaced or rivalled the Registrar General's scheme in terms of

Registrar General's Social Classes

1 Higher professionals, managers and administrative employees
2 Lower professionals, managers and administrative employees.
3a Lower-level non-manual
3b Skilled manual
4 Semi-skilled manual
5 Unskilled manual

frequency of use in Britain, except for the market research industry's similar A, B, Ci, Cii, D, E classification. Sociologists have never believed that either social standing or skill level is the foundation of social class, and their dissatisfaction became vociferous following the change in the official rationale in 1981. An outcome was that in the early 1990s the UK government invited the social science community to propose an alternative to the long-standing Registrar General's scheme. This invitation was extended via the Economic and Social Research Council which commissioned a group based at the University of Essex to consult widely to see if there was a consensus among social scientists on an alternative. There was not total unanimity (there never is in the social sciences), but the recommendation to the government (see Rose and O'Reilly 1997) was that the existing Registrar General's scheme be replaced by a new official classification which is a slightly modified version of a class scheme originally developed by John Goldthorpe for use in his 1972 study of social mobility in Britain (see Goldthorpe *et al.* 1987). In 1998 this scheme was adopted as the UK's new official class scheme (see fig. 10.1) and its first large-scale official use has been in analysing the 2001 census. However, prior to its official adoption in Britain, the Goldthorpe class scheme had already been used widely by sociologists internationally in large-scale comparative studies of social mobility.

This new official UK scheme purports to group together occupations with common market and work situations. The strength of an occupation's market situation can be measured by the rewards that practitioners typically receive; the pay (past and future as well as current), pensions, company cars and other fringe benefits, security of employment, and opportunities for career advancement. Work situation refers to how much autonomy practitioners have, the closeness with which they are supervised, and whether they are in charge of, and have responsibility for, the work of subordinates. It is claimed that when all occupations are assessed in terms of their typical work and market situations we discover that they fall into a limited number of clusters (the classes listed in fig. 10.1). It is then claimed that there are two main clusters of classes. The first (at the

I. i. Employers (large organisations) and senior managers I. ii. Higher professionals	SERVICE/ MIDDLE CLASS
2. Lower managerial and professional	
	INTERMEDIATE CLASSES
3. Intermediate e.g. clerks, secretaries, computer operators	
4. Small employers and own account non-professional	
	WORKING CLASS
5. Supervisors, craft and related	
6. Semi-routine e.g. cooks, bus drivers, hairdressers, shop assistants	
7. Routine e.g. waiters, cleaners, couriers	
8. Never worked, long-term unemployed	

Figure 10.1 The 1998 UK official class scheme.

top of the scheme) is the middle class or service class. These occupations have advantaged work and market situations. They are well paid, risks of unemployment are low, and the incumbents have good chances of career ascent. Those concerned usually enjoy a 'trust relationship' with their employers. They are accorded considerable autonomy and are trusted to apply their knowledge and skills, and to regulate the work of others, in the interests of their employing organisations. The second major cluster of classes, the working class, is towards the base of the scheme (but above class 8, an 'underclass'). The working class is the opposite of the middle class in every sense. Employment relationships are strictly 'contractual'; there is little trust on either side. The jobs are relatively low paid, risks of unemployment are much higher, and there are few promotion opportunities. A point to note is that this class scheme is not consistently linear. The middle class is certainly above the working class but it is not claimed that class 3 is higher than class 4. Rather, these are treated as discrete classes, which co-exist generally in the intermediate space between the middle class above and the working class beneath.

Not all sociologists are happy with this new official UK class scheme. Some prefer to classify people purely on the basis of their work situations (relationships to the means of production in classical Marxist terminology), or according to the extent to which others extract surplus value from their labour (for example Gubbay 1997). Other sociologists would prefer a 'gradational' scheme which dispensed with divisions and groups of occupations, and gave each occupation a precise position along a continuum (see Prandy and Blackburn 1997). American sociologists have tended to favour gradational definitions of class and corresponding schemes, whereas

European sociologists have normally preferred to define class 'relationally', which produces divisions (as in the Goldthorpe scheme). Classes are said to be formed through their inter-relationships (employing and being employed by one another, managing or being managed by another class, etc). 'Relationalists' argue that their definitions lead to the more powerful explanations of things. For example, their definitions purport to identify different classes' distinctive experiences in labour markets and at work, which may nurture distinctive class cultures which may thus lead to distinctive types of political action. However, 'relationalists' are not all agreed on exactly which relationships are crucial in the formation of classes. As explained above, Marxists object to the Weberian (market situation) features in the UK's new official scheme. Marxists insist on separating a capitalist class from the rest, and they want to make distinctions among the latter solely in terms of degrees of exploitation or 'relationships to the means of production' (work situation). However, Marxist sociologists' big problem has always been separating different classes among the vast majority of the population who are not owners.

Fortunately for some purposes, including this chapter's, which class scheme is adopted is not vitally important. They all reveal the same main trends and tendencies. However, in order to discuss the relevance of class to career guidance it is necessary to adopt a particular definition and a scheme, so in the following passages the classes referred to will be those distinguished in the Goldthorpe–new official UK classification.

Changes in the class structure

In Britain there have been three big changes over time in the class structure, all of which have affected young people's career opportunities and the work of guidance professionals. Some, but not all, of these changes have also occurred in other advanced industrial societies. First, throughout the twentieth century the working class was in numerical decline while lower-level white-collar jobs (until the 1970s) and middle-class jobs (which still are) were increasing in number. At the beginning of the twentieth century the class structure was pyramid-shaped: roughly three-quarters of all jobs were working class. At the end of the century roughly a third of all jobs were working class, another third were intermediate and the final third were middle class. So the present-day class structure resembles a pillar rather than a pyramid. The upgrading has been due to industry-shifts and occupation-shifts. The crucial industry-shift has been the reduction of employment in manufacturing and extractive industries such as engineering and coalmining, and the increase in the number of service sector jobs. The UK is now most definitely a post-industrial society in the sense that less than a fifth of all jobs are in the manufacturing and extractive sectors. Overall the service sectors (which include education, health, banking, insurance, and central and local government) contain higher proportions of intermediate and middle-class occupations than manufacturing and extractive businesses. Occupation-shifts have occurred within sectors, especially manufacturing. Technology has reduced the need for manual (working-class) labour and has created new middle-class occupations for managers and technologists who design, maintain and supervise the operation of these socio-technical systems. The results of this class upgrading are that career advisers nowadays find themselves dealing with more young people from middle-class home backgrounds (who tend to have concerned and ambitious parents), and there are more middle-class jobs, and fewer low-level jobs, to present to clients.

The second trend, which began only in the late twentieth century, has been the degradation of swathes of working-class jobs. Skilled jobs have been lost from the contracting manufacturing and extractive industries. There are new working-class jobs in services (in call centres, contract cleaners, security firms, hotels and restaurants, and in domestic service, for example) but these jobs are mostly low-skilled, low status, badly paid and non-unionised. During the last quarter of the twentieth century the UK class structure became elongated. The middle class received the biggest pay increases. Working-class jobs became less likely to keep the holders out of poverty (see Hills *et al.* 2002). There were also increased risks of unemployment. At the end of the twentieth century roughly one out of every six UK households which contained adults of working age had no one in employment. The implications for career guidance have been twofold. First, although we have become a more middle-class society overall, the number of young people from heavily disadvantaged families has increased. Second, there are now a substantial number of working-class jobs which it is difficult to advise any young people to contemplate as long-term occupations.

Some writers, including some of the contributors to this book, believe that a combination of globalisation and new technologies is responsible for the recent immiseration of sections of the working class. Globalisation is said to pit every country's workers against workers in every other country in a desperate competition for investment and jobs which forces down wages and working conditions. However, the degradation of working-class jobs has been more pronounced in countries with long-standing unregulated market economies (such as the UK and the USA) than in countries such as Germany which, despite globalisation, has been able to retain considerable joint regulation of employment by government, employers and trade unions (see Felstead and Jewson 1999). And the same new technologies which can unleash frightening levels of change and insecurity can also open up new opportunities for individuals to construct new portfolio careers and experiment with new identities.

The third set of trends (common to all advanced industrial societies)

Table 10.1 Percentages of sons remaining in same social class as father

	Birth cohort						
	Pre-1900	*1900–1909*	*1910–1919*	*1920–1929*	*1930–1939*	*1940–1949*	*1950–1959*
Service class	51	49	61	69	67	62	73
Working class	76	75	73	67	60	53	50

Source: Aldridge 2001.

has followed the changing shape of the class structure. The growth of the middle class has increased the volume of upward mobility i.e. the proportion of working-class children who are able to get on. Since the 1950s roughly one in two children from UK working-class homes have risen into a higher class. Simultaneously, although the possibility of social demotion continues to stir anxieties in middle-class homes, the risks of these children descending have diminished (see Table 10.1). The reasons for these trends are simple: the larger the middle class, the easier it becomes for those born into that class to remain there, and for individuals born beneath to ascend. There have been major changes in absolute mobility rates, but not in relative rates (the relative chances of those born into the middle class remaining there vis-à-vis those born into the working class reaching the middle class). In absolute terms, working-class children's chances of ascent have improved, thus helping to create one of the twentieth century's great illusions, of society becoming more and more open. In reality, the strength of the links between social origins and destinations has not changed (Roberts 1993). An implication of these trends is that it has become easier for career advisers to assist children to get on. Yet life chances continue to vary widely according to social origins.

Obscure divisions

Young people's career opportunities depend heavily, though not exclusively, on their social-class origins, and by age 16 they are moving along career trajectories that are built and sustained by class-rooted processes. Despite this, young people themselves are unlikely to assess their situations in class terms (see, for example, Lawy 2002; Raby 2002). This is not only because they are unlikely to be familiar with, let alone skilled in using, class discourses (unless they are studying sociology), though unfamiliarity alone would be a sufficient cause. Politicians and the media do not offer daily doses of class analysis: they are more likely to dismiss class as a thing of the past. However, it is also the case that young people's own class positions are indeterminate and must remain so until their youth life-stage transitions are complete. Young people may know their class origins but the majority cannot be certain about their destinations. They cannot but be aware from personal experience that there is a great deal of social mobility in present-day society. So young people from working-class backgrounds are not necessarily being unrealistic when they aim higher. Meanwhile, middle-class families endure anxieties about the schools that their children are attending, their exam performances, and whether their lifestyles are jeopardising their futures. Even adults in present-day Britain are diffident about placing themselves in social classes. They may agree that there are classes, and they may be able to describe them, but they often explain that, for example, 'my parents were working class but . . .', or, 'I suppose people would call me middle class, but . . .' We all appear to be keen to stress our own individuality and hesitate before placing ourselves in any 'boxes' (see Savage *et al.* 2001; Sayer 2002).

In addition to all this, it has become more difficult than in the past for young people to envisage the kinds of adults that they will become. This means that today's young people have better reasons than earlier generations for being unable or reluctant to base identities, including class identities, on what and who they expect or hope to be in the future. Youth transitions have been elongated. Adulthood has been pushed into a haze beyond 16-year-olds' immediate futures. Moreover, most UK children now attend common comprehensive schools where they all study the same national curriculum. Nowadays most young people stay in full-time education beyond age 16. They have reached age 21 before over a half of them have left education and obtained full-time jobs (Organisation for Economic Cooperation and Development 2000). Sixth forms and further education colleges are a mix of young people from all social-class backgrounds and with different prospects. So today's young people are unlikely to see themselves as belonging to any particular classes in ways that set them clearly apart from others in their age group. Most young people are sensitive to, and value their individuality. Most feel personally responsible for the positions that they have reached, and feel able to continue to construct 'choice biographies'. Ambitions are fluid. Many young people prefer indeterminate futures to being committed (with no escape) to particular kinds of future employment. Young people constantly assess and reassess their capabilities and interests, then act accordingly, or so they believe (see du Bois-Reymond 2001).

However, the fact that young people feel class-free and in control does not mean that they really are in charge of the development of their lives. They are in fact all travelling along bounded career and class trajectories. They have been pushed from particular class origins by their parents' aspirations, choices of (and sometimes their ability to pay for) schools for their children, and so on. At the same time, they are being drawn towards particular class destinations by employers' preferences for recruits with particular qualifications, who have attended particular schools and universities, and maybe who have particular accents and types of dress sense. As young people move towards adulthood, their prospects become more and more tightly bounded. In Britain they may all sit, and the vast majority pass, similar batches of GCSEs (or the Scottish equivalents) but only grades A-C confer any advantages in the labour market (McIntosh 2002). Thereafter they can pursue A-levels (highers in Scotland) or vocational qualifications but unless the latter are achieved at Level 3 or above there are unlikely to be any career benefits (McIntosh 2002). If they opt for government supported training, its value depends on whether they are trained by an employer who subsequently retains the trainees (Roberts and Parsell 1992). Those who enter the UK's post-1992 unitary system of higher education discover that there are 'best' and 'other' universities, and that employers who are filling traditional graduate jobs want only the best (Ainley 1994; Brown and Scase 1994). When they enter employment they find that the age-old rule, 'To those who have...' operates with a vengeance. Those who are best qualified to begin with are given the most training and have the best opportunities to gain yet more qualifications (Arulampalam and Booth 1996). The effectiveness of these processes does not depend on young people being aware of their operation. The fact that young people are not highly class aware does not mean that there are no longer any social classes. Class awareness is a possible consequence, but not an automatic consequence, of the existence of class divisions.

Class-blind career guidance

Career guidance is normally steered into class blindness by several forces. First, as we have just seen, clients are unlikely to raise the class issue. Second, government paymasters do not expect, and would be unlikely to tolerate, the intrusion of class. The recipients of guidance are rarely clients in the market sense. There is no mass career guidance service anywhere in the world that runs on a user-pays basis. The state is the purchaser of most career guidance and, like other UK public service professions, in recent years career advisers have been subjected to more and more government-imposed targets and performance indicators. Guidance has become part of wider policy packages designed, on the one hand, to promote economic efficiency, effectiveness and competitiveness, and, on the other hand, to combat exclusion (primarily from the workforce and secondarily from mainstream society in general). Third, as explained below, assisting individual clients, and treating them all even handedly within the variable (by class trajectories) constraints of the everyday worlds in which they live, requires tactical class blindness on the part of career advisers. It should be no surprise, therefore, that the theories, which simultaneously serve as professional ideologies, which career guidance professionals have embraced, have consistently erased class from their fields of vision.

At one time in Britain and in many other places, and still today in some, young people's class destinations, as well as their origins, have had to be taken as given by all concerned. When lower secondary school pupils are divided into academic and vocational tracks which lead to different levels in the occupational structure, career advisers must work within these realities. Under these circumstances differential psychology is likely to offer the most appealing theories. The advisers' task becomes one of finding square holes for square pegs, accelerating what would tend to happen in any case through young people's job-hopping, and minimising long-term mismatches.

When, as in North America since the 1930s, young people are not so clearly class divided, developmental psychology is career guidance's most likely source of theory (Daws 1977; Ginzberg 1972; Super and Jordan 1973). The role of guidance is construed as assisting young people's self-discovery, enabling them to formulate then act on their own conceptions of their interests and abilities, to decide who and what they hope to become, then to try to realise their dreams, reassessing everything at each point along the way (see Egan 1998). This has always been the type of theory favoured by America's high-school counsellors (Armor 1969; Kitsuse and Cicourel 1963) and since the 1960s it has been the role definition favoured by the UK's youth employment officers/careers officers/ career advisers (see Bates 1984; Roberts 1971). It is a theory that accords with most present-day young people's common sense understandings of their own situations. The end result is inevitably that class inequalities are unchallenged.

Since the 1980s UK governments have been imposing a different, but not necessarily incompatible, type of thinking. Governments have urged career advisers to assist or if necessary to cajole young people into climbing the new qualification and skill hierarchies that have been constructed (Manpower Services Commission 1981), thereby lifting themselves beyond the threats of unemployment and social exclusion and up the occupational structure (Department for Education and Employment 2000). Surrounding guidance with this rationale enables targets to be set and effectiveness measured (National Foundation for Educational Research 1996). Unsurprisingly, guidance professionals have been ambivalent. Many see advantages (being able to demonstrate their professionalism and value) but are simultaneously aware that clients' personal development may have to be sacrificed and that success may sometimes hinge on pressing square pegs into round holes. And there is the danger, a real danger, that guidance may be unable to deliver. The enemy is not intractable hordes of young people; rather it is the shape of the class structure.

The best advice for most individual clients is to grasp whatever opportunities are available. There is no contradiction between person-centred guidance and encouraging individuals to comply with economic requirements. Compliance may not always be in the interests of entire classes of people, but guidance deals with individuals, not classes. For individuals, accepting any education and training is usually better in all senses than 'doing nothing'. For some, even the meanest opportunities act as stepping stones to better things, but this is impossible for everyone because of the shape of the class structure, and 'everyone' here includes the majority in the UK 'Connexions' group, those who are said to be most at risk of social exclusion. There is insufficient space above for everyone to ascend. The system needs a flexible and disadvantaged working class. So the opportunities that can be offered to the most disadvantaged young people turn out, for most, to be 'black-magic roundabouts' which keep them in circulation but without lifting them up the occupational structure.

Confronting class

There are two ways in which career guidance might attempt to engage with class inequalities. First, it could embrace the liberal agenda and declare itself on the side of equal opportunities (to become unequal), popularly known as meritocracy. The problem with this agenda is not that it is grotesquely unrealistic. Indeed, it is arguable (but also debatable) that present-day Britain is in fact a basically meritocratic society (Saunders 1990; 1994). The real problem with the agenda is that, as explained above, there is only limited room at the top. Guidance would have to engineer social demotion in order to increase the scope for promotion. In other words, it would have to refuse to assist, and maybe even set its own traps for, young people from privileged backgrounds. The privileged would soon wise-up and resource a more compliant guidance profession. The problems with the liberal agenda are that life at the bottom is harsh and no one wants to be told (and career advisers do not want to tell clients) that they merit nothing better.

Second, guidance could adopt a radical class agenda. It could confront clients with the unjust inequalities of the world of work, the inequalities in rewards and in work situations which cannot be explained or justified in terms of effort or talent because in reality they are products of the unequal power of the different social classes. And here is the conundrum. The security and lifestyles of the relatively privileged managers, professionals and owners (the goals that inspire some young people and which are endorsed by their advisers) depend on the exclusion of others. The lifestyles of affluent middle-class consumers are made possible only by a lower paid working class which will work flexibly in response to the shifting tastes of the better-off, and which will be on duty and stood down as and when demanded. The need to maintain disadvantaged classes prevents everyone clambering up whatever qualification, skill and occupational ladders may be presented. The class interests of the better-off also make it impossible for everyone to enter occupations that match their preferred identities, and are likely to require some round pegs to fill odd shaped holes.

In the 1970s some youth researchers believed that Britain's post-war youth cultures represented at least primitive expressions of working-class consciousness which could be strengthened and politicised through radical cultural work (Hall and Jefferson 1976; Willis 1977). That moment, if it ever existed, has gone. Permitting and resourcing such radical youth work, and related career guidance, would be possible only in a context of a powerful working class which would protect the radical projects. During the closing decades of the twentieth century Britain's working class not only continued its longer-term numerical decline but also disintegrated as a socio-cultural and political entity (Roberts 2001). Challenging the powerful is not a realistic agenda for early twenty-first century career guidance. How can guidance hope to succeed when trade unions and political parties of the left have failed? Maybe class inequalities need to be challenged. Several chapters in this book make this case, but the crucial point remains; career guidance is simply not an appropriate weapon. As other chapters in this book demonstrate, there are other objectives for guidance which are not just worthy but also realisable.

Bibliography

Ainley, P. (1994) *Degrees of Difference*, London: Lawrence and Wishart.

Aldridge, S. (2001) *Social Mobility: A Discussion Paper.* Available HTTP. http://www.cabinet-office.gov.uk/innovation/papers/socialmobility.shtml.

Armor, D.J. (1969) *The American School Counselor*, New York: Russell Sage Foundation.

Arulampalam, W. and Booth, A.L. (1996) *Who Gets Over the Training Hurdle?* Working Paper 96-4, ESRC Research Centre on Micro-Social Change, Colchester: University of Essex.

Bates, I.M.H. (1984) *Curriculum Development in Careers Education: A Case Study*, unpublished thesis, University of Leeds.

Brown, P. and Scase, R. (1994) *Higher Education and Corporate Realities*, London: UCL Press.

Daws, P. (1977) 'Social determinism or personal choice?', *Studies in the Sociology of Vocational Guidance, 1*, Keele: University of Keele.

Department for Education and Employment (2000) *Connexions: The Best Start in Life for Every Young Person*, Nottingham: Department for Education and Employment.

du Bois-Reymond, M., Plug, W., te Poel, Y. and Ravesloot, J. (2001) '"And then they decide what to do next..." Young people's educational and labour trajectories: a longitudinal study from the Netherlands', *Young*, 9(2). Available HTTP. http://www.alli.fi/nyri/young/2001-3/duBois.htm.

Egan, G. (1998) *The Skilled Helper*, 6th edn, California: Brooks/Cole.

Felstead, A. and Jewson, N. (eds) (1999) *Global Trends in Flexible Labour*, Basingstoke: Macmillan.

Ginzberg, E. (1972) 'Towards a theory of occupational choice – a restatement', *Vocational Guidance Quarterly*, 169–176.

Goldthorpe, J.H., Llewellyn, C. and Payne, C. (1987) *Social Mobility and Class Structure in Modern Britain*, Oxford: Clarendon Press.

Gubbay, J. (1997) 'A Marxist critique of Weberian class analyses', *Sociology*, 31: 73–89.

Hall, S. and Jefferson, T. (1976) *Resistance Through Rituals*, London: Hutchinson.

Hills, J., Le Grand, J. and Piachaud, D. (eds) (2002) *Understanding Social Exclusion*, Oxford: Oxford University Press.

Kitsuse, J. and Cicourel, A.V. (1963) *The Educational Decision-Makers*, Indianapolis: Bobbs-Merrill.

Lawy, R. (2002) 'Risky stories: youth identities, learning and everyday risk', *Journal of Youth Studies*, 5: 407–423.

McIntosh, S. (2002) 'Further analysis of the returns to academic and vocational qualifications', *Research Report 370*, Nottingham: Department for Education and Skills.

Manpower Services Commission (1981) *A New Training Initiative: An Agenda for Action*, London: MSC.

National Foundation for Educational Research (1996) *An Evaluation of the Performance of Pathfinder Careers Services*, London: Department for Education and Employment.

Organisation for Economic Cooperation and Development (2000) *From Initial Education to Working Life: Making Transitions Work*, Paris: Organisation for Economic Cooperation and Development.

Prandy, K. and Blackburn, R.M. (1997) 'Putting men and women into classes. But is this where they belong?', *Sociology*, 31: 143–152.

Raby, R.C. (2002) 'A tangle of discourses: girls negotiating adolescence', *Journal of Youth Studies*, 5: 425–448.

Roberts, K. (1971) *From School to Work*, Newton Abbot: David and Charles.

—— (1993) 'Career trajectories and the mirage of increased social mobility', in I. Bates and G. Riseborough (eds) *Youth and Inequality*, Buckingham: Open University Press.

—— (2001) *Class in Modern Britain*, Basingstoke: Palgrave.

Roberts, K. and Parsell, G. (1992) 'Entering the labour market in Britain: the survival of traditional opportunity structures', *Sociological Review*, 30: 727–753.

Rose, D. and O'Reilly, K. (1997) *Constructing Classes*, Swindon: ESRC/ONS.

Saunders, P. (1990) *Social Class and Stratification*, London: Routledge.

—— (1994) 'Is Britain a meritocracy?', in R. Blackburn (ed.) *Social Inequality in a Changing World*, Cambridge: Sociological Research Group.

Savage, M., Bagnall, M. and Longhurst, B. (2001) 'Ordinary, ambivalent and defensive: class identities in the northwest of England', *Sociology*, 35: 875–892.

Sayer, A. (2002) 'What are you worth: why class is an embarrassing subject', *Sociological Research Online*, 7(3).

Super, D.E. and Jordan, J.P. (1973) 'Career development theory', *British Journal of Guidance and Counselling*, 1: 3–16.

Willis, P. (1977) *Learning to Labour*, Farnborough: Saxon House.

Chapter 11

Working with youth at risk of exclusion

Nuria Manzano Soto

Introduction

The term 'social exclusion' has been widely used over the past decades, despite the fact that no agreement has been reached on how to define the concept. It has spread rapidly and is usually related to other aspects of social life such as poverty, social 'deviation' or maladjustment, segregation, rejection and marginalisation. The language of social exclusion serves to integrate a range of aspects as it seeks to explain a complex phenomenon which intertwines multiple variables associated with the following dimensions: economic (poverty, unemployment), cultural (rejection, discrimination), political (citizenship) and social (isolation, segregation, marginalisation, etc.). Consequently, social exclusion can be regarded as the common outcome of various original situations that interrelate and complement each other, generating a vicious cycle of disadvantage (Rubio and Monteros 2002). Ballester and Figuera define social exclusion as a

> process of withdrawal from the social boundaries appropriate to the community in which one lives, with a loss of autonomy in relation to obtaining the necessary resources to live, participate in, and integrate into the society of which one forms part.
>
> (2000: 291)

In other words, social exclusion refers to those people whose access to basic rights and primary opportunities are limited, and who thereby are unable to benefit from full citizenship.

Exclusion is thus defined as being in opposition to integration and inclusion. The existing dichotomy presents a population that, on the one hand, is fully integrated in all sectors of social life, whilst on the other there are citizens who are excluded from training, work, cultural, and other social aspects (Tezanos 1998a). This duality of social being is occurring as a silent phenomenon, becoming embedded in the social fabric, and may affect generations to come if preventative measures are not taken.

In the European Union (EU), social inclusion, and the risk of exclusion, is currently one of the main issues for concern. In the aim of the 'Plan for social inclusion', exclusion is understood as follows (CEC 2001):

- *Low-income and vulnerability*: Eurostat claims that approximately 18 per cent of the population in the European Union (65 million people) live on less than 60 per cent of the average national income.
- It is a *multidimensional phenomenon*: it includes equal access to the labour market, to education, to health, to the legal system, to other social rights, and also to decision-making and participation.
- It is a *structural phenomenon*: the trends, which are currently structuring our societies, besides entailing positive effects, can also increase the risk of social exclusion.

This chapter focuses on those young people who fail at school and 'drop out' at an early age which, when added to other circumstances, places them at risk of becoming socially excluded. It is essential, therefore, to identify situations of vulnerability with a high inherent social risk, and to implement preventative measures aimed at this particular group as failure to reduce such risk may result in a chronic condition, whereby such young people become part of the 'excluded' society.

After establishing a basic conceptual framework, this chapter briefly discusses the process that may lead young people to become socially excluded and outlines the socio-educational profile of a particular group of at-risk young people to illustrate how these groups are sometimes defined. It explores the role of comprehensive guidance programmes, as well as some approaches to the prevention of social exclusion, paying particular attention to their current focus. The policies and plans of the European Union concerning social inclusion are examined, and the chapter argues in favour of a comprehensive schooling system (as a basis for social justice) whereby all students are valued, and taught to become critical learners and thinkers. Consideration is also given to the current debate concerning 'globalising' social justice.

Process and evolution of social exclusion in young people

Exclusion is a dynamic process resulting from the pathways which lead a person from more or less integrated situations to areas of vulnerability and, ultimately, to social exclusion. Castell (1999, in Rubio and Monteros 2002) identifies three areas in this process of exclusion:

- *Area of integration*: characterised by a secure job and solid social and family relations.

- *Area of vulnerability*: characterised by professional and relational instability and inadequate social benefits or assistance.
- *Area of exclusion*: characterised by gradual social isolation and expulsion from the labour market.

These areas, however, appear quite simplistic, seeming to emphasise the notion that *secure* paid employment is the basis for integration (although they also take into account family and social relations), whilst other situations are regarded as socially excluding. Alternative lifestyles, for instance in relation to employment (see Introduction to this book by Irving and Malik), are not even considered. Clearly these areas could be further explored, allowing for different gradients within and between the categories.

Most discussions around social exclusion are similarly concerned with the attainment of educational credentials and subsequent labour market participation, lacking any significant critical analysis. These issues will be taken into account in this chapter, but considering work as a basic right (not as subservient to the global economy), and from the stance that young people should become critical learners and workers, engaged in active citizenship and able to question inequitable social and labour market practices (see Chapter 2 by Irving). Many groups are denied real participation in society, and this should be an aspect that is fully explored in schools.

This 'integration-exclusion' continuum (see fig. 11.1) involves a series of intermediate steps that push groups towards either exclusion or integration. This is dependent on the paths available to young people in their

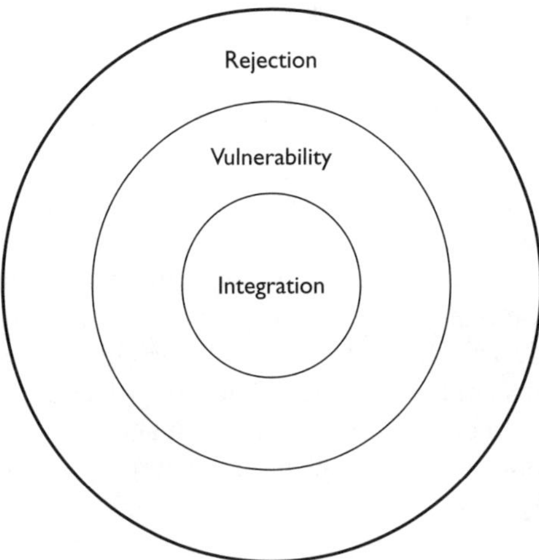

Figure 11.1 Area of rejection/integration.

Source: Garcia Serrano and Malo 1998: 138.

transition into adult life, both from the *economic–workforce* point of view as well as from the *social and family* point of view.

Ways of transition into adult life which most frequently occur amongst young people who are 'excluded'[1] are:

a Unstructured trajectories: a series of conditions converge to bring about risk situations that hinder the social integration of a young person.
b Precarious trajectories: a youngster follows pathways that jeopardise his/her emancipation as a consequence of the new organisation of a casualised labour market in which precariousness and job rotation are increasingly frequent.
c 'Successive approach': this is the most common method of transition amongst young people, whether from the middle or working classes. The person has a series of social and career expectations which are not fulfilled, thereby following different pathways, through a method of trial and error. There is a continuous and gradual adjustment between initial expectations and acceptance of partial achievements.

(Casal 1996)

However, regardless of the career, personal, or social paths chosen by a young person, the origin of exclusion can be generally traced (Castell 1997: 1999) to adverse conditions in the labour market (unemployment, precarious work, informal economy, emphasis on meritocracy, etc.) and the rupture of personal relations within his/her immediate environment (family, friends, etc.). Added to this is the discrimination experienced by many groups in mainstream society.

Socio-educational profile of young people at risk of social exclusion

Social exclusion is usually the final stage of a gradual process. Therefore, it should be tackled in its early stages, which generally coincides with the teenager's failure at school and dropping out of education. In Spain, the cultural association Norte Joven (a non-governmental organisation) works with young people who have dropped out of school without attaining the basic qualifications and who, due to additional circumstances, are considered 'socially vulnerable'. Norte Joven suggest that at-risk youths will usually display some of the following characteristics (Asociación Cultural Norte Joven 2002):

- Age-range between 14 and 25.
- Many come from shattered families with a low socio-economic status (desertion/over-protection).

- Recurrent history of school failure (and very often personal), which influences self-esteem and motivation.
- Acquired defencelessness (towards learning, engagement in interpersonal relations, seeking work and, in general, confronting the adult world).
- Lack the necessary skills to 'succeed' in school (little motivation to achieve, low resistance to frustration, scarce control over situations, etc.). This should also be interpreted as a responsibility of the schools which fail to adapt their norms to children from diverse backgrounds, thereby hindering their 'success'.
- Few opportunities and lack of appropriate models to learn accepted patterns of social behaviour.
- Sustained social disadvantage, inadequate family relation patterns and under-development of basic skills.
- Negative vision of work and employers (work equals exploitation and boredom), derived from what they, or others close to them, have experienced.
- Brought up in the street (aggressive social roles, survival of the strongest, etc.).
- Some previous experience with alcohol and/or drug abuse.
- Increasing number of young people from ethnic or cultural minorities (Roma, certain immigrant communities) among those at risk of exclusion.

The problem with the above description is that the characteristics mainly focus on the individual and their socio-economic origin or family status. There is little reference to the likely impact of other institutions or society in general (e.g. school, the labour market, a capitalist economy, etc.). Nevertheless, they must be understood within the context of this association's scope and may be useful in identifying potential risk situations. The presence of these 'vulnerability' characteristics in a particular group increases the probability of its members' social maladjustment and reduces their chances of participating fully in society and accessing their basic social rights. Risk situations, however, should never be considered as the result of isolated causes; they are part of a wider context, in which there is a higher probability that certain events might occur. Intervention to prevent risk situations means reducing the probabilities of this occurrence (Vélaz de Medrano 2002).

These adolescents bring with them not only the disadvantages[2] of their social origin, i.e. low socio-economic status, economic precariousness, etc., but also the *inequalities* generated by a school system and a society which legitimate and reproduce differences in origin. Through the adoption of a constructivist and multicultural perspective in their educational provision and career guidance activities (see Chapter 5 by Malik and Aguado, and

Chapter 13 by Reid), schools can endeavour to create a less discriminatory and more inclusive environment. Attempting to bridge the gap between socially embedded disadvantages and inequalities will contribute to greater opportunities for students. Educators and career guidance practitioners play a key role in addressing students' diversity both within the formal and non-formal education systems, and by working collaboratively with other educational agents (teachers, mediators, social workers, etc.).

Educators and guidance practitioners should require a profound knowledge of the factors that increase the risk of exclusion, but this should not stem from a deficit model whereby the student's characteristics and family background are held responsible for their 'failure'. Contextual factors, and a critical analysis of the current social and economic order, must be taken into account if the dominant liberal discourse is not to pervade the actions and programmes implemented to reduce such risk.

The role of guidance programmes in the struggle against social exclusion

Young people who risk social exclusion have ample experience of school and personal 'failure', and they usually confront the adult world with an *acquired defencelessness*. It is argued that the education system has the obligation to create the necessary opportunities for all students to engage in a significant learning process, and to facilitate the transition into adult life. But this should not only aim at providing them with the necessary skills to 'succeed' in education and in the labour market, as defined from a technocratic perspective. It is essential to promote active participation in society and to enable all students to challenge inequitable practices (see Chapter 2 by Irving, and Chapter 12 by Hernández and Muñoz), engaging in the promotion of social justice.

The prevailing discourse and practices aimed at preventing social exclusion focus mainly on assisting youth to overcome personal barriers, which are considered to hinder the transition into working life. Most initiatives which endeavour to reduce exclusion are based on the implementation of programmes to develop competencies previously identified as 'deficient'. These often relate to the acquisition of 'appropriate' life skills and basic competencies for social and labour insertion such as learning strategies, social and labour skills, self-concept, self-esteem, motivation for achievement, exploring future prospects, attitudes, values and norms.

Acknowledging that preparation for work (amongst other aspects) and the acquisition of basic competencies are necessary, we must question who determines what is appropriate, and whose point of view dominates, and which cultural framework underpins the programmes implemented. Comprehensive guidance programmes which aim to reduce social vulnerability in terms of self-esteem, self-awareness, social skills, developing initiative/autonomy, informed decision-making, etc. are essential yet should be framed by a wider educational perspective that incorporates critical and multicultural perspectives. The following approaches are usually adopted to address social exclusion:

1 *'Empowerment' of the individual:* This is considered a systemic approach (when individually focused it also, allegedly, takes into account the context), and is the most commonly applied strategy to prevent school failure and social exclusion, by enhancing the person's resources to 'succeed' in life. Research has shown that it is very important for a young person to have strategies to effectively enable them to use their own abilities and be aware that they have them. Strategic thinking influences success in learning and, consequently, self-confidence and motivation. The aim of this approach is to give people the power to act effectively in transforming their lives and their immediate environment, by: a) strengthening personal identity; b) developing personal awareness; c) facilitating access to information; d) supporting their leadership; e) contributing to increased power in making decisions (Ballester and Figuera 2000: 309). It is essential to bear in mind the cultural worldviews of the individuals, and how their identity is mediated.
2 *Community approach:* This is a new way of interpreting situations related to social risk, considering the community as capable of generating change processes which not only act upon risk factors/environmental protection, but also on the individuals. Using this approach means that the whole of society or the community is jointly responsible for the resolution of problems derived from situations of social risk; it means being aware that the community as a whole experiences these situations and, consequently, the entire community should act in search of solutions. The educational institution acts as facilitator of community participation and fosters a fluent collaboration with the rest of the community: family, municipalities, mass media, social and health services, etc.
3 *Competency-based approach:* Programmes aimed at developing competencies are widely used in preventing social risk; they enable the young person to confront risk situations and to overcome social vulnerability, providing that they are carried out within the framework of community programmes with a wider scope. These programmes should promote actions to minimise the influence of risk factors and, at the same time, to maximise the influence of protection factors.

In accordance with this latter approach, programmes focus on developing a series of general competencies and, depending on the needs of the group, certain specific skills. The following is a synthesis of the general and specific competencies and skills which are generally addressed.

General competencies

These should be part of an individual's range of personal resources and include:

a *Avoiding acquired defencelessness:* This is an acquired sentiment of 'scarce ability' whereby a person perceives themself as less capable than others. They assume that their individual capabilities cannot be altered and, consequently, cognitive distortion occurs, as well as a lack of motivation.
b *Attributive style:* Refers to how a young person explains things which happen to themselves – who is blamed for their failures and to whom their achievements are attributed (whether oneself, or to an external causes) – and being aware of it.
c *Coping strategies:* These are general dispositions which lead an individual to think and act in a more or less stable manner when confronted with different stressful situations.
d *Strategies for self-effectiveness:* Beliefs in one's own ability to plan and carry out the necessary actions to achieve certain goals and outcomes. A strong feeling of personal effectiveness is needed to persevere in the achievement of goals (although this will inevitably be mediated by external factors).
e *Learning strategies and metacognitive skills:* According to Beltrán (1993) the objective of these strategies is to know *what* we have to do in order to learn, to know *how* to do it and to *control* it whilst doing it; together with the awareness, control and regulation of these strategies.
f *Specific abilities:* Certain abilities will be developed, depending on what a youngster lacks. Some of the most frequent social skills are communication skills; assertiveness skills; self-assessment skills; skills for coping in the environment; and skills for co-existence (Asociación Cultural Norte Joven 2002).

This approach should, however, be combined with a community approach, so as not to place all the responsibility on the individual. The design and implementation of comprehensive guidance programmes should bear in mind the different issues addressed in other chapters of this book if they are to reduce social exclusion and promote social justice. It is important to avoid a deficit model which holds the individual responsible for their personal circumstances, and to adopt a critical stance emphasising the importance of the context, and promoting wider educational aims that go beyond the development of narrow life, social and employability skills. Active citizenship, environmental activism, and a critical awareness of the labour market and society in general must not be overlooked.

At present there is a tendency to speak more in terms of inclusion than exclusion because it implies *preventing* social risk. The struggle against social exclusion must be endorsed by educational policies (as well as by economic and social policies) to cater for the educational and social needs of all students, enabling them to participate fully in society, in a constructive and critical way.

There are a range of programmes and training initiatives in Spain (Asociación Cultural La Kalle y Arquero 1995; MEC 1990, MECD 2003a) and elsewhere (Casal *et al.* 1999) that seek to reduce social exclusion. These are primarily institutionally based, and designed to reduce academic failure at school, to prevent youth unemployment, and to promote social inclusion. Most, however, focus on the perceived deficits of the individual, attainment of educational credentials and acquisition of employability skills, without questioning the existing economic and social order. Very few take into account contextual factors nor emphasise the importance of critical social participation.

Casal *et al.* (1999) suggest that if education is to respond positively to the needs of all students, alternative or 'second opportunity' schools that operate outside of mainstream provision are fraught with potential problems. They argue that this alternative or 'second opportunity' initiative entails a three-fold risk by 'offering a second stigmatized opportunity, offering devalued certificates and, finally, relieving the education system of the responsibility to fulfil the needs of its youth' (Casal *et al.* 1999: 41). It appears that if the social exclusion of students is to be effectively addressed, a better course of action would be to ensure that 'problem' students do not lose their first opportunity from the outset, as reinsertion becomes very difficult for those labelled as failures.

European policies and plans for the social inclusion of young people

All Member States of the European Union (EU) share a common concern with the issue of school failure, with the fact that many young people do not have final end qualifications from school, and with the high drop out rate. Several organisations affirm that the number of young people who leave school prematurely progressively increases with age (Eurydice 1998; CES 2001; MECD 2001). In Spain, the Ministry of Education (MEDC 2002) admits that the student failure rate in schools is currently between 25 and 30 per cent.[3] Clearly, the number of young people who are at 'risk' of social exclusion is increasing progressively.

According to the most recent data, 18 per cent of the population in the EU run the risk of falling into poverty and social exclusion.[4] As far back as 1992, the EU report 'Towards a Europe of Solidarity' (CCE 1992) declared that this phenomenon had a structural character, because mechanisms to exclude part of the population from economic and social life were infiltrating the social fabric. Some of these mechanisms, which still exist today, are the inequalities generated by the globalising approach to employment, given that the productivity of capital can grow without work (Manzano 2002). Exclusion from employment also exacerbates other aspects of exclusion in relation to education, housing, living conditions, etc. Moreover, according to Tezanos (1998b), this problematic situation is intensified as many European societies are experiencing a crisis in their social welfare provision, unleashing a diversification in the policies of social security benefits, giving way to different types of discrimination. Prevention of social exclusion is thus presented as one of the most pressing structural challenges of the EU.

Every Member State has adopted a series of measures to prevent or reduce this problem in accordance with its own needs. The majority of these policies are the responsibility of each individual state, and implemented locally. Action at a European level is aimed at supporting the national and local efforts of member states to modernise policies and mechanisms, which promote social inclusion. However, calling for a common strategy, at the Council of Europe in Lisbon in 2000, member states of the EU promised resolutely to combat poverty and social exclusion, by pursuing the following strategic objective over the next ten years: 'to become the most competitive and most dynamic knowledge economy in the world, capable of a lasting economic growth, accompanied by quantitative and qualitative improvement in employment and greater social cohesion' (Consejo de Europa 2000: 43). It is striking to note how the neoliberal discourse permeates the discourse on social cohesion and inclusion.

With this in mind, each government elaborated a 'Plan for Social Inclusion'. All of these agreements are based on the recognition that, whilst employment is crucial for inclusion, there are many ways in which people can be excluded by factors which have nothing at all to do with employment. The battle against social exclusion should imply a cross-section of social policies (housing, health, education and training, transport and communications, social benefits) and a co-ordination of all these services. Thus, the different strategies of the EU can converge in a common effort which is evident in a range of reports: 'European Strategy for Employment'; 'Strategy for combating all type of Discrimination'; 'Community framework Strategy in favour of Equality between Men and Women'; and 'Community Strategy for fighting against Social Exclusion'. They highlight that all sectors of society need to work together to achieve the objectives outlined above (CEC 1999; 2001).

Adopting a comprehensive model of social justice: the influence of globalisation

Graded schooling which is organised inflexibly into homogeneous age or ability groups, using a standardised teaching methodology, applying identical learning rhythms for everyone, and promoting academic tracking at an early age, demonstrates the high value currently placed on the transmission of knowledge. There is little evidence to suggest that it is concerned with the promotion of meaningful learning for all. As an outcome of this, the less privileged fail, and diverse cultural identities are blurred.

By contrast, truly comprehensive schooling is flexible, endeavouring to overcome the classification and segregation of students. Teaching methodologies are sensitive to the different rhythms of each individual, and the teacher's explanations are not as important as the active engagement of each learner (both individually and co-operating with others). Thus the teacher designs, stimulates, guides and evaluates this process, in co-operation with the students (Pérez Gómez 2002).

One of the main goals of the comprehensive educational reforms in Spain in recent years has been to eliminate internal divisions during the period of compulsory and common schooling. It has been demonstrated that the early choices pupils make can be biased and therefore jeopardise those who enter the school with social disadvantages, or does not present a faithful reflection of the true abilities of the pupils (Fernández Enguita 2002).

A comprehensive approach to schooling and guidance delivery, drawing on the work of Vélaz de Medrano (2002), identifies the following:

- *Adopting measures to address diversity*, avoiding the homogenisation of groups for the sake of performance and efficiency. This implies the need to be aware that all pupils are likely to experience and engage with the learning process differently.
- *Active implication of the entire school community*, in the process of teaching and learning with a group of heterogeneous pupils.
- *Diversifying teaching processes*, using inclusive strategies that promote a critical and active approach to learning and which enable all pupils to reach the minimum aims of the curriculum.
- *Opportunities for mediation*, teachers should act as mediators to facilitate the learning of their pupils; students can be peer mediators with their classmates; guidance practitioners should mediate with family, teachers, school administrators and community services.
- *Opportunities for co-operative work*, where pupils can work collaboratively to achieve their aims, fostering interaction, communication, problem-solving, critical and divergent thinking, confidence, acceptance, support within the group, and a high personal and emotional involvement. All of these aspects are of prime importance to the person, in relation to the group.

The biggest challenge presented by the former Spanish educational reforms, implemented in the 1990s after the LOGSE (MEC 1990) came into force, was the option for comprehensive education at the compulsory secondary education level. 'It was a difficult challenge because it was necessary to combine comprehensiveness with heterogeneity, confront the school tradition and considerably improve the professional training of many teachers in Secondary Schools' (Pérez Gómez 2002: 68).

The current reforms (MECD 2003b) return to an academic education, defining certain minimum levels, offering different curriculum options at an early age, classifying pupils, and so forth. What it actually does, beneath the veneer it presents as a platform for the promotion of equality of opportunity, is to conceal the premature diversification of pupils 'depending on other aspects – social condition, culture, ethnic group – which go beyond the criteria of performance and ability' (González González 2003).

The comprehensive school requires more resources and dedication than the selective school. It is a more expensive option for society, if it is to be state-subsidised, and is more demanding for teachers and guidance practitioners. Therefore, it is only possible to implement if there is an ample political and social commitment to a holistic education.

This contrasts with the idea of education that is presented from a globalised point of view, or presented as a pragmatic reality in response to the global economy in which we live.[5]

> The neo-liberal policies which the globalized market sustains have displaced educational policies from being a State commitment, to the ambit of private decisions [. . .] favouring the ideology which seeks to link the school system – curriculum, specialities, groups, etc. – to the labour system and to the needs of economic productivity, putting social inequalities at risk.
>
> (Gimeno Sacristán 2001: 134)

In other words globalisation, without the conditions for inclusion, increases inequalities and leads to the social exclusion of certain groups. For this reason, some argue that one of the most important challenges at present is to globalise social justice and solidarity, just as the market is globalised, and even to make them both compatible. This is currently a contentious position as it defends an ethic-economic posture in which the mechanisms of the market and the ethical requirements of social justice are blended together (Conill 2001). From this perspective,

> it is necessary to find a meeting point – between the 'principle of economic rationality' which searches to optimize expenditure in relation to benefits, and the 'principle of social cohesion' which, from a perspective of social justice, searches for equality, for inclusion of all citizens and social intervention on the margin of economic profitability of expenditure, among other goals.
>
> (Casal 1996: 315)

This perspective contributes to a crucial contemporary debate concerning the ethics of social justice and its relationship with the marketplace. Yet is this meeting point at all possible, or even desirable? The implications of these statements require an in-depth analysis and further exploration of the underlying assumptions if issues of social exclusion, citizenship rights and democratic participation are to be fully uncovered and addressed.

Notes

1 These have increased over the past years mainly to: a) The period of economic recession and its effect on the labour market; b) the impact of 'information capitalism' and of the technological paradigm; c) and, mainly, the new social model arising from the irreversible tendency towards a 'global economy' which is determining the occupational structure, the organisation of work, both formal and non-formal training, etc.

2 Vélaz de Medrano points out the differences between the terms Difference, Disadvantage and Inequality. She asserts that 100 per cent of pupils are diverse, either because of individual differences (which would be referred to as *Difference*) or because of contextual differences or socio-economic origin (which would be denominated *Disadvantage*, in the case that they are negatively affecting learning), and *Inequality* (in the case of the school legitimating and reproducing the differences of origin).

3 Failure in school is measured by the percentage of pupils who finish schooling without the Certificate of ESO (Compulsory Secondary Education). The latest Report *'Figures on Education in Spain. 2003 Edition'* of the Spanish Ministry of Education (MECD 2003a), states that 36.8 per cent of pupils accumulate academic deficiency prior to the fourth year of the ESO.

4 Data obtained from the Report on *Integration of excluded people*. Web of the Employment and Social Affairs Bureau http://europa.eu.int/comm/commissioners/diamantopoulou/ (last accessed 15 December, 2003).

5 In a *global economy*, the 'social citizenship' tends to give way to a 'private citizenship' (Alonso 1999) causing the social contract, which advocates the right to work and protection against social risks, to deteriorate (Rubio and Monteros 2002).

Bibliography

Alonso, L.E. (1999) 'Crisis de la sociedad del trabajo y ciudadanía: una reflexión entre lo global y lo local', *Política y sociedad*, 31: 7–35.

Asociación Cultural La Kalle y Arquero, M. (1995) *Educación de calle. Hacia un modelo de intervención en marginación juvenil*, Madrid: Editorial Popular – Comunidad de Madrid.

Asociación Cultural Norte Joven (2002) *Habilidades socio-laborales para la prevención de toxicomanías*, Madrid, ANJ: Comisión Europea (CD Rom).

Ballester, L. and Figuera, P. (2000) 'Exclusión e inserción social', in P. Amorós and P. Eyerbe (eds) *Intervención educativa en inadaptación social*, Madrid: Síntesis.

Beltrán, J. (1993) *Procesos, estrategias y técnicas de aprendizaje*, Madrid: Síntesis.

Casal, J. (1996) 'Modos emergentes de transición a la vida adulta en el umbral del siglo XXI: aproximación sucesiva, precariedad y desestructuración', *REIS-Revista española de investigaciones sociológicas*, 75: 295–316.

Casal, J., García, M. and Planas, J. (1999) 'Escolarización plena y "estagnación"', *Cuadernos de Pedagogía*, 268: 38–41.

Castell, R. (1997) 'La exclusión social', in Proceedings of the International Meeting, *IV Encuentro internacional sobre Servicios sociales. Exclusión e intervención social*, Valencia: Fundación Bancaixa, pp.187–196

—— (1999) *La metamorfosis de la cuestión social*, Barcelona: Paidós.

Comisión de las Comunidades Europeas (1992) *Hacia una Europa de la solidaridad. Intensificación de la lucha contra la exclusión social y promoción de la integración*, Bruselas: CCE.

Commission of the European Communities (1999) *Report on Round Table Conference 'Towards a Europe For All: How Should the Community Support Member States to Promote Social Inclusion?'*, Brussels (6–7 May): CEC.

—— (2001): *Commission Staff Working Paper 'e-Inclusion Report. The Information Society's Potential for Social Inclusion in Europe'*, Brussels: CEC.

Conill, J. (2001) 'Aspectos éticos de la globalización. Justicia, solidaridad y esperanza frente a la globalización', *Documentación social*, 125: 225–242.

Consejo de Europa (2000) *Objetivos en la lucha contra la pobreza y la exclusión social*, Bruselas, 30 de noviembre de 2000.

Consejo Económico y Social (2001) *La pobreza y la exclusión social en España: propuestas de actuación en el marco del Plan Nacional para la Inclusión Social*, Madrid: CES, Colección Informes.

Eurydice (1998) *Medidas adoptadas por los Estados Miembros de la Unión Europea para ayudar a los jóvenes sin titulación*, Bruselas: Unidad Europea de Eurydice/Comisión Europea.

Fernández Enguita, M. (2002) 'En torno al borrador de la LOCE. Los itinerarios, los abiertos y los encubiertos', Key-address presented at the *7º encuentro de profesionales de la orientación escolar. Centro de apoyo al profesorado de Aranjuez. Dirección de Área Territorial Madrid Sur* (September).

García Serrano, C. and Malo, M.A. (1993) El comportamiento económico de los excluidos: un modelo para la política social, in VVAA. *Pobreza, necesidad y discriminación*, Madrid: Popular.

Gimeno Sacristán, J. (2001) 'El significado y la función de la educación en la sociedad y cultura globalizadas', *Revista de educación*, Special Issue, 121–142.

González González, MªT. (2003) Las investigaciones contradicen los objetivos de la ley de calidad y su apuesta por los itinerarios. Key-address presented at the *7º encuentro de profesionales de la orientación escolar. Centro de apoyo al profesorado de Aranjuez. Dirección de Área Territorial Madrid Sur* (September).

Manzano Soto, N. (2002) 'Iniciativas de la Unión Europea que promueven la prevención de la inadaptación y de la exclusión social', in C. Vélaz de Medrano (ed.) *Intervención educativa en sujetos con desadaptación social*, Madrid: UNED.

Ministerio de Educación y Ciencia (1990) *Ley Orgánica General del Sistema Educativo* (LOGSE), 1/1990, de 3 de octubre de 1990. Madrid: MEC (BOE de 4/10/1990).

Ministerio de Educación, Cultura y Deporte (2001) *'Cifras de la educación en España, las estadísticas e indicadores. Edición 2001'*, Madrid: MECD.

Ministerio de Educación, Cultura y Deporte (2002) *'Cifras de la educación en España, las estadísticas e indicadores. Edición 2002'*, Madrid: MECD.

Ministerio de Educación, Cultura y Deporte (2003a) '*Las cifras de la Educación en España. Edición 2003*', Madrid: MECD.

Ministerio de Educación, Cultura y Deporte (2003b) *LEY ORGÁNICA 10/2002, de 23 de diciembre, de Calidad de la Educación* (LOCE). Madrid: MECD – Boletín Oficial del Estado (BOE) núm. 307 de 24/12/2002. Available on 'PDF' format at http://www.mecd.es/leycalidad/index.htm (last visited: 15 December 2003).

Pérez Gómez, A.I. (2002) 'Un aprendizaje diverso y relevante', *Cuadernos de Pedagogía*, 311: 66–70.

Rubio, MªJ. and Monteros, S. (Coords.) (2002) *La exclusión social. Teoría y práctica de la intervención*, Madrid: Editorial CCS.

Tezanos, J.F. (1998a) *Tendencias de dualización y exclusión social en las sociedades avanzadas. Un marco para el análisis*. Textos de Sociología, n° 4, Madrid: UNED (Working Document).

—— (1998b) *Tendencias en exclusión social en las sociedades tecnológicas. El caso español*, Madrid: Sistema.

Vélaz de Medrano, C. (2002) *Intervención educativa en sujetos con desadaptación social*, Madrid: UNED.

Chapter 12

Social justice and equality of opportunity for Mexican young people

Julia Hernández Hernández and Bernardo Antonio Muñoz-Riverohl

Introduction

Considering our professional experience as educational counsellors and given our knowledge of the social realities in which young Mexican people grow up, it is with great interest that we have accepted the invitation from the editors to participate in this important book.

In our chapter we will discuss a range of issues in relation to Latin America in general, and more specifically the current situation in Mexico. Consideration will be given to the opportunities available to Mexican youth that will enable them to develop their full potential, and to become critical citizens. Although there are many different factors that contribute to the present scenario, we will focus on two issues of central concern, education and work.

Prior to any discussion of these key concerns, it is necessary to describe the existing demographic and social conditions in Mexico, within the wider context of modernisation and globalisation, as these shape the kind of opportunities that young people are able to access if they are to live with dignity. These conditions and opportunities provide the real evidence of the existence, or absence, of a specific social justice project beyond the official discourses or the ideological debate generated around this legal and political category.

In the first section, we describe the difficult panorama faced by Latin American youth with regards to education and work. This brief description serves to ascertain the demographic and social circumstances in which young Mexican people live, and how they relate to opportunities in education and work: two of the most urgent social needs of young people in present society. Finally, we move on to present an agenda for action that will assist career educators and guidance counsellors to respond positively to the imposed 'realities' of our time, and ensure that their practice continues to advocate for socially just outcomes.

Our Latin American setting: segregation of young people

Throughout the world young women and men face a difficult situation. According to figures from the Organisation for Economic Co-operation and Development (OECD 2002a), there are 180 million unemployed people worldwide. It is estimated that by the year 2010 there will be a need for 500 million new job vacancies, the amount required to cover for the shortage of jobs up until then, and accommodate the demand at that time. The OECD also estimated that the rate of unemployment for young people between 15 and 24 years of age has nearly doubled between the period of the late 1980s and 1999, and is still tending to increase (OECD 2002a: 28).

During this latter period of intense globalisation, neither the promise of increasing job opportunities, among other important social needs, nor the economic projects aimed at sustainable development have been fulfilled. The number of unemployed people ('parados') in Spain, Italy, Germany, France, etc., as well as large demonstrations against neo-liberal economic policies and unemployment conditions, were indicators of the situation at the turn of this new century. With regard to the world of equality and social justice promised by the neo-liberals, 'the continental economic and commercial agreements under the banner of free trade (in its more violent and imperialistic version), represent the new "*metharelato*" or the new lie' (Lyotard 1987: 3).

In the meantime, the latest historical, economic and political events in Latin America are worrisome. At the dawn of a new millennium, we can draw on two critical examples to illustrate this. Firstly the attempts of *coup d'état* against the legally constituted Venezuelan government presided over by General Chavez; and secondly the economic, social and political sequels left behind by the economic crisis in the Republic of Argentina, which will probably delay the implementation of the populist policies undertaken by president Luis I. Lula da Silva. This might also further extend to the weaker economies in Central and South America.

This situation is caused, to a large extent, by the impact that the hegemony of global capital organisations and markets is having on the social, political and cultural life of different countries. Globalisation, the modernisation process in the organisation of work, and the growth of vast commercial markets (among some other key historical events) coalesce and serve to transform the contemporary reality.

The Uruguayan writer Eduardo Galeano (1999) draws our attention to the unfair distribution of wealth worldwide: only 20 per cent of the world population benefit from the work of others. For example, in Mexico the great social barriers that prevent this country from entering the so-called 'first world' are evident as extreme opposites prevail: 40 per cent of the population lives in poverty, 30 per cent suffers extreme poverty, whilst wealth is primarily distributed amongst 300 families.

Concerning employment, the situation in Latin America is also of concern. There are 70 million unemployed people in this continent. Regarding young people, the rate of unemployment during the early 1990s was 7.9 per cent, doubling up to 16 per cent in 1999 (in Latin America there are approximately one hundred million young people between 15 and 24 years of age). It is also worth noting that poor or materially disadvantaged youth represents two thirds of the total unemployed and marginalised population. For example, among the poor and extremely poor sectors, the rate of unemployment is 24.6 per cent. This significantly exceeds the 11.5 per cent of young people who are located within more affluent socio-economic levels (OECD 2002a).

Even for Latin American youngsters who can get a job, their material situation is not very promising. Out of every one hundred active workers, only seven are classified as young, and they earn half the minimum wage received by an adult (IWO 2002).

Regarding the relation between education and work, we observe that in spite of the cutbacks to investment in education undertaken by most Latin American governments, and despite the huge growth of the informal economy in which no credentials or qualifications are required, the amount of educational accreditation, or years of schooling, is still an important factor in obtaining a better paid job. For example, job positions that were occupied by people with more than ten years of schooling increased by 2.5 per cent, whilst those in which the workers occupying them had lower qualifications with under six years of schooling were reduced by 2.9 per cent (CONAPO 2001). The average income of employed people with higher education qualifications is 4.6 per cent greater than the income received by those who have only completed a basic education. Moreover, workers who completed secondary education earned 46.3 per cent more than those who left school at the end of their period of elementary education (CONAPO 2001).

Concerning education, it is well known that it presents a serious social problem in Latin America. Only 20 per cent of children enter basic education. Out of this, 40 per cent fail the first grade, and almost half attend school irregularly. As a consequence, the proportion of students that complete elementary education is very low: out of every one hundred children who enrol, only forty-four finish elementary school (Martinez 2002). The impact on secondary education is clear, since only half the teenagers enter this higher educational stage.

Latin American youth are those most affected by the economic crisis, in particular young people with the lowest qualification levels. Consequently it is not strange to find that young people in this category are economically disadvantaged, having the lowest economic incomes and performing nonqualified, subsistence jobs. Not surprisingly, most poor young people are inclined to engage in criminal activity, violent behaviour and participate in substance abuse of some kind. 'In Mexico, for example, 50 per cent of youngsters live in urban marginal zones of the country, and this situation increases the possibilities of criminal actions, violence, etc' (Garza 1999: 7). It is clear that the hegemonic impact of global capital jeopardises young Latin Americans.

Mexico, a country of young people

Mexico cannot escape the unfair realities imposed by the globalisation of capital and markets. Whilst the present government claims that the Mexican economy is in ninth position, alongside the developed economies of the world, Mexican young people do not believe the substance of this official discourse. For the majority, the poor social and economic conditions in which they live are evident, and this serves to provide a clear indicator of the kind of actual opportunities that are available to them.

A key issue to consider when analysing the social and economic context in which young people develop, is how this relates to demographic features. Bearing in mind that Mexico is mainly a country of young people, consideration must be given to the extent to which demographic considerations influence the policies of the Mexican government, and whether it relies on a short, medium and/or long-range plan to provide education, health and jobs for youth.

A remarkable fact of Mexican demography over the last thirty years is the decrease in the infant population, which continues to fall. For example, 2.1 million births were registered during the year 2000; however it has been estimated that within seven years the birth rate will decrease to 1.9 million, and by 2020 it is estimated that this will further reduce to 1.7 million (CONAPO 1999). Mexican society is highly aware of the decrease of the infant population, whilst the youth population grows and increases the demand for more secondary and higher education, and calls for a bigger supply of jobs.

The National Council of Population in Mexico has grouped the population into four age segments: pre-school (children under 6); basic school age (6 to 14 year-old children); labour (15 to 64-year-olds); third Age (65+ years old). The population decrease in the pre-school segment is significant, and has resulted from the effectiveness of family planning policies. 'In 1970 there were 22.2 million children in this segment, whereas there are 12.7 million nowadays. It has decreased by nearly 50 per cent' (CONAPO 1999: 34).

The number of young children continues to fall and is starting to have its impact on education. Attention to children in the pre-school segment has increased, and education is not encountering the same difficulties as a decade ago, when the provision of educational services for children of pre-school age did not satisfy the demand. Now, pre-school provision tends to balance with the demand for schooling.

In the basic school segment student numbers are increasing. In 1970 there were 12.8 million children, whereas now it has increased to 20 million. This number responds to a logical inertial increase, due to the transition of children from the pre-school stage.

In the labour segment we find a bigger population increase. Whilst in 1970 the population was 9.2 million, in 2002 it rose to 20.5 million. This segment is more dynamic compared with the previous two, since it is growing at an annual rate of 0.75 per cent. Based on these figures, it is estimated that in about seven years, the population will reach 21.2 million people, its highest level, yet in the years to come it will start to decrease.

Within the labour segment we can clearly identify a sub-segment encompassing young people between ages 15–24. This boundary in the labour segment is important (there could even be further divisions), not only because of the obvious differences between both generations, but also because work-job-related problems for the sub-segment of those aged between 25 and 64 are more pressing in Mexican society. In 1970, this sub-segment was made up of 15.2 million people, whereas in 2002 it had increased to 43.4 million. Due to the inertia of population increase, in 2030 there will be about 69 million people, and it is estimated that at this point it will have peaked, after which, it will start to fall gradually.

The segment comprised of people older than 65 presently stands at up to five million, and represents 4.9 per cent of the total population. The annual growth rate increased from 1.4 per cent in 1980 to 3.7 per cent in 2002. In proportional terms, the data presents the following statistics. In 2002, one out of twenty Mexican people was located in this segment and, according to demographic trends, in the year 2020 it will be one out of eight, whilst thirty years later it will be one out of four (CONAPO 1999: 40). In spite of the accelerated growth rate, the Mexican government has not implemented any short, medium or long-term social projects to cater for the growing needs of people in this segment.

It is clear from the previous analysis that the current situation and demographic trends entails a series of social conditions that cannot be ignored, such as the demand for increasing secondary and higher education provision, or the need for more jobs to prevent a bigger social deterioration.

It is worthwhile to acknowledge that the demographic situation has significantly impacted on the provision of education. We must not forget the problematic social situation that exists at the secondary and higher education levels, partly because of the increased demand by young people to enter these levels, but mainly due to the irregular investments in education, which have been decreasing for the past twenty years. There is an urgent need therefore for the development of governmental policies in relation to the labour segment. This does not mean that the provision of quality education for the pre-school and school segments have already been consolidated. On the contrary, this goal is still far from being achieved due to an array of social and labour problems, amongst others, which create several obstacles and serve to drive children away from school.

The lack of opportunities to enter university

The impact of demographic trends has started to change the education scenario. Whilst educational provision has advanced in relation to the first and second segments, due to demographic inertia and a reduction in the numbers of children, serious difficulties exist in the labour segment to satisfy the educational demand.

As a consequence of demographic inertia, the population has decreased in both the first and second segments, while it increases in the others. It is estimated that during the first thirty years of this century the youth population between 15 and 24 years of age will grow remarkably. As a result, the demand for secondary education will increase to about 70 per cent, whereas the demand to enter higher education (university) will be around 50 per cent (INEGI 2002).

The adult population in the 25 to 64 age span shows a similar trend. The main problems faced by this sub-segment are access to work, and participation in low wage employment. Although many graduates between 25 and 35 are interested in undertaking post-graduate courses, most of them are under pressure to improve their income; labour wages have lost 60 per cent of their value and the rate of unemployment increased dramatically in the last five months of 1999 (CONAPO 1999).

Limited job opportunities for young people

The Mexican researcher and political analyst, Gerardo Nieto, states that the labour market is 'suffering a deep transformation. In the global era, the so-called "life-long jobs" are disappearing, jobs that in some societies warranted the individuals a place in the society and secure economic provisions for the household' (Nieto 2002: 5). In Mexico, there are mainly two sectors experiencing this situation: the primary sector (related to farming production) and the secondary sector (industrial–manufacturing). The manufacturing sector is particularly at risk of disappearing altogether. For example, last year manufacturing industries lost 574,000 jobs, with 246,565 (almost half) belonging to the 'maquila' (assembly) industry.

Nieto provides data concerning the increase of unemployment:

> according to the National Institute of Statistics, Geography and Computer Sciences (INEGI, by its acronym in Spanish), in September 2002, the rate of open unemployment rose to 3.05 per cent, which meant an increase of 122 thousand unemployed people with respect to August of the same year, and an increase of 272 thousand in the course of that year.
>
> (Nieto 2002: 6)

This was the highest rate of unemployment since February 1999, higher for men than for women. For men the rate rose to 3.1 per cent, whereas for women the rate was 2.96 per cent. The rise in unemployment confirms Mexico's economic weakness. During the first semester of 2003, a significant increase of unemployment occurred and the rate rose to 5 per cent.

The history of unemployment in Mexico is dynamic and critical. Professor Nieto considers that in the last twenty years Mexican governments have failed considerably to create jobs. Between 1980 and 2000, out of 23 million Mexicans trying to access the formal labour market, only 6 million found employment. The remaining 17 million moved into other markets in order to subsist. Around 10 million entered the informal economy, while the other 7 million migrated to the United States where they annually contribute to the Mexican economy by means of remittances of over 12 billion dollars (Nieto 2002: 8).

According to the National Council of Population, the demand for jobs during the present decade will be for about 1.2 million Mexicans, on average, per year. Consequently the economically active population, which at present represents about 43.8 million of workers, will rise to 55 million by 2010 and to 64 million by 2020 (CONAPO 2001).

Young people in the 15–34 age group are most affected by unemployment. Between August and September 2002, the unemployment rate in this age range increased by more than 16 per cent. Gerardo Nieto declares that

> unemployment among young people is four times higher than the percentage of unemployed people who are older than 34 years. In this segment of population, it can be seen as a regression of job opportunities. They do not lack academic qualifications. Quite the opposite, a high percentage of them have some kind of professional qualification but they are unemployed, underemployed or in precarious working conditions. Young people are suffering the greater weight of economic recession, due to the absence of co-ordination between the educational and work sectors and the lack of a plan that takes advantage of the millions of youths who enter the labour market.
>
> (Nieto 2002: 12)

Are opportunities and social justice for young people possible?

The figures and percentages shown above are overwhelming. The conditions to enable Latin American and Mexican young people to develop fully are not easily apparent. In fact, quite the opposite is evident which paints a pessimistic picture of the future. Many obstacles must be overcome in Mexico, among them: a better and fairer distribution of wealth; a recovery of the primary sector of the economy; improvements in the public health system; and the expansion of educational opportunities enabling more young people to enter the secondary and higher levels of education. Currently in Mexico, only 19 per cent of the population have the opportunity to enrol in college, as opposed to 50 per cent of youths in the United States, and 70 per cent of Canadians.

Under these circumstances, there is a need to ask whether it is possible to speak about opportunities and social justice for Mexican young people? However, let us try to briefly and meaningfully address this question.

When we talk about equality of opportunities for young people, we do not refer only to those who have had the privilege of obtaining academic qualifications and acquiring the necessary competencies to perform efficiently in the labour market. We also include those who, for whatever reasons, abandoned school or dropped out of the school system early. All young people have the right to employment, regardless of whether they have complete or incomplete educational credentials.

This right must also include individuals with special needs, i.e. physically or mentally (dis)abled people, or those who continue to be rejected and discriminated against by their employers. In most of Latin America, women still do not benefit from full citizenship rights, or have access to equality of opportunities. Moreover, it is necessary to highlight that the social and legal category 'equality of opportunities' requires updating and adaptation to reflect the independent social movements of civil society. Equality of opportunities, as a modern mechanism for the full achievement of democracy, not only has an unresolved task in extending and consolidating the opportunities for women and for the (dis)abled, it also has a social debt to repay with reference to ethnic and cultural diversity (Rawls 1996).

Until about thirty years ago, dealing with the needs of the 'many' as universal, against the differentiated needs of the 'few', seemed to be a demonstration of social justice and democracy. From the 1970s onwards, the category of 'social justice' (Rawls 2002), and consequently the social discourse about equality of opportunities, has included cultural diversity. However, in the dynamics of social daily life there is still little tolerance or acceptance of counterculture movements which are headed by young people, such as 'dark', 'scatos', 'punk', etc. A similar situation occurs with movements that struggle for the recognition of sexual orientation and preference, which still face rejection from conservative societies, such as that which exists in Mexico.

Another example of segregation and social injustice is the situation in which the indigenous peoples of Latin American live. In Mexico, for example, the executive, legislative (parliamentary) and judicial authorities do not recognise the ancient and legitimate forms of indigenous (native) organisation. It is internationally known that during the first minutes of 1994, in the state of Chiapas (located in the south-eastern part of the Mexican Republic), the Zapatista Army for National Liberation (EZLN, by its acronym in Spanish) declared war on the Mexican government. It was also at this precise moment that Mexico 'opened its doors' to the North American Free Trade Agreement (NAFTA) which involved the United States and Canada.

At the cry of 'Ya basta!' ('That's enough!'), the EZLN claimed the right of over fifty ethnic groups to live with dignity as people, to be recognised and respected as Mexicans, with entitlements that included the rights to work, education and health. This movement highlights the struggle that Latin American natives have been engaged in for almost five centuries in their attempts to avoid their extermination, exploitation and segregation.

In Mexico, the rights to education, work and health, as well as freedom of expression, are among a number of basic democratic constitutional rights that are formally guaranteed in the national constitution. However, these principles and commitments of the state are not being fulfilled due to constraints in the budget that is allocated to social issues (health, education, housing), and which Mexican politicians have been gradually reducing during the past twenty years.

Political justification for investment in education below 8 per cent of the Gross Domestic Product (GDP), the amount recommended by the UN, have been endorsed by the alleged 'fear' that it will produce a condescending or patronising state that takes responsibility away from the people, and restricts service development. By way of this pretext, the Mexican government is actually justifying the privatisation of education and public health services. As a result, it is likely that only those people with the financial means to pay for such basic services will have access to privately funded services and facilities.

If we add to this the fact that the Mexican economy depends on the sale of its hydrocarbons and the services offered by the country; that its manufacturing production is still far from being competitive in the vast markets; and that its farming and food industries are in poor condition; we have some basic elements to deduce the lack of opportunities that young people have to develop fully as critical citizens in current society.

Towards the practice of a critical and alternative educational guidance

Schools have a tendency to avoid any discussion about the realities of life. They fail to present opportunities for any deep analysis or raising of awareness of Latin American and Mexican 'reality'. The contents of basic subjects such as social sciences, science, maths, etc., are too theoretical and 'encyclopaedic', taught in an isolated way, with no relation at all to the actual situation of the country. Students' awareness of major national problems is not fostered in schools as these seem to have a 'bureaucratic' function, more concerned with the completion of school credits than with the promotion of critical thinking. Moreover, schooling is gradually moving away from its humanistic foundations that have given it its modern significance. Schools nowadays appear to be dominated by an excessive and dangerous pragmatism, of which the priorities are to cater for the trinomial production–consumption–competition.

At the higher education level, public universities in Mexico are under a great deal of pressure to shift the focus of their teaching and research to technological contents. Conservative industrialists, encouraged by the new government, continuously claim that a university curriculum which places a greater emphasis on the development of technological contents is what is required in the 'new' economy. Knowledge and research in other fields that are important for social development, such as basic science, health sciences, social sciences and the humanities, are thereby relegated and awarded a secondary status.

It is within this difficult context that the educational guidance services in Mexico must operate, and currently are encountering serious problems. Approximately 60 per cent of counsellors do not hold the academic qualifications required to deliver guidance to young people; there are not enough resources available to enable them to train; and the availability of educational guidance services is likely to be restricted given the forecast increase in demand. The inertia and old problems that have characterised Mexican educational guidance in particular have become even more serious in the last ten years, as a consequence of the troublesome structural situation that the country is going through.

Educational guidance (and counselling) is generally delivered only within schools. This is in contrast to the provision available in most western nations (OECD 2002b), where it operates in a range of settings, and may be publicly and/or privately funded. In Mexico, guidance is part of the school curriculum, and its purpose has traditionally been to address learning difficulties, vocational or career choice, etc., in order to offer alternatives to those perceived 'problems' that prevent individual development, or appropriate socialisation of the student. In this respect, Mexican educational guidance cannot be understood or considered outside the school setting, as it is an important part of the educational process.

Consequently, since the school environment bears a strong influence on educational guidance, the educational counsellors' discourse and guidance delivery is limited and fails to engage with a wider understanding of social realities. For example, it is still naively believed that encouragement, good will and the identification of a student's skills, interests and personality traits are enough to assist them in choosing the best career options. Any discussion or raising of awareness about the difficult conditions that characterise the labour market is avoided, whilst the social causes that can bring about family disintegration, addictions, violence and criminal behaviour are completely ignored.

We believe, however, that educational guidance services must acknowledge the wider challenges that teenagers and young people face, not only those related to emotional and academic aspects, but also in relation to the social, cultural and political spheres (see Chapter 2 by Irving). Teachers, with the assistance of educational counsellors, must educate and encourage students to be open-minded and critical thinkers, promoting a critical awareness and understanding of how social reality is constructed and presented. This will allow students to gain a critical insight into, and an understanding of, dominant discourses, thereby enabling them to develop strategies that help them mount challenges to injustice and identify the potential for change, instead of reproducing the 'symbolic violence' (Bordieu 1986) of an unfair and inequitable economic system.

Guidance delivery and educational curriculum that is naive, uncritical and which reinforces the narrow economic imperatives that are often associated with globalisation should be discarded if the interests of social justice and equality are to be progressed. To conclude this chapter therefore, we put forward the following agenda for consideration. Our goal is to move guidance practice and the educational curriculum away from a model based on psychological premises, towards a more holistic approach that is critical and socially located. This will contribute to a process that enables young people to construct their world views and social realities in relation to their own lived experiences and those of their peers.

To conceive of guidance as a practice that facilitates awareness

The role of the counsellor is relevant in promoting students' awareness of social and individual values that contribute to the improvement of relationships with others in the complex dynamics of society. Moreover it recognises and accepts that ethnic and social diversity should occupy a central place. The identification of these core values implies that counsellors will develop a multicultural perspective (see Chapter 13 by Reid), be seen to act in a socially just and equitable way, and ensure it is implicit in all aspects of their work.

To incorporate gender equality into guidance delivery

Counsellors have a responsibility to understand, internalise and promote equality with particular reference to gender. There is a need to explicitly emphasise the inclusion of women in all aspects of social and political life. This will help to counter the social exclusion that continues to be experienced by many women throughout the world, and more specifically in many Latin America countries where a 'macho' culture continues to thrive.

To promote the civil rights of young people

A major goal of counselling is to contribute to education for citizenship, which includes the promotion and advocacy of young people's civil rights (a task that UNAM, National Autonomous University of Mexico, is promoting with determination and rigour). These imply the observance of a series of principles concerning respect and recognition of social justice, which might possibly contribute to reduce the existing gaps between social groups, including gender, and an awareness of responsibilities *and* rights.

To incorporate a deep understanding of social diversity

This important concept cannot be understood if tolerance and respect are not seen to be put into practice in all aspects of the educational curriculum, and guidance counselling practice. If cultural, sexual, or any other type of social diversity is to be accepted, it is essential to accept that all individuals should have the right to express themselves freely, and to be able to do so overtly. Where limits on social and individual freedom are imposed these should be based on a collective good derived from responsible freedom, and not assumed as an individual birthright. In a world that is dynamic and in a constant state of flux, equity must be continuously pursued, promoting the active inclusion of all individuals, regardless of gender, religion, social class, sexual preference, or ethnicity.

To promote the right to social and work opportunities

The right to employment is also an important aspect of our analysis. Today the lack of employment opportunity is one of the crucial problems faced by the economic system, and this affects the work expectations and aspirations of college students in particular. In this context, economic recession hinders the development of employment opportunities, notwithstanding the increasing demand. Thus, an analysis of the labour market, and of available work opportunities is important (even though these are becoming increasingly limited as a result of globalisation). In this respect, one of the functions of counselling is to promote the right to fair treatment and remuneration in the workplace. This takes us beyond the basic need to prepare students to become useful or 'satisfactory' employees who perform high quality work.

Regarding career education and development, besides providing students with the necessary tools and strategies to attain the cognitive and emotional competencies required in their professional development, it is essential to ensure that they receive information on the current status of occupations. Further to this it should assist students in their decision-making processes, and include critical thinking as a core competency. We contend that educators and guidance counsellors must foster the critical capacity of students, enabling them to engage as active citizens and workers. This must be a key part of the process of 'learning for work'. They should not ignore their students' individual and collective humanity, or their right to express themselves constructively and directly in the face of inequality and social injustice, which are recurrent themes in this age of cannibalism and symptoms of extreme capitalism.

Bibliography

Bordieu, P. (1986) 'The forms of capital', in J.E. Richardson (ed.) *Handbook of Theory of Research for the Sociology of Education*, Westport: Greenwood Press.

Consejo Nacional de la Población (1999) *Atlas Demográfico de México* CONAPO: Mexico (Demographic Atlas of Mexico).

Consejo Nacional de la Población (2001) *Tendencias demográficas en Latinoamérica* (dossier), CONAPO: Mexico (Demographic Trends in Latin America).

Galeano, E. (1999) 'Incertidumbre y pobreza en América Latina', in *La Jornada*, diario de 28 de Septiembre, sección 'El mundo', p.26.

Garza, G. (1999) 'La megaciudad de México' (dossier), CONAPO: Mexico.

Instituto Nacional de Estadística e Informática (2002) *Cuaderno de Estadística de Educación en México*, INEGI: Mexico (Notebook on Educational Statistics in Mexico).

International Work Organisation (2002) *Section on Mexico, Annual Report for 2000–2002*, Organización Internacional del Ttrabajo: Mexico.

Lyotard, J.F. (1987) 'Reglas y Paradojas', *Universidad de México*, XLII, 437: 3–9.

Martínez Rizo, F. (2002) 'La desigualdad educativa en México', *Este País*, 19 (October), p.60 (Educational inequality in Mexico).

Nieto Lopez, G. (2002) 'Demanda laboral y perfil profesional. Resultados de dos estudios de caso', Informe de Investigación, Dirección General de Orientación y Servicios Educativos, Universidad Nacional Autónoma de México: Mexico (Labour demands and career profile. Results from two case studies. Research Report).

Organisation for Economic Cooperation and Development (2002a) *2002 Report*, OECD: New York.

Organisation for Economic Cooperation and Development (2002b) *Country and Thematic Policy Reviews in Education, Career Guidance Policy Review*, Online. Available HTTP. http://www/OECD.org/els/education/careerguidance/ (accessed 4 February 2004).

Rawls, J. (1996) *Theory of Justice*, Fondo de Cultura Económica: Mexico.

—— (2002) *Justice as Equity*, Paidos–Ibérica: Madrid.

Chapter 13

Beyond the toolbox

Integrating multicultural principles into a career guidance intervention model

Hazel L. Reid

Introduction

Whilst multiculturalism is well established within counselling and psychotherapy, its principles are less likely to be located within the intervention models used in the training of career guidance practitioners. Training does pay attention to equal opportunities but often this remains politically neutral and does not consider the multi-layered subjects of social justice and multiculturalism. Both are frequently viewed as a concern with ethnicity rather than with a range of variables linked to social context. This chapter discusses multiculturalism in the context of guidance and considers the traditional approach of a three-stage model, questioning its potential to meet the needs of a diverse client group. It suggests additions to a three-stage model to cater for the needs of clients whose 'world-views' are different from each other and different from the practitioner. The chapter ends by suggesting a way forward for the training of careers practitioners.

The context of career guidance in the UK

A range of disciplines sited in the social sciences informs career guidance in the UK. Although in practice it is difficult to separate career theory and guidance theory, a distinction is useful to clarify what this chapter means when talking of guidance theory.

> Theories of career development are attempts to describe, explain and predict what happens. Theories of guidance are attempts to think how we might sensibly intervene in what happens. The former is concerned with what is: the latter with what might and should be.
>
> (Law 1981: 152)

This chapter is concerned with the intervention models used in the training of career guidance practitioners in the UK. It will focus on the work of one higher education training institution but will make a number of general points, which aim to be relevant to the whole sector in the UK and potentially elsewhere.

When discussing career guidance training in the UK it is important to acknowledge the influence of Rogers' (1961) person-centred approach. This approach is embedded in psychology and counselling. Career advisers in the UK have not worked in a therapeutic context, although the work of 'additional needs' career advisers differs from that of generic advisers. However, this is changing with the development of the Connexions service in England, and via other initiatives designed to meet the inclusion agenda in the other home nations in the UK. This work began with a 'refocusing' agenda (Reid 1999) that predates the development of the Connexions service (D*f*EE 2000).

The Connexions service was designed to draw personnel from a number of 'youth support services', for example the Careers Service, parts of the youth service and a range of other specialist agencies concerned with youth welfare, in order to provide an integrated service. The service has lead to the creation of a new youth worker known as a personal adviser. In England the majority of career advisers working with young people in careers companies that are now part of the Connexions model, are known as personal advisers.

Even though the other countries in the UK have rejected the Connexions model, addressing the government's inclusion agenda is a key motivator for change in their operational structure and delivery (ICG 2002). Levitas (1998) discusses the differences in meaning of inclusion and exclusion; this discussion is useful for gaining an understanding of the political 'social inclusion' agenda in the UK. She views exclusion as endemic in all modern societies and suggests that definitions can be organised around three key concepts: a redistributionist discourse (RED) where inclusion will only be achieved with a redistribution of material goods: a social integrationist discourse (SID) where it is not necessary to change the status quo, but those excluded need to increase their employability skills for work: and a moral underclass discourse (MUD) where the excluded are perceived as a threat to the cohesion of society, with the root cause being lack of the correct values towards work and citizenship.

Levitas posits that 'New Labour' has moved away from RED to an inconsistent use of MUD and SID. Levitas suggests that by stating that exclusion is not about poverty the government is able to justify action that does not address poverty directly (the move away from RED). Whilst insightful, this can be viewed as a 'grand conspiracy', which overlooks the benefits that a 'holistic' Connexions service can bring. There will be many genuine examples of how Connexions personal advisers have 'enabled' the young people they work with. That said, empowerment of whole groups of disadvantaged young people is something else. Roberts states, 'guidance may assist but it cannot be the main answer to the disadvantages that arise from the wider socio-economic inequalities' (2002: 9).

Integrated guidance practice – supplying the tools for the box

Nonetheless, whilst there is a clear need for a critical debate about what may be a socially constructed problem, practitioners do have to get on with the job. What models are careers advisers using within this inclusive agenda? Many will be using the models learned in their initial training albeit with them having been adapted with experience in practice.

The analogy of the toolbox is useful here. In the training of career advisers a basic framework is given to provide the trainee with a structure on which to build their skills. In its simplest terms the process taught provides the structure of the box. The internal compartments can represent the knowledge, competence and experience of the practitioner. The lower sections are filled with underpinning theories and the upper sections with a range of guidance and counselling skills.

But what models are used in the training of practitioners in the UK? Although the Qualification in Careers Guidance has specific educational and professional aims and intended learning outcomes, defined by the awarding body, course centres use different approaches in their teaching. Many, but not all, teach guidance theory and skills using the Egan three-stage 'Skilled Helper Model' (Egan 1998). The alternative route to qualification for the statutory sector via National (or Scottish) Vocational Qualifications (training whilst in work) also uses a three-stage approach influenced by this process model. Process models have been criticised for recommending practice that is based on white, hierarchical, male assumptions of individual development. Although these approaches emphasise the importance of empathy, they offer little advice on how to empathise with people from different cultures or from marginalised groups (Reid 1999). Based on counselling models that tend to be built around individual problem solving, these approaches can mask the wider causes of inequality. The view is that individual, 'personal' intervention will help individuals to break out of the spiral of disadvantage which is in some way caused by their own inaction (Irving 2001).

If practice hopes to resonate with the real lives of individuals, career guidance training needs therefore to examine with some seriousness the discourses around equal opportunities, social justice and multiculturalism.

We must acknowledge that 'race' is a social construct that many think transcends all other social variables because of its visibility (Carter 1995; Moodley 1998). The historical identity of many 'black' people has been told through a European and colonial subjectifying 'gaze' and is only now being re-written by the people themselves. Clearly a western view of what counts as useful guidance may not match the needs of someone from a different culture where values accorded to family and community relations, values placed on time past, present and future, and the relationship with the natural world, may be at odds. This is also the case *within* cultures where a model based primarily on talking about oneself and individual decision-making can leave some clients craving direction.

Before continuing, let's be clear about what is meant by multicultural here. A multicultural approach is not an exclusive discussion of the impact of race, but means developing an awareness of the potential impact of *any* social variable (e.g. age, gender, social class). The view of multiculturalism being advocated in this chapter should not be confused with a liberal assimilation project that aims to create 'insiders' out of 'outsiders'. Nor should it be confused with a pluralist view that believes that 'anyone can make it', given enough opportunities. For example having an educational activity for minority groups to display and take pride in their cultural heritage may be well meaning, but does little to ameliorate the effects of years of oppression (Kincheloe and Steinberg 1997).

It is also important to recognise that multiculturalism can be used to repress marginalised groups by maintaining their separateness and subordination, so an awareness of the potential to stereotype individuals is essential.

But, whilst acknowledging the power of labelling individuals, refusing to discuss group identity in the belief that individual agency is more important than social context, can undermine the collective experience of marginalised people and diminish the real effects of unequal power relationships. Such posturing can be disempowering for the individuals that we seek to support.

Many of the guidance approaches that are used assume a high level of resourcefulness in clients. The experiences of marginalised clients will be different and their capacity to effect change will be influenced by the social context. Outside the cocoon of the guidance interview, a client's ability to make things happen in the larger context of their life will depend on their access to social and economic power.

Returning to the significance for career guidance training, the multicultural approach within counselling and psychotherapy has produced work that emphasises the importance of social context. The work of Ivey *et al.* (1997) and Sue *et al.* (1996) in counselling and psychotherapy, and Bimrose (1996) in guidance, supports both an integrated and multicultural approach. An integrated approach advocates the use of particular strategies as relevant to the client's needs. This leads to a collaborative relationship where negotiated decisions are made about what works best for the client. A multicultural approach will help practitioners to understand their clients' real rather than presumed needs.

Equal opportunities or social justice?

So, if career guidance is fuelled by an inclusion agenda, guidance needs to include an exploration of clients' perceptions of their gender, family, school, community, and historical or socio-economic positions. How are career advisers in training in the UK prepared for this?

On the Qualification in Careers Guidance programme there is a unit that explores equal opportunities, values and ethics. This exploration will cover personal and professional understanding of these terms, and include an understanding of how anti-discriminatory legislation and related codes of practice operate within career guidance work. Some course centres extend this understanding to include a critical understanding of the concept of social justice, which moves beyond the idea that the same access to opportunity is sufficient to create equality. This may include a study of the complex relationship between power and knowledge, and how this affects the way knowledge about disadvantage is produced, accepted and rejected.

Other course centres or training programmes do not go that far and may offer an approach that is stuck in outdated notions of equal opportunities. The concept of social justice however, aims to move towards a society that is anti-oppressive, where the distribution of social benefits is based on fairness. This moves beyond the notion of 'the same for all' and recognises that many will need much more support and resources than others. A 'same for all' approach can be criticised for recommending interventions based on assumptions about shared goals and values. Within practice this viewpoint seeks to adapt behaviour to fit with the prevailing discourse in any society about what is normal. This suggests that there is one universally held goal, rather than acknowledging a plurality of diverse goals of equal value.

Although focused on difference, there is a pluralist assumption in the above that an acceptance of difference does not challenge the dominant western ideology. The experiences of marginalised groups become depoliticised, devalued and hidden. By contrast, critical multiculturalists work to expose the hidden processes that ensure that marginalised groups remain on the periphery despite meritocratic policies to promote equality of opportunity (Kincheloe and Steinberg 1997). An examination of the discourses around inclusion and exclusion then becomes important in order to expose those hidden processes. Policy and practice can ignore the silenced voices of the marginalised unless the taken for granted assumptions in the dominant equal opportunities discourse are questioned. Thinking that career guidance can in some way be a neutral activity divorced from 'politics' is faulty (Irving and Marris 2002). Policy dictates practice, and impartiality as an ideal may be untenable when working with clients who need a partial helper (i.e. biased in their favour).

Pagliano (2000) discusses changes to a career guidance curriculum in Australia, which was found to be limited to traditional methods no longer suited to the changes experienced in multicultural practice. He discusses the need for students to be immersed in the situated lives of their own and their clients' understandings, and details the use of approaches that help to question and deconstruct many of the taken for granted assumptions that inform guidance training and guidance practice. The work for trainees is challenging but the aim is to ensure that they will be able to 'hit the ground running, no matter where they are sent' (Pagliano 2000: 109).

This approach echoes the views of Kincheloe and Steinberg:

> The neglected realm of politics, of political literacy as it relates to everyday life, the workplace and the economic domain and to race and gender, becomes more important than ever. Any attempt to study the nature of social justice must be grounded on a familiarity with the political, that domain of social study that analyses the way power is produced and distributed.
>
> (1997: 103)

Multicultural principles in the counsellor's toolbox

Moving on, Bimrose (1996) points to the discussion offered by D'Andrea and Daniels (1991) of four main approaches in counselling training programmes in the United States. These are relevant to guidance and could be used to evaluate the development of multicultural approaches within career guidance training and practice. Adapted for guidance these stages are:

1. Culturally entrenched: here a process model along with the core counselling skills based on active listening, genuineness, empathy and respect, are all that is needed to be able to work with the client. From a position of unconditional positive regard, practitioners are viewed as being able to rise above any cultural or social differences between themselves and the client.
2. Cross-cultural awakening: here cultural differences are acknowledged but similarities are looked for to diminish difference in a liberal attempt to offer the same guidance across groups. The focus is on applying the same model and the same skills such as empathy and respect.
3. Cultural integrity: this becomes more progressive in that a range of approaches may be considered that allow for cross-cultural communication skills, built on knowledge of different groups. In other words consideration is given to what works best for particular clients.
4. Infusion: this would incorporate multicultural goals in all areas of the

curriculum. Multiculturalism becomes embedded into all areas in the training programme not just the skills-related elements.

Clearly cultural competence on the part of the career guidance practitioner begins in acknowledging the cultural values that inform their own worldview. This is needed to avoid a 'them and us' approach to diversity which sees some groups as 'other', or as people described in deficient terms, i.e. the disaffected, the disengaged, the difficult-to-help or non-English speakers, non-indigenous people. Of course, what we see in others depends very much on where we stand to look. Our particular stance needs to be understood in terms of its social and historical origins.

Sue *et al.* (1995) have developed a matrix that classifies what they view as cross-cultural skills and competencies for counsellors. Under the headings of: a) *awareness of own assumptions, values and biases,* b) *understanding the worldview of the culturally different client,* and c) *developing appropriate intervention techniques and strategies*, they consider the aspects of, *beliefs and attitudes*, *knowledge* and *skills.* The matrix is detailed and readers are directed to the original for that detail, but for career guidance practice we could perhaps summarise in the following way. A practitioner who is culturally competent:

- Ensures they are aware of their own biases and limitations and are knowledgeable about how these affect the guidance process.
- Recognises the range of social variables that lead to cultural difference and are knowledgeable about the effects of oppression, racism, discrimination and stereotyping on themselves and others.
- Understands differences in communication styles and their impact.
- Is open about the guidance process and actively seeks the client's understanding about the purpose of the interaction and their view about ways of working together.
- Actively engages in training and education opportunities to enrich their understanding and effectiveness for working with culturally different groups.
- Is aware of the impact of negative reactions and treatment experienced by culturally different groups and seeks to understand this, and not devalue that experience.
- Understands how and why traditional and established approaches may be inappropriate and seeks out research and other material that will enrich their understanding.
- Engages in outreach work with clients outside of the normal work setting to broaden their understanding.
- Respects clients' beliefs, values and views about what guidance can offer and what their community can offer, and is aware of any conflicting values they may have.

- Values the language of the client and does not judge a language or manner of speech as an impediment to the guidance process, and will refer when their (the practitioner's) linguistic skills are inadequate.
- Recognises that institutionalised methods of assessment may be unhelpful and create barriers.
- Is aware of discriminatory practices at the individual, social and organisational level.
- Makes genuine attempts to advocate with, or lobby on behalf of, clients to overcome relevant discrimination.
- Extends their communication skills so that they are not limited by a singular cultural approach.
- Are open to alternative ways of helping, including using the resources of the client's community.

There is a danger that stereotypical assumptions are made about individuals on the basis of assumed or perceived group membership. Before any assessment of the client's needs takes place, the practitioner must appraise the client as an individual within a cultural and social context. This implies taking time to understand the client's philosophy of life, beliefs, values and assumptions. Effective use of time is a key element to build into the guidance process and its importance in the pursuit of multicultural competence cannot be over emphasised.

A three-stage process model for guidance interviews

Although Fouad and Bingham (1995) have developed a seven-step career counselling model for working with minority ethnic clients, Egan's Skilled Helper approach (1998) will be more familiar to career guidance practitioners and training institutions. The three stages may be worked through with a client over a series of interviews, albeit that each interview will have a beginning, middle and end. Career advisers working as personal advisers with the 'harder-to-help' may have the time allowance to conduct several interviews. However, this should not be assumed as often the young person does not want to commit to that investment in time and may only be seen once or twice.

The tutors at The College of Guidance Studies[1] adapted the Egan model for use in career and educational guidance settings (Fielding and Vautier 1994). It is this model that the chapter will now look at to see if multicultural competencies can be integrated into the framework it offers. Like any model its scope is limited but it aims to provide a foundation for novice practitioners onto which they can build other approaches as their experience develops. It is therefore an integrated approach and tutors encourage trainees to adopt an open mind to 'new' approaches for their continuous professional development.

Stage 1 – Negotiating the Contract and Agreeing the Agenda

- Carry out introductions and explain role
- Help clients to understand the possibilities within the interaction
- Enable client to identify their current situation and guidance needs
- Identify and prioritise objectives for the interaction
- Establish agenda

Stage 2 – Developing Issues and Identifying Goals

- Investigate relevant issues
- Use information to broaden the client's perspective
- Help client to reflect on the implications of choice
- Enable client to establish preferred options/goals

Stage 3 – Planning Action

- Help client to identify possible action
- Assist client to evaluate courses of action
- Help client to choose a course of action
- Timetable action

Figure 13.1 The GOGS three-stage model of guidance interactions.

Source: Fielding and Vautier 1994).

Like the Egan model the COGS model has a number of steps in each stage, and recognises that clients may not always make linear moves through each stage. These steps require particular activities and skills, which are part of the detail not included here, but Figure 13.1 gives a simplified version of the model. The model has also been adapted for use in guidance group work settings.

A way forward – integrating multicultural principles

Stage one – process and skills

Stage one is perhaps the most important part of any interaction – get it wrong and the rest of the interview is likely to be ineffective. We begin negotiating the contract from the minute we meet the client, as we start to build rapport. Stage one takes time and should not be rushed. The client needs time to 'tell their story', and involving them as early as possible in interactive talk in stage one can help to set the tone of the interview. We need clients to talk about what they do know, i.e. if we use the metaphor of a journey, 'where they are now', before we ask them to talk about things they may not know, i.e. ' where they would like to go and how they are going to get there'.

In order to clarify the issues we need to give the client space to tell their story. This is a vital step where we need to encourage clients to tell their stories in their own way. But we need to remember that for some individuals, from our own or different cultures, this will feel odd, unexpected and uncomfortable. Negotiating the contract then does not mean getting the client to see the sense in doing it our way, but is about involving the client from the start of the meeting and asking them about meaningful ways of working together. It is also about explaining and being transparent about our approach and being open to adopting a different approach.

The relevance of getting the client to tell their story is often underestimated by trainees, and indeed often gets rushed in busy practice. The tendency is to brush over the client's perceptions and understanding of their own situation in an impatience to make progress and move the client on. In multicultural settings if we do not take time to find out about our client, and to understand things from their perspective, we are in danger of treating them as stereotypes rather than as individuals. Unless we do this, the issues that are focused on are likely to be the ones identified by the adviser rather than the client.

Evidently, empathy is essential and is understood to be a core skill. But empathy is easy to display when culture is shared but less easy to achieve in cross-cultural communications. Cross-cultural here is not just about ethnicity, it can refer to communication between adults and young people in any culture. Empathy is a way of 'being' with a client and not a skill that a practitioner switches on and off at the right time.

Cross-cultural misunderstanding can also derail rapport-building, crucial for empathic responses. Ivey *et al.* (1997) state that culturally appropriate nonverbal communication is essential if the outcomes of counselling are to be successful. It would be an impossible task to learn all the social messages contained in body language across different cultures, but at the very least we need to be aware of common problems. Ivey *et al.* discuss these in greater detail but we can consider the following general points:

1 Misattribution: we can assign the wrong or unintended meaning to non-verbal behaviour. This is of course two-way; we can also send the wrong signal.
2 Misunderstanding the context: 'rules' about behaviour in formal and informal settings can vary across cultures.
3 Missing signals: gestures and body language are often subtle and can be missed by a person from a different culture. (Similarly words may be the same but the meaning can alter with the use of pace, cadence and emphasis.)

An important task for the practitioner is to be alert to the value they place on the above through the exploration of their own body language, cultural values and beliefs. They will then be better able to suspend judgement when assessing the meaning of nonverbal and verbal cross-cultural communication. We need to reach conclusions about meaning on what seems normal for our client, not normal for us. This will take time and suggests the need for careful, not rushed, steps in stage one.

There are also differences in amounts of eye contact deemed appropriate plus differences in: how to sit (opposite, at an angle, side-by-side); the use of space and closeness; amounts of touching; voice levels and the importance of time structuring, i.e. keeping to appointment times. It would be the practitioner's responsibility to become familiar with these aspects if working often with particular groups, but what can we do generally to improve our multicultural competence?

It is vital that we are aware of our own nonverbal and verbal communication style in order to be alert to differences between any client and ourselves. Although difficult, we could try the technique of mirroring to match our own way of communicating to that of the client we seek to help. Clearly this is only a first step, as a deeper understanding of the meanings of a particular cultural communication style requires direct engagement for a fuller immersion in order to avoid superficial use of this technique.

Stage two – process and skills

When working cross-culturally we need to be sure we build flexibility into our model and ensure that we share information appropriately, using the skill of challenging in culturally sensitive ways.

For example, a model derived from a humanistic/existential worldview sees individuals as having agency to make and implement their own decisions. It would be inappropriate to challenge a client about individual indecision if they see the family and the community as the decision-making 'agent'. So, we need to pay attention to the social context of the client and work towards goals that are meaningful for them. In helping clients to see new perspectives we should not ignore their current knowledge and understanding about what is possible.

Stage three – process and skills

The purpose of this stage is to give clients clear ideas about how they can achieve the goals agreed in stage two. Goals will only be attainable if they are specific and clear to the client. The action that follows must be meaningful for the client and 'doable' in terms of the social context of their lives. The exploration and evaluation of possible steps is important for clients, so that they develop meaningful strategies. Again when working cross-culturally the adviser needs to suspend judgement and avoid the temptation to impose ideas on the client. When working with disadvantaged groups there is a greater need to advocate on behalf of the client and not to assume the client will be able to overcome the significant barriers they may face in implementing action. All of the above, incorporating multicultural competencies, can be explored and practised in training via role-play and other methods.

What else can training do to increase multicultural competency?

The chapter has already discussed the need for an investigation of the political nature of guidance work and for an exploration of how power shapes discourses within the field. But what are the other practical activities that can promote multicultural competency? Most courses will involve a period of placement activity. This can be used to increase self-awareness of their own cultural values if trainees are encouraged to spend time in an agency with people that are culturally different. A follow up activity would be to reflect on these differences and log them in some way, perhaps through a reflective portfolio.

Trainees can be encouraged to visit unfamiliar cultural groups to discuss their views about the purpose and process of guidance and to share their new knowledge of the group with their peers, or alternatively, to invite group representatives to speak to peers on the topic. Tutors may do the latter, but could trainees be encouraged to own the process more?

Not everyone finds writing a reflective portfolio enjoyable or even helpful, but many professional courses expect some kind of reflective account of learning to take place. It is possible to achieve this in different ways other than some endless paper chase; can course requirements encompass creative ways of doing this? For example, by utilising more narrative approaches, with the use of video recording or art works.

It is also important that the skills needed to become a reflective practitioner are developed via the use of research articles and other journals. Courses will aim to develop the ability of the trainee to become a critical consumer of research findings. However post-qualification, academic journals may be difficult to access when in the workplace, but there are now a growing number of useful career research websites that trainees and practitioners can visit. Professional institutions can help to identify these in the periodicals they produce.

Conclusion

Multicultural competency is more than an understanding of relevant anti-discriminatory legislation and ethical codes. Beyond what individuals do, this needs to include the integration of multicultural principles at the organisational level. And a reminder here at the end of the chapter that in advocating a multicultural approach we are including those that are disadvantaged by a range of social variables. Our policy and practice in both training guidance practitioners and delivering services to clients, needs to be positively anti-oppressive rather than passively based on equality of opportunity.

We also need to avoid labelling individuals and expecting certain behaviour due to perceived membership of particular groups. A person may fall into a number of social groups, and as such categories are socially constructed. Nevertheless the most significant group aspect is likely to affect, positively or negatively, the life chances of an individual.

In terms of social justice we need to find new ways of working with a diverse population. This will become even more important with the new workforce arriving from Eastern Europe and elsewhere, from cultures that do not share a colonial past with their 'host' country.

Trainers of career guidance practitioners have a responsibility to work beyond their traditional 'tool box' models. Multicultural principles need to be embedded in any training programme, not merely 'bolted on', for meaningful integration to take place. We will not achieve social justice in the twenty-first century if we continue to promote models that belongs in the past.

Note

1 COGS, now the Department of Career and Personal Development at Canterbury Christ Church University College.

Bibliography

Bimrose, J. (1996) 'Multiculturalism', in R. Bayne, I. Horton and J. Bimrose (eds) *New Directions in Counselling*, London: Routledge.

Carter, R.T. (1995) *The Influence of Race and Racial Identity in Psychotherapy*, London: Wiley.

D'Andrea, M. and Daniels, J. (1991) 'Exploring the different levels of multicultural counselling training in counsellor education', *Journal of Counselling and Development*, 70: 78–85.

Department for Education and Employment (2000) *Connexions: The Best Start in Life for Every Young Person*, London: DfEE.

Egan, G. (1998) *The Skilled Helper*, 6th edn, California: Brooks/Cole.

Fielding, A. and Vautier, E. (1994) *Guidance Explored: An Integrated Approach to Guidance Interventions*, unpublished, Swanley: The College of Guidance Studies.

Fouad, N.A. and Bingham, R.P. (1995) 'Career counselling with racial and ethnic minorities', in W.B. Walsh and S.H. Osipow (eds) *Handbook of Vocational Psychology: Theory, Research and Practice*, New Jersey: Lawrence Erlbaum Associates.

Institute of Career Guidance (2002) 'Career guidance: one aim, three routes', *ICG Briefing Paper*, December, Stourbridge: Institute of Career Guidance.

Irving, B.A. (2001) *Transforming Career Guidance Training: Towards a Socially Just Approach*, paper presented at an education staff seminar, James Cook University, Australia.

Irving, B.A. and Marris, L. (2002) 'A context for Connexions: towards an inclusive framework', in Institute of Career Guidance (ed.) *Career Guidance. Constructing the Future: Social Inclusion, Policy and Practice*, Stourbridge: Institute of Career Guidance.

Ivey, A.E., Ivey, M.B. and Simeg-Morgan, L. (1997) *Counseling and Psychotherapy: A Multicultural Perspective*, 4th edn, Needham Heights: Allyn & Bacon.

Kincheloe, J.L. and Steinberg, S.F. (1997) *Changing Multiculturalism*, Buckingham: Open University Press.

Law, B. (1981) 'Community interaction: a "mid-range" focus for theories of career development in young adults', *British Journal of Guidance and Counselling*, 9(2): 142–158.

Levitas, R. (1998) *The Inclusive Society? Social Exclusion and New Labour*, Hampshire: Macmillan Press.

Moodley, R. (1998) '"I say what I like": frank talk(ing) in counselling and psychotherapy', *British Journal of Guidance and Counselling*, 26(4): 495–508.

Pagliano, P. (2000) 'Careers guidance preparation: (re)constructing the future', in Institute of Career Guidance (ed.) *Career Guidance. Constructing the Future: A Global Perspective*, Stourbridge: Institute of Career Guidance.

Reid, H.L. (1999) 'Barriers to inclusion for the disaffected: implications for "preventive" careers guidance work with the under-16 age-group', *British Journal of Guidance and Counselling*, 27(4): 539–554.

Roberts, K. (2002) 'Introduction', in Institute of Career Guidance (ed.) *Career Guidance. Constructing the Future: Social Inclusion, Policy and Practice*, Stourbridge: Institute of Career Guidance.

Rogers, C. (1961) *On Becoming a Person*, Boston: Houghton Mifflin.

Sue, D.W., Arrendondon, P. and McDavis, R.J. (1995) 'Multicultural counseling competencies and standards: a call to the profession', in J.G. Ponterotto, J.M. Casas, L.A. Suzuki and C.M. Alexander (eds) *Handbook of Multicultural Counseling*, California: Sage.

Sue, D.W., Allen, E.I. and Pederson, P.B. (1996) *A Theory of Multicultural Counseling and Therapy*, Pacific Grove, CA: Brooks/Cole.

Chapter 14

Challenging careers

Perspectives from auto/biographical research

Linden West

Introduction

I want to reflect on notions of career and guidance in what has been described as a 'postmodern', 'globalised' world in which, for many, predictable career trajectories have broken down. This is a world which places immense strains on people through processes of individuation and having to cope with unprecedented change. Economic liberalisation and individuation mean that people, like it or not, have to take greater responsibility for the circumstances, rules and direction of their lives. But, paradoxically, in the weakening of historic social scripts that shaped people's lives, there are more opportunities for experiment with our identities, however unequal opportunity structures remain (see Roberts this volume). Managing a career, in a broad biographical sense, in such a paradoxical world, requires the capacity and resources to make meaningful choices and to constantly re-orientate oneself afresh (West 1996; Alheit and Dausien 2002). The questions at the heart of this paper are what enables individuals to become, even in oppressive situations, more active agents in their lives, including challenging injustice; and what are the implications for the guidance community?

The context

The implications of a changing culture for peoples' biographies are immense. Whereas in previous agrarian and industrial societies, people lived according to more or less clearly defined social scripts, economic change can mean these may quickly unravel or become redundant. The new global economic order involves fund managers, banks, corporations as well as millions of individual investors, transferring massive sums of money from one part of the globe to another, at the flick of a switch. Traditional economies, communities and shared biographical expectations can fracture overnight.

Many working-class men, for instance, in the traditional industrial communities of Britain, have lost conventional roles, and may struggle to cope with lost status. Intimate family relationships, including those between fathers and sons, can be dramatically affected as old opportunity structures collapse and the lifeworlds these sustained disappear. For those in paid work, under the impact of neo-liberal economics and managerialism, the increasing demands on time alongside growing occupational insecurity can increase psychological pressure across social groups. If most people want some degree of security, they are told, in the neo-liberal mantra, that this is illusion in a cut-throat competitive world (Elliot and Atkinson 1998).

Ulrich Beck (1997) has observed that individuals face a range of insecurities at a time when the welfare state is in retreat and people have lost faith in national governments or corporations to address their concerns. The political agenda, in this view, is dominated by a pervasive neo-liberal consensus, in which responsibility and risk have shifted from the state to the individual and families. Individuals under the banner of lifelong learning are 'encouraged' to take greater responsibility for preparing themselves for the flexible career. Or, face the consequences of exclusion. And those most marginalised by economic and cultural transformations are morally and financially cajoled into taking jobs, however short-term, unskilled and low paid, or into training, however purposeless. Learn, or lose benefits; 'upskill', or lose your job (Field 2000). What role is there for guidance in this insecure and, as some see it, morally authoritarian environment (Coffield 1999)?

Guidance in crisis

A neo-liberal world of social fragmentation, increased insecurity and growing inequality has precipitated uncertainty among many professional groups about their role and values, not least as the state also increasingly seeks to regulate professional practices. There is a growing debate about how the guidance community should respond, for instance, to the imperatives of the neo-liberal training and educational agenda. Has the discourse of flexibility and adaptability to the new world order, in which, (so the argument proceeds) there is little or no alternative, penetrated the stories 'guidance' tells itself about its purpose and the message, in turn, to be conveyed to clients? There can, some suggest, be an uncritical, even triumphalist acceptance of the liberalised labour market in which the virtues of flexibility, portfolio careers, and '5 to 9' jobs are trumpeted (Watts 1996; Colley 2000; Collin 2000). Practitioners are under perpetual pressure to facilitate 'realism' in their clients, which, in effect, can become a form of social control (Colley 2000). Privatisation of many careers services and commercial imperatives have compounded, so the argument proceeds, these pressures. Some workers may feel they have little choice but to do the bidding of those in power in a hard, low trust environment, dominated by targets, prescribed outcomes and ubiquitous regulation. Notwithstanding, the critics insist the guidance community is in danger of losing professional bearings as Rogerian values, always fragile in a low status profession, succumb to harsh realism. There is, the argument proceeds, however difficult, a need for a more critical, empowering, and even political commitment, especially among the marginalised, to encourage clients, for instance, to challenge the quality of choices available to them and how they are treated more widely in their lives (Collin 2000); if, that is, client-centredness is to amount to more than empty rhetoric.

The development of the Connexions service in the United Kingdom could bring the issue to a head. There is pressure, fuelled for example, by moral panic over teenage pregnancy or the violence of young working class unemployed men, to use Connexions to discipline, in Foucault's sense, young people, making them fit for the flexible labour market. The assumptions made about young people seem to derive from deficit models, in which they, and their fecklessness, lack of skills or morality, are the root problem. Structural inequalities, poverty and, arguably, the pervasive power of capitalist consumerism to exploit human vulnerability and need, most particularly among the poor, are excluded from the analytical equation. Yet Connexions could provide precious transitional space in which highly marginalised youngsters and adults can take stock, question and take some risks with their career, on slightly more of their own terms.

I want to bring to the debate evidence from 'auto/biographical' research among marginalised adults and young people who are seeking to compose and recompose their careers in difficult, demanding, social and economic conditions (West 1996; 2002). I use two case studies (both distinct but also illuminating common themes across many biographies) to explore the 'cultural psychology' of making choices about career and its parameters as well as to consider the possible role of guidance workers in such processes. The analysis challenges narrow conceptions of career but also some underlying assumptions about human motive, capability and the self, which have been influential in the guidance world. A basic argument is that the self, i.e. who we are and might be, is not fixed, essential and/or susceptible to simplistic classification into personality types, but is deeply contingent, developmental and relational in character. This is a self that is easily paralysed by primitive anxiety at times of transition and uncertainty, about, for instance, its capacity to cope or whether it can ever be good enough in the eyes of others. Such a perspective, drawing on feminist psychoanalysis, has, I argue, profound consequences for how we think about guidance and how workers should think about their role.

The biographical turn

There has been a turn to biographical methods in research in diverse contexts, including addressing the nature of career and processes of change management. The intention has been to engage with those at the heart of such processes and to encourage them to tell their stories (Chamberlayne *et al.* 2000; Crossan *et al.* 2003). This, in part, represents a commitment to empower the marginalised and give them a greater sense of voice. The term 'auto/biography' is used to emphasise the dimension of power in research but also how we draw on others to make sense of our narratives as well as vice-versa (Stanley 1992). Researching the lives of adult learners and young people made me realise how much, in asking questions of others, about learning, managing change and the struggle for some agency in a life, I was asking questions of myself. Michelle Fine (1992) argues for the reflexive and self-reflexive potential of experience, in which the knower is part of the matrix of what is known, and where the researcher (and guidance worker?) needs to ask in what way has s/he shaped the processes of research (or guidance?). For me, this included analysing how gender, class and early family experience shaped my career trajectory and feelings as a man, including the neglect of emotional life (West 2001).

I undertook three major auto/biographical studies over the last decade. The first, beginning in the early 1990s and lasting four years, focused on what motivated particular individuals in marginalised communities to enter Access to higher education programmes. And what enabled them to 'keep on keeping on' in what could be difficult, oppressive situations (West 1996). A second study, using a similar methodology, explored doctors and learning in difficult, demanding inner-city locations, at a time of profound uncertainty in the profession (West 2001). The third involved a group of highly disaffected young people living in marginalised communities in East London. It examined their stories about the impact of a parenting and community arts programme on identities, senses of self and career aspirations (West 2002).

Two case studies

I want to introduce the first case study, Jim, at this stage (all names are pseudonyms). He was a working-class man who entered an Access to higher education programme in a further education college. He lived in Thanet, on the furthermost edge of South East England, a place of economic insecurity, pockets of intense poverty, and a fragile, casualised labour market. Jim, like others in the research, was made redundant on a number of occasions. His story is of taking risks and finding some agency at the sharp and painful edge of the new economic order. His narrative of rebuilding a career evolved, over a period of four years, to encompass the central role of significant others, and of higher education and of fishing in strengthening his sense of self as well as providing space to re-consider his identity, as husband, father, worker and learner.

Gina is a highly disaffected and disturbed young mum, at one time dependent on hard drugs, who lives on a marginalised public housing estate in East London. She participated in a community arts programme. Her story illustrates how supportive others, and the space provided by the community arts, offered resources to enable her to reconsider her career and strengthen her sense of self, however contingently. Both stories challenge, I suggest, narrow, one-dimensional definitions of career as well as some overly 'psychologistic', rationalistic, essentialist and asocial assumptions about the self and human capability, which can dominate the careers world (Edwards 2003).

Jim

The work with Jim, alongside twenty-nine other learners, involved seven interviews over the four years of the study. The cyclical and longitudinal nature of the process enabled, as suggested, strong relationships to form and a sense of dialogue to develop, in which we shared our stories and their interpretation. Men, like Jim, in working-class communities where historic occupational structures and the biographical predictabilities have shattered, can easily become trapped in pretences of coping and psychological defensiveness. Men, especially, may struggle to handle the emotional aspects of lost status, given their relative investment in public roles and how they have been taught to repress anxiety and deny vulnerability (Samuels 1993).

What is interesting about Jim was that he was managing to rebuild his career, in the broadest biographical sense, rather well. He was 35 when we first met, with a wife and two sons. He had a relatively successful time as a painter and decorator, which came to an abrupt end with redundancy in the middle of the 1990's recession. He felt insecure, he said, for most of his working life and knew what it was like to drift. Over three years in higher education, he trained as a radiographer, and distanced himself from his previous identity, as he grew more confident in himself and of making a success of the new project. At first, in the early stages of the Access programme, he was fearful of severing ties with the building trade but this gradually changed as he progressed towards a degree.

His decision to break with the building industry and enter an Access programme, in the early interviews, troubled him greatly. He felt on the margins of two worlds, of college and a previous career, but identified more with the latter. He thought he was taking risks before he believed he could cope. He felt guilty at not providing for his family and struggled with the impact of redundancy, higher education as well as the research. He was anxious about studying and there were constant hints of needing to justify his actions to self as well as others. It was the apparent impossibility of finding another job, which led him towards college and radical change. Had he found work in the building trade, and prospects had been reasonable, for all his reservations, he would probably have continued as before. But he tried and failed in an increasingly fragile economic environment. He might also, he said, have drifted into a career of drink and depression.

In an early interview Jim mentioned, in passing, that his sister had taken an Access programme and she encouraged him to do the same. Towards the end of the research the story developed and he said that he would never have started the degree, or completed it, without her support and challenge. She encouraged him and he was able to identify with her as a role model:

> when she was young, things were a little more torrid. She has been a kind of inspiration to me really. Probably if she hadn't done the course in the first place then I wouldn't have done it you know. Probably because I just wouldn't have thought of doing it more than anything else but it is nice to see somebody in front of you for a bit of guidance.

She helped him believe in himself.

Particular students and teachers helped too, as did fishing and the development of stronger relationships with his sons:

> I look forward to it from one week to the next ... It is a love without a doubt. There is something about that time of day. There is a feeling about it ... You look around, mist on the water, sun coming up, all the wild life jumping out ... There is just a magic about that time of day ... feeling of excitement, get your gear out, can't get it out fast enough, can't wait to get started ... To talk to people who haven't fished, or maybe who have fished and didn't enjoy it, you can't get across your feelings for it properly.
>
> ...Still makes me shake when I catch a good fish and I have caught a lot of good fish, but it still gives me the shakes still. Strange, but I am not alone, there are a lot of people like me ... I feel when I am out there that I am most myself.

There was no stopping Jim in this moment and a quiet reticent man came alive in telling the story. Fishing was what he was good at, as well as, increasingly, radiography, and the balance constituted a new sense of career. Paid work was only part of the picture. Relationships, with his sons and his wife, had become more important. She had educational qualifications and was deeply frustrated at home and in her job as a part-time waitress. They were continuingly negotiating their 'careers' and their relationship improved. She began an Access programme and he was sensitive to her difficulties and frustrations. He was enjoying his family more as he felt better about himself. Higher education, fishing and an important relationship provided space to take some risks with his identity.

Gina: 'cottoning on'

Gina lives in East London, which has been an especial casualty of globalisation and neo-liberal economics as well as, in part, a beneficiary too. From the 1970s East London has been subject to a massive process of de-industrialisation, dramatised most obviously in the closure of the docks but also affecting other traditional trades and industries. Large pockets of what has been termed 'yuppification' co-exist with depressed public housing estates suffering racial violence, drug abuse and growing youth employment. It is a place of widespread educational under-achievement and social exclusion, poor health and poverty (Bardsley *et al.* 1998). East London symbolises, in an acute form, the divided, unequal state of contemporary neo-liberal England.

Gina participated in a parenting and community arts project organised by a body called Theatre Venture. The aim was to engage, via outreach work, disaffected learners in the visual arts and to encourage them to progress into formal arts education or the labour market. The project was ambitious and involved recruiting groups of educationally alienated young men and women (West 2002). Gina participated in a series of workshops called '*Cotton-on*', targeted at young mothers aged 14 to 19. The focus was experiences of pregnancy and parenthood using the visual arts, textile design in particular, but also sculpture, printing, photography and video. In-depth interviews were held with Gina at an early stage of the project and towards the end.

Gina told me that no one had ever really listened. She felt pressurised to participate in education and get a job and yet also wanted to enter college. But she had her child to think of and felt confused, muddled and under pressure, from all sides. Her introduction to the Centre where the Workshops were based was due to the encouragement of a sympathetic Health Visitor. At first she was upset at leaving her daughter in the crèche but she relaxed. She changed, she said, as a result of the parenting programme. There was a time, she insisted, when she could not tolerate mess, in the home or anywhere else, and everything had to be kept in order: 'I hate mess, and everyone goes on at me to let her feed herself'. She had never let her baby play on the floor, in case she got dirty, while upstairs other children were *'romping about'*. She was more at ease now.

She liked the Centre and the peer education project, while *Cotton-on* had given her ideas for the future:

> I would like to go back to college, do an Art A level, but I don't know if I am going to be able to do it at A level ... Because it is getting

> crèche places and it is full time, I may have to do a BTEC first. Eventually I want to go back to my media...

Gina told me in the first interview that she had begun a GNVQ in Media Communications and Production. It was *'just basic media stuff'*, she said, somewhat disparagingly, but she dropped out when pregnant. There was a great anxiety about returning to college, given other pressures in her life, even though, as she put it, she was determined to do so for her daughter.

Three months later, Gina was working intensely on a sculpture:

> When I was pregnant and I didn't really get very big. I made myself a little pregnant belly from a washing basket to put your washing in. I used chicken wire and plaster of Paris and painted it up funny colours. They kind of expressed my mood when I was pregnant, bit dark, dull colours, bit cold.
>
> Yes ... I don't know people who are looking at it probably won't get it, but to me it's a hangover for anger.

Pregnancy was hard and troubling, and she felt, at times, unreal since she did not look pregnant. She was depressed and *'really ill throughout'*. Her mood was translated into the sculpture. She was trying, she said, *'to get across that, the darkness'*. There was no head on the sculpture, either; it was a headless torso, which, she said, was deliberate:

> So there is no head, and I suppose, as I was pregnant I didn't really feel. I suppose all I was, was a baby carrier. That is what I felt. There is no head and no legs because I wasn't actually a person. Like a baby machine. So just middle, just boobs and a belly.

She found sculpting therapeutic: she needed, she realised, to express her feelings about the pregnancy, and of being *'a baby machine'*. But she was past some of that now and the Centre provided a key. She was starting to use brighter colours too, more *'yellows and reds'*, which symbolised feeling better about herself and more alive.

She thought *Cotton-on* was good. She enjoyed it and it gave ideas for a future career. She wanted to enrol on an art course, maybe do an A level, and the workshops offered a range of relevant experience. She applied to do a graphic design course at her local college but was still doubtful about going through with it. She always liked art but an A level might be too much, too soon. It was a big commitment given her present life and responsibilities. There were different and conflicting voices inside her head. She had done GCSE Art at school and she got an A there, which she really enjoyed. But College was another story, a step too far just now.

She dreamed of working for a magazine, doing the page layouts and digital designing. She had gone to a 'Futures Fair' and a careers worker gave her a brochure. She needed to act soon, she said. But she simply could not take too many risks at present, since there was a baby to worry about.

The importance of relationships was at the heart of her narrative, for better as well as worse. A relationship with a youth leader, for instance, who acted as a surrogate parent as well as the art tutor who encouraged her 'to go for it'. Gina talked a great deal about her life history and a pattern of broken relationships, depression and loss of hope. There had been a 'turning point' in her life, she observed. She was sitting at home, one day, and her brother asked what was on television. She could

> reel off the whole of daytime TV, TV guides and I thought, oh my god, how sad. That is all I do, sit at home watching TV, the same shows every day at the same time. I knew it was a bit sad.

Her whole life had been sad, she mused, and she did not want her daughter living that way. It motivated her, Gina, to want to learn, and she enjoyed engaging with others in the group. She talked animatedly about formulating and presenting a case to the local council for more single-parent friendly housing and was deeply involved in peer sex education programmes for schools. She felt good, empowered and enlivened by this and was surprised at what she was able to do, including for others. She found, in short, some voice and agency. She had, on her own admission, a destructive and rebellious side, when she wanted to do nothing and disengaged from the group. Yet she was progressing in her life, in many and diverse ways, including psychologically and, in effect, politically, as she began to challenge the behaviour of those in authority.

Building a career, in the case of Gina, viewed through a biographical lens, has many dimensions. Progression encompassed intimate relationships, political activity as well as education. Ambivalence about college or doing art has to be understood, at least in part, as the consequence of deep-seated anxiety about her capacity to cope or whether she could ever be good enough for or liked by others, or deserved any respect at all. Doing art and the relationships surrounding this, in which she felt listened to, respected as well as understood, perhaps for the first time in her life, were central to her progression. Story telling, and devising a new, more vibrant and reflexive narrative, was also important, both in sculpting and even in the research, as she felt listened to by me. Stories are the prime means by which we can create more meaning, direction and agency in a life. There are important lessons here for guidance and for thinking about what guidance workers actually need to do.

On becoming a subject

For a young woman like Gina, but also Jim and others in the research, progression and the struggle to build a new identity, however precariously, on more of their own terms, requires considerable courage. Risk taking is hard when people feel fragile, inadequate and riddled with anxiety about whether they can cope, will be accepted, liked or are even likeable. A person, any person, needs to feel sufficiently believed in to enter a new community of practice, such as higher education or an arts group, and to exploit the space and resources on offer. They have to be able to see themselves, however fleetingly, in the eyes of others as well as self, as a learner in higher education, a radiographer, budding artist or political activist. They have to be able to tolerate the deep ambivalence of moving from the safety of the periphery and of the familiar towards embracing a new identity and membership of a different group (Ainley *et al.* 1999). Engaging with what is new and different, and investing of self in the process, can easily evoke intense anxiety about failure and rejection and of being found wanting all over again.

Hollway and Jefferson (2000), drawing on the clinical work of psychoanalyst Melanie Klein, argue that anxiety is fundamental to the human condition and that unconscious defences come into play when a self and identity are threatened. Klein argued that defences against anxiety operate in relationships between people, both in early as well as subsequent experience, particularly when something unfamiliar and unsettling is encountered. Defences can include disparaging what may be offered, or a self's capacity to learn and/or staying on the periphery of a group, maybe acting out in destructive, self-defeating ways. But defences can be lowered, over time, as significant others, a sister, teacher, art tutor, therapist, researcher and/or a guidance and Connexions worker, contain some of the anxiety and provide sufficient reliability, psychological consistency, unconditional acceptance, challenge as well as inspiration. This can enable people like Jim or Gina to enter a transitional space, whether in art, higher education, a new relationship or in challenging the treatment of single mums by a local council, and take some risks with their identities, find some agency and create a stronger self in the process.

The psychoanalytic theory of the self, which underlies this perspective, is in sharp contrast to the overly essentialist, individualistic, unitary and rationalist self, which has been influential in careers and guidance theory (Edwards 2003). The psychoanalytic self, in feminist object-relations theory, for example, is deeply and perpetually contingent, born in the quality of relationships in which it is embedded and whether these relationships provide sufficient legitimacy, nourishment, reassurance as well as appropriate challenge. We develop, or shrivel, in shared spaces of affective intercourse, in which there is fundamental overlapping of one and another.

The infant, for instance, can be said to exist in the gestures and meaning of others. Processes of communication, or risk taking and learning, cannot be reduced to participants in isolation (Diamond 1998). As with an infant, a young person or adult, at moments of vulnerability, can feel frightened, potentially overwhelmed and incapable and thus retreat from engagement, however unconsciously. Conversely, if the affective space is good enough, and there is sufficient acceptance, support and encouragement, then a person can move from the edge, and over-defensiveness, into a fuller engagement in life.

Conclusion, and beginnings?

How does this analysis relate to guidance and guidance workers, including what they need to do and know? Clearly, the idea of career needs to be conceptualised more holistically, informed by a biographical imagination, especially in a fragmented, individualistic and consumerist society, in which older social scripts of class, family and locality have weakened; if that is, clients are to be central to the work, rather than at an extreme, reduced to the status of commodities that have to be better marketed in a hard, neo-liberal world. Conceiving a career in the wider biographical sense also involves challenging conventional distinctions between private and public worlds or between progression narrowly conceived and other aspects of the lifeworld. Moreover, if career is to be conceived more holistically, so too must the activities of guidance workers, which as Herr (1997) argues, must encompass a continuum of intervention processes which range from facilitating self and occupational awareness, an imaginative exploration of different possibilities and the learning of career planning skills to a fusion of career and personal counselling. To which might be added a commitment to fairness and social justice. Truly being alongside a young person like Gina, and understanding the world through her eyes, is always and inevitably a political act necessitating, among other things, challenges to deficit models of people and their lives; being truly alongside, in fact, often brings deep respect and even admiration for the capacity of particular individuals to 'keep on keeping on' in the most testing of experience. All this might not change a whole world, or shake the pervasive class inequalities that shape opportunity structures, but it can make a real difference to one life.

Such an analysis may evoke mixed reactions among guidance workers ranging from 'we do this already' to apprehension about what is required. To work effectively with someone like Gina requires the ability to listen and engage authentically while also dealing with anger, projection and acting out. It necessitates self-knowledge, political commitment as well as technical knowledge. I want to illustrate my point, by way of ending, with reference to a GP, Dr Daniel Cohen. He, too, was under pressure to meet targets and follow clinical guidelines in what he termed a ten-minute, instrumental culture. He worked in a difficult area of inner-London, among many fragile, even disturbed, people. But he passionately believed in narrative-based, person-centred, and empowering medicine. He suffered psychological difficulties in his own life, in a profession that has tended to neglect, even disparage, the psychological aspects of the work. Yet, for Daniel, self and cultural awareness, alongside the more technical and scientific aspects of being a doctor, was at the core of being a more effective practitioner (West 2001).

He told me about a Somali woman refugee who came to the surgery. She was an asylum seeker and a 'problem' for the authorities. Daniel gave her some of the time and attention she craved. One day she brought him a gift and he was immensely moved. It was, he felt, a symbol that he was providing 'a secure base' in the sense of support and unconditional regard. She felt listened to and understood for the first time in this country. They ended up having 'the most extraordinary conversation . . . about Darwinian evolution in relation to why were her children getting asthma and eczema . . . when children didn't get it in Somalia and the way the immune system might be adapted for one environment'. He found himself having a conversation that was part of her becoming a person again and she was able to act in new, more assertive, yes, and political, ways with the authorities.

All of us, whatever our profession or background, have experience of feeling lost, bewildered, angry, stupid, rejected, misunderstood, redundant and/or inadequate. 'Globalisation' and the uncertainties, anxieties as well as new possibilities this brings, can unsettle us all. Each of us need space and good enough relationships to enable us to cope, take risks and challenge the stories others may impose upon us. Reflecting on our own autobiographies, as professionals, in training, continuing professional development and psychotherapy, as Daniel Cohen did, can enable us to connect more effectively and auto/biographically with the other who may be struggling on the margins of the new liberal order. Therein lies, perhaps, the big 'auto/biographical' challenge to the guidance community: remembering and learning from the fragile humanity we all share, in an uncertain and increasingly insecure world but one offering new opportunities too.

Bibliography

Ainley, P., Cohen, P., Hey, V. and Wengraf, T. (1999) *Studies in Learning Regeneration*, London: UEL Centre for New Ethnicities Research.

Alheit, P. and Dausien, B. (2002) 'Lifelong learning and biographicity', in A. Bron and M. Schemmann (eds) *Social Science Theories in Adult Education Research, Bochum Studies in International Adult Education*, 3: 211–241. Munster: LIT.

Bardsley, M., Baker, M., Bhan, A., Farrow, S., Gill, M., Jacobson, B. and Morgan, D. (1998) *The Health of Londoners, a Public Health Report for Londoners*, London: Kings Fund.

Beck, U. (1997) *The Reinvention of Politics: Rethinking Modernity in a Global Social Order*, Cambridge: Polity Press.

Chamberlayne, P., Bornat, J. and Wengraf, T. (eds) (2000) *The Turn to Biographical Methods in the Social Sciences: Comparative Issues and Examples*, London: Routledge.

Coffield, F. (1999) 'Breaking the consensus: lifelong learning as social control', *British Journal of Educational Research*, 25(4): 479–499.

Colley, H. (2000) 'Deconstructing "realism" in career planning: how globalisation impacts on vocational guidance', in Institute of Career Guidance (ed.) *Career Guidance: Constructing the Future, a Global Perspective*, Stourbridge: Institute of Career Guidance.

Collin, A. (2000), 'A reconceptualisation of career: implications for careers guidance and education', in Institute of Career Guidance (ed.) *Career Guidance. Constructing the Future, a Global Perspective*, Stourbridge: Institute of Career Guidance.

Crossan, B., Field, J., Gallagher, J. and Merrill, B. (2003) 'Understanding participation in learning for non-traditional adult learners: learning careers and the construction of learning identities', *British Journal of Sociology*, 24(1): 55–67.

Diamond, N. (1998) 'On Bowlby's legacy', in M. Marrone (ed.) *Attachment and Interaction*, London: Jessica Kingsley.

Edwards, A. (ed.) (2003) *Challenging Biographies: Relocating the Theory and Practice of Careers Work*, Canterbury: Canterbury Christ Church University College.

Elliot, L. and Atkinson, D. (1998) *The Age of Insecurity*, London: Verso.

Field, J. (2000) *Lifelong Learning and the New Educational Order*, Stoke-on-Trent: Trentham Books.

Fine, M. (1992) 'Passions, politics and power', in M. Fine (ed.) *Disruptive Voices, the Possibilities of Feminist Research*, Michigan: the University Press.

Herr, E. (1997) 'Career counselling: a process in process', in *British Journal of Guidance and Counselling*, 25(1): 81–93.

Hollway, W. and Jefferson, T. (2000) *Doing Qualitative Research Differently*, London: Sage.

Samuels, A. (1993) *The Political Psyche*, London: Routledge.

Stanley, L. (1992) *The Auto/biographical I. The Theory and Practice of Feminist Research*, Manchester: University Press.

Watts, A.G. (1996) 'Socio-political ideologies in guidance', in A.G. Watts, B. Law, J. Killeen, J. Kidd and R. Hawthorne (eds) *Rethinking Careers Education and Guidance: Theory, Policy and Practice*, London: Routledge.

West, L. (1996) *Beyond Fragments, Adults, Motivation and Higher Education; a Biographical Analysis*, London: Taylor and Francis.

West, L. (2001) *Doctors on the Edge: General Practitioners, Health and Learning in the Inner-city*, London: Free Association Books.

West, L. (2002) *Glimpses Across the Divide*, London: London Arts and the University of East London.

Index

achievement 12, 65, 88–90, 92, 110–11; academic 68; of career aspirations 101; educational 67, 123; factors 28; low 63; student 119, 122–3; under- 192
ageism 20
anti-oppressive practice 20, 184
assessment 59–61, 63–4, 94–5, 179; mainstream methods of 64; pre-assessment 94; schemes 79; self-assessment 67, 150; techniques 63
awareness 19–20, 50, 64, 108, 125–6, 168–9, 175, 178, 196; class 138; critical 126, 150, 168; cultural 59, 197; opportunity 19, 77; political 95; raising of 76, 167–8

biographical methods 189

capitalism 100–1, 111, 155, 170; liberal 36; welfare 7, 25–6, 28–30, 33–7
career behaviour 93–4; women's 86–7, 90–3, 95
career development 41, 44, 49–50, 91–2, 94, 96, 116–18, 124; theory 49–52, 87, 172; women's 88, 91–6, 100
career education 5, 15–17, 19–21, 76–7, 79–80, 114–16, 118–19, 122, 124, 170; culturally sensitive approach to 78, 82; curriculum 114–18, 121–22, 124; materials 83; (for) Muslim girls 72, 80–1; programmes 77–9, 94; reconstructed model of 19
career guidance 17, 25, 93, 116, 130, 147–8, 178; class-blind 138–9; critical framework 26, 38; economic value of 29; influences on practice 27–8; intervention models used in training 172–3, 175, 179; multicultural approaches within training 177, 184; relationship with welfare capitalism 28, 30–7; relevance of class to 134–5, 140–1; socially just practice 35, 176; theory 139, 172
career education and guidance 1, 4–7, 10, 18–21, 57, 61, 76–7
career exploration 68, 77–8, 93
career management 18, 20, 77–8, 109; life- 96
career options 60, 94, 168
career theory 6, 14–15, 27, 88, 93, 100, 172
careers work 41–2, 48; opportunity-structure theory 41, 50
choice(s) 2, 6–7, 13–5, 36, 46, 51, 57, 72–3, 75, 80, 87, 137, 180; biased 153; career 27–9, 33, 35, 45, 68, 72, 89–90, 92, 126, 167; degrees of 41, 53; individual 14, 20, 25, 80, 110; enablement of 41–3; making choices 4, 16, 34, 41, 75–7, 94–5, 186, 188; occupational 104
citizenship 3, 8, 74, 173; active 17; critical political 14; education 19, 169; full rights 74, 143, 155, 165
collaborative: action 19; partnerships 66; relationship 175; service programs 124; work 57
collective 6, 16, 19, 37, 72, 73, 170, 175; collectively oriented 62; culture 73, 78; good 3–4, 14, 169; interests 20; rights 2, 83; wellbeing 100
communication skills 150, 179
competence-based models of training 17
competition 3, 12, 20, 82, 119–21, 135, 167; global competition 1–2, 37, 111
competitiveness 11, 114, 120, 138,

comprehensive schooling 57, 144, 153
compulsory education 17, 80
compulsory schooling 1, 56
Connexions 17, 42,173, 188; worker 195
cooperative work 153
critical citizens 56, 158, 166
critical learners 16, 144–5
critical understanding 19, 176
critical thinking 67, 167, 170
cultural competence 178
cultural diversity 7, 56, 59–61, 67, 69, 83, 165
culture 6, 27–8, 42–3, 46, 48–9, 51, 53, 59, 64, 66, 68, 72–6, 78–83, 95, 106, 134, 141, 154, 169, 174–5, 181, 184, 186; dominant 16, 74; majority 13, 60; Maori 34; school 57, 60, 69
curriculum 59–61, 67, 72, 114, 116–17, 121–4, 137, 154, 167–8, 178; culturally specific 68; ethnocentric 72; inclusive 65, 69; informal *(hidden)* 57, 66–7; mainstream 119

decision making 105, 126, 144, 149; career 90, 93; individual 175, 182; needs 93; processes 13, 68, 95, 170; skills 126–7
democracy 2, 121–2, 165
democratic engagement 7, 14, 17
democratic and inclusive society 11, 21
dependency 34, 52; *welfare* 30
disabilities 7–8, 34, 78, 114–15, 117–122, 124–7; learning 58, 63, 120; physical 21, 58
disablism 20
disadvantaged: classes 140; families 135; people with disabilities 120–1, 127; students 58, 115–17; young people 160, 173
discrimination 60–1, 67–8, 73–4, 77, 80, 82, 89, 109, 146, 179; anti- 12, 101, 130; effects of 16, 178; formal 92; job 115; knowledge of 94; sex 91; forms of 20, 78, 101, 106, 152
domination *see* oppression

emancipatory ideologies 130
employability skills 2, 20, 126–72, 150, 173; development of 5, 17
employment 2, 5, 15–16, 29–34, 88, 103–5, 119–20, 123, 132–5, 137–9, 163–5, 192; equality 110; equity 100, 115; exclusion from 152; gendered segregation in 104; insecurity 10, 111; opportunities 16, 81, 96, 169; paid employment 3, 12, 18, 36, 95–6, 101–2, 121, 145; participation in 107; patterns of 87–8; women 91, 106, 109
empowerment 149, 173
equality 10, 31–2, 77, 82, 92, 109–10, 122, 159, 168, 176; of opportunity 11–12, 18, 21, 115, 154, 184; of opportunities 57, 60, 165
equity 19, 56–7, 61, 100, 102–4, 109, 115, 169; neo-liberal approaches to 110; promotion of 66–7, 69, 116, 122
ethnicity 7, 12, 41, 51, 72, 78, 92–3, 104, 172, 181
evaluation of students 65
expectations 4, 49, 51, 63, 65, 75, 90, 118, 188; biographical 186; career 146; family 42; gender 95; success 59; work 89, 169

feminist psychoanalysis 188
freedom 41–9, 51–3, 96, 106, 166; of choice 28, 36, 105; individual 11, 169

gender 12–13, 35–6, 72–3, 76, 80–3, 89, 91, 93–4, 102–3, 110, 176; disparities 104, 106; equality 103, 107–8, 169; gap 105, 108; role socialisation 75, 90, 92, 95
global capital 2, 10, 159, 161
global economy 11, 145, 154–5
globalisation 1–2, 30, 34–5, 56, 100–1, 110–11, 119, 127, 135, 154, 158–9, 151, 197; effects of 121; process 25

'Honest broker' 25, 28, 37
human capital 11
human rights 100, 102–5, 107, 109–11

identity 67, 73–4, 80, 83, 90, 104, 149, 190, 195; group 63, 175; historical 174; self- 13, 16
inclusive curriculum *see* curriculum
inclusive society 14, 21, 74, 83
individual choice *see* choice(s)
individual responsibility 78, 103
inequalities 5, 11, 56–8, 63, 69, 106, 110; class 139–41, 147, 152, 154, 196; sources of 60–1, 66; structural 2, 12, 16, 18, 188

inequitable practices 12, 56, 69, 148
injustice(s) 36, 67, 126; challenging 6, 21, 130, 168, 186; social 6, 34, 166, 170

labour market 4, 11, 15, 33, 76, 134, 138, 147–8, 165, 192; causalised 146, 189; changing 2, 120, 163; critical exploration of 15, 168; engagement in the 3, 11–12; entry to 77; equal access to 144; flexible 34, 188; formal 164; global 5, 10, 29; inequitable practices in the 12, 17; liberalized 187; opportunities in 5, 18; participation in 11, 16, 31, 37, 145
liberalism 21, 111
lifelong learning 29, 32, 76, 95

marginalisation 61, 109, 143; at risk of 18
marginalised groups 174–6, 188–9
meaningful learning 66, 153
meritocracy 140, 146
meritocratic 2, 12; policies 176; principles 11; society 140
mono-cultural society 69
multicultural competence 182
multiculturalism 74

neo-liberal: agenda 102, 187; discourse 152; economics 2–3, 187, 192; individualistic conception 2; limitations of approaches to equity 110; macro-environment affecting career guidance 35; policies 154, 159; world 187, 196
neo-liberalism 101–2, 108–10
new Right 25

oppression 6, 12–13, 73; effects of 175, 178; forms of 20

parental involvement 62
participative dialogue 21
personal barriers 18, 148
poverty 1, 4, 32, 34, 36, 107, 110–11, 135, 143, 151–2, 160, 173, 188
power 12, 111; relations 4, 6; unequal 140, 175–7, 183, 188–9

race 2, 12, 41, 72–3, 76, 78, 89, 92, 94, 174–5, 177; inequality 36
racism 1, 20, 67, 101, 178; in the labour market 76
religion 51, 72, 74–6, 78, 80, 82, 169
religious: affiliations 83; beliefs 3, 13, 73; practices 106
role models 124; career 68

school failure 59, 147, 149, 151
self-awareness 15–16, 68, 77, 125, 148, 183, 196–7
self-determination 3, 28, 33, 124–6
sexism 20, 91, 101
social autonomy 34
social change(s) 6, 10, 91, 93, 108; agents of 126
social class 2, 36, 41, 51, 73, 76, 89, 92, 94, 130–2, 136–8, 140, 169, 175
social cohesion 1, 3, 116, 152, 154
social democratic approach 31–3, 36
social exclusion 139–40, 143–6, 149–52, 154–5, 169, 192; *see also* marginalisation
social inclusion 11, 37, 77, 144, 151–2; agenda 12, 173; policies 32, 76
social justice 6, 17–19, 36–8, 56, 60, 74, 93, 95–6, 103, 115–16, 121–2, 158–9, 165, 169, 174, 184, 196; agenda 130; alternative visions of 12; concept of 10, 176–7; critical-recognitive perspective 10, 13, 18; democratic and participative form 14; distributive model of 11; *economic* demands and 25–6; 'globalising' 144, 154–5; principles of 60, 127; promotion of 66, 83, 95, 120, 148, 150
social mutuality (state sponsored provision) 11
social order 11, 17, 121, 151
social sequestration 53
status quo 20
success 2, 11–12, 18, 20, 33, 74, 88–9, 92–3, 110, 139, 147, 149; academic 60, 67; postschool 123; school 3, 59, 67–9
symbolic violence 168

understanding of self, work and opportunity 18
unemployment 105, 131, 135, 139, 143, 146, 151, 159–60, 163–4

voluntary non-employment 34

vulnerability 44, 144–5, 147, 188, 190, 196

wealth 3, 32, 41, 53, 69, 165; redistribution of 11–12, 31; unfair distribution of 159–60

wellbeing 100–3, 105, 107, 109–11
well-connectedness 41
welfare 3, 11–12, 25, 30, 34, 152, 173, 187; provision 26, 29, 31–4, 36; *to work* strategies 29, 31